Global Trends in Human Resource Management

Global Trends in Human Resource Management

Edited by

Emma Parry
Cranfield School of Management, UK

Eleni Stavrou
University of Cyprus, Cyprus

and

Mila Lazarova
Simon Fraser University, Canada

First published 2013 by
PALGRAVE MACMILLAN

Palgrave Macmillan in the UK is an imprint of Macmillan Publishers Limited,
registered in England, company number 785998, of Houndmills, Basingstoke,
Hampshire RG21 6XS.

Palgrave Macmillan in the US is a division of St Martin's Press LLC,
175 Fifth Avenue, New York, NY 10010.

Palgrave Macmillan is the global academic imprint of the above companies
and has companies and representatives throughout the world.

Palgrave® and Macmillan® are registered trademarks in the United States,
the United Kingdom, Europe and other countries.

ISBN 978–0–230–35483–8

This book is printed on paper suitable for recycling and made from fully
managed and sustained forest sources. Logging, pulping and manufacturing
processes are expected to conform to the environmental regulations of the
country of origin.

A catalogue record for this book is available from the British Library.

A catalog record for this book is available from the Library of Congress.

10 9 8 7 6 5 4 3 2 1
22 21 20 19 18 17 16 15 14 13

Printed and bound in the United States of America

Contents

v

List of Figures and Tables

Figures

Tables

Notes on Contributors

Editors

Emma Parry is Reader in Human Resource Management at Cranfield University School of Management, UK. Her research focuses on the impact of contextual factors on human resource management (HRM), specifically the impact of national context and sector in shaping HRM and the impact of demographic and technological change. She is also a Visiting Research Fellow at Westminster Business School. Emma leads a number of global research projects, including Cranet, a worldwide network of over 40 business schools that conduct comparative research into HRM and 5C, which, in collaboration with academics from 30 institutions around the world, examines cultural differences in attitudes towards career development. Emma is a UK representative on the global team for the Center of Aging and Work at Boston College, USA. She is the co-editor of *Managing an Age-Diverse Workforce* (Palgrave Macmillan 2011) and has published in the *International Journal of Management Reviews*, *Long Range Planning*, *International Journal of Human Resource Management* and *Human Resource Management Journal*. She reviews for a number of journals and is on the editorial board of the *Journal of Managerial Psychology*. She speaks regularly at academic conferences.

Eleni Stavrou is Associate Professor of Management at the University of Cyprus. She received her Ph.D. at George Washington University. Her articles have appeared in the *Journal of Organizational Behaviour*, *Journal of Business Ethics*, *Entrepreneurship Theory and Practice*, *British Journal of Management* and *International Human Resource Management Journal*. Her research focuses on work–life issues, strategic and comparative human resource management and intergenerational transitions in family firms.

Mila Lazarova is Associate Professor of International Management and also Director of the Centre for Global Workforce Strategy at the Beedie School of Business, Simon Fraser University, Canada. She received her Ph.D. in Human Resources and Industrial Relations from Rutgers, the State University of New Jersey. Her research focuses on expatriate management, comparative HRM, careers and career management, and the changing role of the HR department in organizations. Mila has published in *Academy of Management Review*, *Organization Science*, *Journal of International Business Studies*, *Journal of Organizational Behavior*, *Journal of World Business* and *International Journal of Human Resource Management*, and has contributed numerous book chapters in edited volumes. She has been awarded the Excellence in Research Award from SFU Business. Mila reviews for over a dozen academic journals and is currently on the editorial boards of the *Journal of International Business Studies, Journal of World Business, The International Journal of Cross-Cultural Management* and the *Human Resource Management Journal.* She holds an Outstanding Reviewer Award from the International Management Division of the Academy of Management.

Contributors

Ruth Alas is Head of the Department of Management at the Estonian Business School. Her research focuses on change and innovation management, crisis management, employee attitudes, learning abilities, organizational culture, leadership, business ethics and corporate social responsibility.

Julia Brandl is Professor of Human Resource Management and Work at Innsbruck University School of Management, Austria and holds a doctoral degree from WU Vienna. Her current research focuses on understanding how firms deal with failures in HRM and the feminization of the HR profession. Her work has been published in *Human Resource Management, Human Resource Management Journal* and *Journal of Management Inquiry.*

Chris Brewster is Professor of International Human Resource Management at Henley Business School, University of Reading, UK and also a Visiting Professor at Radboud University, Nijmegen in the Netherlands, Vaasa University in Finland and Paris II. He has written or edited more than two dozen books and 175 articles.

Ilona Bučiūnienė is the Vice Dean of Ph.D. Studies, Chairman of the Doctoral Committee, and a member of Senate at ISM University of Management and Economics, Lithuania. She teaches courses in HRM and research methodology. Her research focuses on responsible HRM and leadership, HRM–performance linkage and aging.

Bart Dietz is an assistant professor in the Department of Organisation and Personnel Management, Rotterdam School of Management at Erasmus University. His research focuses on the management of salespeople.

Paul Gooderham is a professor in the Department of Strategy and Management at the Norwegian School of Economics. His research interests are international HRM, multinational companies and transfer of business advice to SMEs.

Birgitte Grøgaard is an assistant professor at the Haskayne School of Economics, University of Calgary. Her main research interests are international strategies and subsidiary roles.

Henrik Holt Larsen is a professor in the Department of Organization at Copenhagen Business School. His research interests are strategic and international HRM, competence development, career development, managerial and management development and assessment interviews.

Zsuzsa Karoliny is an associate professor at the University of Pécs, Hungary, from where she graduated, obtained her Ph.D. and where she delivers management courses for every level of student attending the Faculty of Business and Economics.

Rūta Kazlauskaitė is a professor at ISM University of Management and Economics, Lithuania. Her research areas include international and comparative HRM, responsible HRM, HRM–performance linkage, employee work-related attitudes and corporate social responsibility. She is the editor of the *Baltic Journal of Management*.

Michael Koch is a Ph.D. candidate at EMLYON Business School. He received a masters in Human Resource Management and Industrial Relations from the University of Paris 1 Panthéon-Sorbonne. Prior to becoming an academic, he worked in an international consultancy.

Andrej Kohont is a researcher and teacher at the Faculty of Social Sciences, University of Ljubljana, Slovenia. He has been involved in a number of Slovenian and international research projects (topics: international HRM, competence management, labour market and public employment services, VET, bologna reform, quality in higher education, career centres and employability of students). He is a vice-president of the Slovenian HR Association.

Paul E.M. Ligthart is an assistant professor of strategy in the Department of Business Administration of Nijmegen School of Management, Radboud University of Nijmegen. Besides his expertise in research methodology and applied statistical analysis, his main research focuses on the strategy effects of configurations of HRM policies and practices, and configurations of innovation activities in the manufacturing industry.

Tina Lindeberg is a consultant at the IPF Institute of Uppsala University, which is a management institute focusing on research and executive management training. Tina is a major in HRM and has been a member of Cranet since 1996.

Bo Månson is a senior consultant at the IPF Institute of Uppsala University, a management institute tasked with disseminating the results of research to practitioners in both private and public sector organizations, mainly in Sweden. Bo has a masters in political science and has worked on organizational development and HR issues mainly in governmental agencies. He has been a member of Cranet since 1996.

Wolfgang Mayrhofer is Professor of Business Administration and holds a Chair in Management and Organisational Behaviour at WU Vienna, Austria.

Previously, he held teaching and research positions at the University of Paderborn and the Dresden University of Technology, both in Germany. His research interests focus on international comparative research in HRM and leadership, careers and systems theory. He has co-edited, co-authored and authored 26 books and more than 150 book chapters and peer-reviewed articles.

Odd Nordhaug is a professor in the Department of Strategy and Management at the Norwegian School of Economics. He researches career development, competence development, general management, HRM, organization theory and international and comparative management.

Andrew Pendleton is Professor of Human Resource Management at the University of York. He has written widely on employee share ownership, employee ownership and corporate governance.

Hilla Peretz is a senior faculty member in the Department of Industrial Engineering and Management, ORT Braude College, Israel. Her research interests concern HRM, particularly cross-cultural HR. She has written a number of papers on cross-cultural HR published in the *Journal of Applied Psychology* and *Journal of Cross-Cultural Psychology*.

József Poór is Professor of Management in the Faculty of Economics and Social Sciences, Szent István University, Hungary, where he teaches a variety of management courses. He obtained his Ph.D. from the Hungarian Academy of Sciences, Budapest. He is also Professor of Management at Selye Janos University, Komarno, Slovakia.

Erik Poutsma is Associate Professor of Labour Relations in the Department of Business Administration of Nijmegen School of Management, Radboud University of Nijmegen. He has many years of experience conducting research in the areas of technological change, entrepreneurship, HRM and employee participation. His main research interest is in international comparative research of the domains HRM and employee involvement.

Astrid Reichel is an assistant professor in the Department of Management at WU Vienna, Austria. She received her masters and doctorate in business and social sciences from the University of Vienna. Her research focuses on status, power, organization and professionalization of HRM, international and comparative HRM and careers. Her work has been published in *Human Resource Management*, *International Journal of Human Resource Management* and *Human Resource Management Review*.

Ágnes Szlávicz is an assistant professor at the Faculty of Economics Subotica, University of Novi Sad, Serbia, where she lectures on organizational behaviour and HRM. She obtained her Ph.D. at Szent István University, Gödöllő,

Hungary in 2010. Her field of interest is employee satisfaction and topics of IHRM.

Sinikka Vanhala is Professor of Management at Aalto University School of Economics, Finland. She mainly researches HRM, employee wellbeing, and gender in management and leadership.

Acknowledgements

We thank the members of the Cranet Network for their hard work in collecting survey data and in making being a member of the Network such an enjoyable experience. In particular, we would like to thank the contributors of the chapters in this text and those network members who helped us by reviewing chapters. Special thanks are due to Jayne Ashley for her tireless work in editing and formatting the typescript.

Introduction

Human Resource Management across Time and Context: Comparative Research and Global Trends in HRM

Emma Parry, Eleni Stavrou and Mila Lazarova

Increased foreign direct investment across the world and the trend for operating across national borders mean that organizations are now expanding into a variety of geographical locations. In this context, managing human resources has become increasingly dynamic and complex. Employers have to deal with the demands of managing people in different national settings and to understand the context in which they are operating by developing human resource management policies and practices that are appropriate for their specific location (Brewster, Mayrhofer & Morley, 2004). To this respect, multinational enterprises (MNEs) and their subsidiaries must seek a balance between the implementation of HRM practices that conform to the legitimate expectations and requirements of their host environment and the pursuit of more distinctive practices in their foreign subsidiaries based on those employed at home or best practices learned from other sources (Gunnigle et al., 2001).

These demands require an understanding of how HRM policies and practices may differ across countries and how the development of management practice may be affected by different institutional and cultural contexts. As Gooderham and Nordhaug (2011) have argued, HRM choices that organizations make should be examined as the product of a mix of exogenous cultural and institutional influences and endogenous organization-level processes. These are likely to reflect not only geographic proximity but also institutional and cultural factors (Brewster, 1995; Stavrou, Brewster & Charalambous, 2010). Therefore, alongside the trend for internationalization, interest in research that promotes knowledge about how people are managed in different countries has increased in recent years. However, while the importance of human resource management to organizations has been acknowledged widely, comparative research on how HRM is most effective within context is somewhat fragmented, with studies conducted in one or few countries providing mainly a snapshot of policy and practice (Stavrou, Brewster & Charalambous, 2010). In order to inform management practice effectively, it is essential that scholars produce systematic research that compares HRM practices, their antecedents and their effects both across countries and over time in order to allow global managers to understand these factors when developing practices in MNEs and their subsidiaries.

This book addresses these needs and provides a rigorous examination of HRM trends in a large number of countries across the globe by drawing on data from 'Cranet', a comprehensive study of HRM policies and practices across different countries, conducted over more than 20 years. Cranet (the Cranfield Network on International Human Resource Management) was formed in 1989 to meet the need for information on HRM practice and performance across Europe and now the world. Coordinated by Cranfield School of Management in the UK, Cranet is a collaboration of universities and business schools located in six continents and over 40 countries and communities. The Network carries out a regular international comparative survey of organizational policies and practices in HRM across the world and provides benchmarks for a systematic comparative analysis of HRM trends within and across employing organizations. The data produced by these surveys are unique in both coverage of country contexts and length of time for which data have been collected.

The book contains contributions from members of the Cranet network who are leading scholars in international comparative HRM within their countries. Each chapter is based upon a sample of the data collected from these regular surveys of HRM practice. The use of these data, combined with the substantial knowledge of the Network members as chapter authors, has allowed us to provide an invaluable collection of analyses of HRM practice both over time and in different national contexts so that we can examine the interplay among HRM cultural and institutional factors.

The Cranet survey

The Cranet survey has been conducted seven times since its inception in 1989. Table I.1 (taken from Kabst & Wehner, 2011) shows the countries and communities participating in the survey in each data collection period. The chapters in this book are based mainly on the data collected in 2004/5 and 2008/9. Each chapter stipulates individually which countries and questions were included in their analyses.

For each survey round, the questionnaire was developed using an iterative process based on past literature on HRM policies and practices, past versions of the questionnaire and discussions of the Cranet research team (see Table I.2 for the six sections of the questionnaire). It was first developed in English and then translated into the language of each country by a local HRM expert. The questionnaire was then translated back into English by a different HRM expert in each country to ensure consistency, validity and reliability in responses.

Table I.1 Members of Cranet and years of survey

Country/Community	Participation in year of survey						
	1990	1991	1992	1995	1999	2003/2005	2008/2010
Australia				•	•	•	•
Austria			•		•	•	•
Belgium					•	•	•
Bulgaria					•	•	•
Canada						•	•
Cyprus					•	•	•
Czech Republic			•		•	•	•
Denmark		•	•	•	•	•	•
Estonia						•	•
Finland			•	•	•	•	•
France	•	•	•	•	•	•	•
Germany	•	•	•	•	•	•	•
Greece			•		•	•	•
Hungary						•	•
Iceland						•	•
Ireland			•	•	•		•
Israel					•	•	•
Italy		•		•	•	•	
Japan					•		•
Lithuania							•
Nepal						•	
Netherlands		•	•	•	•	•	•
New Zealand						•	
Norway		•	•	•	•	•	•
Portugal			•	•	•		
Russia							•
Serbia							•
Slovakia						•	•
Slovenia						•	•
South Africa							•
Spain	•	•	•	•	•	•	
Sweden	•	•	•	•	•	•	•
Switzerland		•		•	•	•	•
Taiwan							•
The Philippines						•	•
Tunisia					•	•	
Turkey			•	•	•	•	
Turkish Cypriot Community						•	•
United Kingdom	•	•	•	•	•		•
USA						•	•
Sample size	5349	6267	5317	6306	9394	7914	6557
% private sector	71	69	67	65	73	67	73

Any differences found after the back translation were addressed after discussion between the research team and the partner in each country, in order to ascertain that the questions in each survey retained their intended meaning. It was first pilot tested locally in each country (Cushner & Brislin, 1996) and shared with local HRM executives to make sure that the meaning was accurate.

The final survey was subsequently conducted by the Cranet representative in each country. Since a comprehensive database of all organizations in each country was not available, each country team developed a mailing list of potential respondents in their country. In most countries a commercial or governmental database was used but in some countries databases from professional associations were used. Potential respondents were contacted by letter or email and subsequently sent a copy of the questionnaire. To encourage response, non-respondents were later sent a reminder.

The unit of analysis was the organization, and surveys were sent to the highest-ranking corporate officer in charge of HRM. In line with Arthur and Boyles (2007) and Kumar, Stern and Anderson (1993), the use of key informants is appropriate in research about HRM at the organizational level. This approach allowed us to survey a very large number of organizations, promoting generalizability. The questions asked were deliberately designed to rely on factual information about HRM within the organization. For example, 'Is the appraisal data used to inform decisions in the following areas: pay?' Furthermore, to discourage 'guessing', respondents were advised to leave blank any questions for which they did not know the answer.

The specific data selections and analyses used by our authors will be discussed separately in each chapter.

Table I.2   The sections of the Cranet questionnaire

Section	Topic	Explanation
1	HRM activity in the organization	Basic information about the HR function and the organization itself
2	Staffing practices	Methods for recruitment, selection and downsizing as well as action programmes for particular diverse groups
3	Employee development	Training design and implementation, appraisals and career development
4	Compensation and benefits	Information about the provision of pay and benefits
5	Employee relations and communication	Influence of trade unions, employer's associations and communication methods
6	Organizational details	Organizational details and information about the individual respondent

An overview of the chapters

The chapters are divided into three sections. In Section One, we take a broad approach in examining the evolving role of the human resources (HR) function, across the countries and communities in our sample. In Chapter 1, Lazarova, Mayrhofer and Brewster provide a longitudinal analysis of the profile of HRM work and Senior HR Managers, examining how the role of HRM has changed over time. Lazarova et al. conclude that the nature of the HR function has changed little in the past 15 years, aside from the increased formalization of HR practices and an increased presence of HR on the Board of Directors, but decreased involvement of the HR function in developing corporate strategy. The chapter sheds doubt on the rhetoric that the HR function has transitioned into one that is more strategic. Chapter 2, by Reichel, Brandl and Mayrhofer, expands on this analysis by investigating the feminization of HRM and its relationship to strategic integration and status. Reichel et al. demonstrate that the proportion of HR jobs taken by women has generally increased over time, but, contrary to expectations, did not find a negative effect of feminization on the status or strategic integration of the HR function. In Chapter 3, Kazlauskaitė and Bučiūnienė look at the increasing emphasis on corporate social responsibility (CSR) and responsible human resource management in Europe. They find a positive association between CSR policy formalization and engagement in responsible HRM action programmes, leading to the conclusion that CSR was not just rhetoric in organizations but is taken seriously by employers. Kazlauskaitė et al. also found an impact of contextual factors such as organization size, industry and national setting to affect the adoption of CSR practices. In our final chapter in this section, Chapter 4, Poutsma, Dietz, Ligthart and Delery examine the relationship between HR systems and firm performance. Poutsma et al. reinforce previous findings that configurations of HR practices can have a positive effect on organizational performance, particularly if they are made up of complementary calculative and collaborative HR practices.

In Section Two, looking at regional trends in HRM, we have four chapters. In Chapter 5 Kazlauskaitė, Bučiūnienė, Poor, Karoliny, Alas, Kohont and Szlávicz examine the changes occurring in HRM in an under-researched area of the world – that of Central and Eastern Europe. Interestingly, they refute the idea of a common HRM landscape within CEE countries and instead find significant differences between them. In Chapter 6, Alas and Vanhala investigate the potential convergence of HRM trends in Estonia and the nearby Nordic countries. Alas and Vanhala find not only directional similarly between Estonia and the Nordic region, but also an indication that HRM practice within these countries might eventually converge at a single endpoint. This is followed in Chapter 7 by an analysis of HRM in Scandinavia, provided by the Swedish and Danish Cranet partners, Lindeberg, Månson and Larsen. Similar to Chapter 5, Lindeberg, Månson and Larsen suggest that, while a characteristic Scandinavian management style does exist, distinct differences also exist among Scandinavian countries with regards to HRM. In Chapter 8, Gooderham, Grøgaard and Nordhaug provide a slightly different analysis – a comparison of Norwegian and North American HRM regimes with a view to examining how the divergence in HRM between these countries has an impact upon Norwegian multinational enterprises (MNEs). Gooderham et al. provide further evidence of the impact of national context and the implications of this for MNEs, having found considerable differences between the Norwegian and North American use of HRM, with North America focusing to a greater degree on the use of calculative HRM practices. Using interviews, Gooderham et al. add some depth to the Cranet data, and find that the use of Norwegian-style HRM practices within a North American setting (or vice versa) could produce mixed and sometimes negative outcomes.

Section Three of this book, which contains four chapters, takes a closer look at HRM by focusing on specific HR practices or areas of HRM. Chapter 9, written by Poutsma, Ligthart, Pendelton and Brewster, examines the development of financial participation in Europe over the past 15 years. Poutsma et al. compare the incidence of two forms of financial participation over time, providing an in-depth discussion of the context in each of the countries studied and the resulting impact of this context on the use of financial participation schemes. In Chapter 10, Peretz examines the use of human resource information systems (HRIS) and the impact of cultural fit on the relationship between HRIS and employee outcomes. Interestingly, Peretz's results show that national culture affects the use of information technology in the HR area and that absenteeism, and, to a lesser degree, turnover are influenced by the level of fit between societal culture and HR-related information technology practices. Finally, in Chapter 11, Koch looks at the use of flexible working practices across a number of national contexts and examines how these practices relate to organizational performance. Not only does this chapter demonstrate different use of flexible working arrangements across different national contexts, but it also provides important insights into the outcomes of these arrangements for organizations. Specifically, Koch concludes that non-standard work patterns have a positive impact on organizational financial performance, but that this impact is cancelled out by increased levels of employee turnover.

Many themes emerge out of the aforementioned chapters. But the most intriguing question that overrides all others is not what the 'right' HRM practices are, but which are the practices in each of many diverse contexts and how they relate this context to each other and important outcomes on multiple levels, and how they develop over time. We hope that after reading the chapters in this book, the complexity and fascination of HRM research and practice will energize further research and a greater dialogue on the diversity in HRM. There is still much to be learned.

References

Arthur, J. & Boyles, T. 2007. 'Validating the human resource system structure: A levels-based strategic HRM framework'. *Human Resource Management Review*, 17: 77–92.

Brewster, C. 1995. 'Towards a "European" model of human resource management'. *Journal of International Business Studies*, 26: 1–21.

Brewster, C., Mayrhofer, W. & Morley, M. 2004. *Human Resource Management in Europe: Evidence of Convergence?* London: Butterworth Heinemann.

Cushner, K. & Brislin, R.W. 1996. *Intercultural Interactions: A Practical Guide* (2ndedn). Thousand Oaks, CA: Sage Publications.

Gooderham, P.N. & Nordhaug, O. 2011. 'One European model of HRM? Cranet empirical contributions'. *Human Resource Management Review*, 21(1): 27–36.

Gunnigle, P., Murphy, K., Cleveland, J., Heraty, N. & Morley, M. 2001. 'Human resource management practices of US-owned multinational corporations in Europe: Standardization vs. localisation'. *Advances in International Management*, 14: 259–84.

Kabst, R. & Werner, M. 2011. 'Methodology'. In *Cranet Survey on Comparative Human Resource Management: International Executive Report 2011*. www.cranet.org.

Kumar, N., Stern, L. & Anderson, J. 1993. 'Conducting inter-organizational research using key informants'. *Academy of Management Journal*, 36(6): 1633–51.

Stavrou, E., Brewster, C. & Charalambous, C. 2010. 'Human resource management and organizational performance in Europe through the lens of business systems: Best fit, best practice or both?' *International Journal of Human Resource Management*, 21(7): 933–62.

Section One
The Evolving HR Function
and Role

1

'Plus ça change, plus c'est la même chose': A Longitudinal Analysis of HRM Work and the Profile of Senior HR Managers

Mila Lazarova, Wolfgang Mayrhofer and Chris Brewster

Introduction

Understanding national differences in handling HRM matters is a key area of international management studies (Ricks, Toyne & Martinez, 1990) and is at the heart of the burgeoning field of comparative HRM (see the contributions in Brewster & Mayrhofer, 2012b). There is now considerable evidence that HRM varies significantly between countries, cultures and institutional settings (see, for example, Croucher et al., 2010; Larsen & Mayrhofer, 2006; Scholz & Böhm, 2008). How significant these differences are depends on whether they are evidence of the embeddedness of HRM in national contexts or of varying stages of development and the different pace of learning of organizations from different contexts. The latter would imply that as globalization increases, these differences would become less pronounced.

From a theoretical point of view, there have been two sets of theories that analyse the differences between nations or clusters of nations. One, building on the concept of national culture, including the work of Hofstede (Hofstede, 1980; Hofstede, 2001; Hofstede & Minkov, 2010), Schwarz (Schwartz, 1992, 1999) and the members of the GLOBE project (Chhokar, Brodbeck & House, 2007; House et al., 2004) argues that specific dimensions of national culture – which vary between nations and groups of nations – influence individuals and collective actors such as organizations. National cultures influence personal and collective values, and these in turn influence individual and organizational behaviour. The second approach, institutional theories, takes a different point of view. These theories view societal institutions as core distinctive characteristics of the respective environment. All social interactions are embedded in this specific setting and have to take into account the formal and informal rules and norms governing a specific setting (Hollingsworth & Boyer, 1997). To be sure, there are quite different and equally successful ways of organizing economic activities (and management) in any capitalist economy (Amable, 2003; Hall & Soskice,

2001; Whitley, 1999). But the important thing is that organizations and the way that they operate and work best are embedded in particular national, or groups of national, environments. A key question concerns whether these differences are receding over time with the processes of globalization or whether they remain deeply distinctive.

This chapter contributes to this research by examining how the process of managing human resources has developed over time in different country clusters around the world with a special focus on Europe. We focus on key characteristics of the HRM department itself rather than on HRM practices (for that, see Mayrhofer et al., 2011). We provide a descriptive longitudinal analysis that seeks evidence of the widely discussed shift towards more 'strategic' human resource management. Specifically, we examine whether the configuration of the HRM department and the profiles of senior HRM specialists have converged in select (mainly European) countries. To do this we draw on data from the Cranet surveys. Furthermore, reflecting a *contextualist* approach (Brewster, 1999), we discuss national differences resulting from the interplay of institutional determinants. By examining trends across time, we contribute to the convergence–divergence debate in international HRM (Brewster, Mayrhofer & Morley, 2004).

Given the nature of our sample, our chapter takes a largely European perspective. In Europe, the question of converging or diverging developments in management practices in general and HRM practices in particular has been debated for some time (e.g. Almond, Edwards & Clark 2003; Mayrhofer et al., 2011). This is partly fuelled by the emerging role of the European Union as a major global player, developing and gradually implementing a social policy that applies to all the countries in the European Union and is now widely accepted also in the surrounding states. In turn, this can be regarded as increased institutional pressure creating a push towards convergence of approach to HRM in Europe.

Changes in the world environment

Since the early 1990s, the political, economic and social landscape has changed substantially. In the political sphere, major developments include the collapse of European communism in 1989/90 and the re-emergence of a number of sovereign states which rapidly moved towards capitalism. The greater integration and the expansion of the European Union, with its commitment to the free movement of goods, capital and people, was also significant. Economically, we have witnessed an accelerated pace of globalization, reordering of economic powers, waves of economic expansion and economic decline, several global financial crises, each more severe than the preceding one, volatile currencies, rising competitive pressures across industries and shifts in dominant industries (see, for example, Djelic & Quack, 2003; Drori, Meyer & Hwang, 2006; Tsoukis, Agiomirgianakis & Biswas, 2004).

Developments in the area of information and communication technology changed the way business is conducted in ways not seen since the Industrial Revolution (for a radical view on this, see Friedman, 2007) and, arguably, contributed to the financial meltdown that started in 2008. From a social standpoint we have seen significant changes in migration patterns: at the end of the first decade of the twenty-first century there were an estimated 215 million global first-generation migrants (a 40 per cent increase from 1990, see *The Economist*, 19 November 2011) in the aftermath of the fall of the iron curtain, the 'flow to the North' between Mexico and the USA and the substantial increase of Indians and mainland Chinese living outside of their home countries. All of these changes have created a new context for HRM.

These macro-level changes in the political, economic and social landscape affect organizations in various direct and indirect ways, and have an impact on the role of the HRM function and on how HRM work is being conducted. Researchers have suggested that the HRM function is undergoing such a transformation and, indeed, has been undergoing such transformation for the better part of the last two decades (Brewster & Mayrhofer, 2012a). This includes, first of all, the change from personnel to human resource management in the early 1990s. While not in complete agreement on the invariable characteristics of HRM, many scholars would concur that when compared to personnel management HRM emphasizes the integration of personnel policies across functions (Lengnick-Hall & Lengnick-Hall, 1988); and, with corporate strategy (Schuler & Jackson, 2007), stresses the role of line managers (Larsen & Brewster, 2003); has a clear focus on the link with organizational performance (e.g. Becker & Gerhart, 1996; Wright et al., 2005); promotes a shift from collective to individual relationships within the organization (Rasmussen & Andersen, 2006); and indicates a reorientation from a more humanistic to a clearly business-oriented value system (Holbeche, 2002; Price, 1997). While there has been substantial critique both of the HRM concept and the rhetoric associated with it, particularly in Europe (e.g. Guest, 1990; Legge, 2005), HRM has become the dominant perspective (Legge, 2005). In parallel, given the high proportion of operating costs consumed by human resources – the people working for the organization – the relative ease of adapting the spending on those resources and the unique value that they provide, it has been argued for some time that HRM might be expected to take centre stage in organizations (e.g. Pfeffer, 1998; Ulrich & Brockbank, 2005), with a concomitant increase of the strategic potential and role of HRM (Schuler & Jackson, 2007).

So, in this chapter we are interested in whether the macro-level changes and the transformation from personnel to HRM is reflected in changes of the key indicators of (1) the role of the HRM department and (2) the characteristics of the senior HRM specialists in selected country clusters. In the next section, we outline the expected changes in HRM in more detail.

Changes in HRM

Increasing strategic importance of HRM

Practitioner and academic literature and rhetoric have it that a strategic orientation of HRM is key to success and a major characteristic of HRM (Greer, 2001; Schuler & Jackson, 2007; Ulrich, 1997; Ulrich & Brockbank, 2005). To that end, the HRM department has a long-term orientation and links HRM objectives to business objectives (Truss, 2003: 50). In addition, the most senior HR manager is an integral member of the top management team. Thereby, the HRM department participates in corporate planning processes that may have more or less obvious outcomes for people management in the organization, right from the beginning. Since most decisions have an HRM element either directly or indirectly as an outcome, firm performance should improve (see, for example, Welbourne & Cyr, 1999).

If this rhetoric is reflected in reality, we would expect that several key changes have taken place over the last two decades. First, given the focus on strategic activity and the consequent much-bruited outsourcing of transactional HRM, the rise of electronic support (e-HRM), and the pressure for line managers to accept more responsibility for HRM (Brewster et al., 2006) that is an intrinsic element of the notion of strategic HRM in the literature, (1) *the size of the HRM department relative to the total number of employees should decrease.* In line with this, we expect that (2) *the extent to which HRM responsibilities are assigned to line managers will have increased.* We should note here that the assignment of HRM responsibilities to line managers has been perceived as both an opportunity and a threat for HRM departments (an opportunity as HRM responsibilities are being 'given away' (Guest, 1987) to allow HRM managers to focus on strategic – as opposed to routine transactional – tasks; or a threat, with HRM expertise being 'given up' (Blyton & Turnbull, 1992), potentially marginalizing HRM professionals as people whose work can be done by anyone). However, in terms of overall human resource *management*, there is a shared opinion that devolvement is part of the strategic approach to HRM, a recognition that HRM work is important and should be embraced by all managers in the organization. The literature has suggested that a more strategic approach to HRM will be associated with higher levels of assignment of responsibility to line managers. It is not our goal to judge the merits of each of these predictions here. Rather, we are interested in documenting whether devolvement has increased over the course of the last two decades.

Changes in the relative size of the HRM department in the level of assignment of responsibilities to line management would be accelerated by the mimetic pressure emerging from so-called best practice examples from the consultancies, the popular business press and management gurus. This is also coupled with higher economic pressure on non-productive ('over-head') functions to be as lean as possible (Brewster et al., 2006).

Next, we might expect (3) *an increase in formal and written expressions of strategic intention over time.* The past decades have been characterized by a surge of standardization, streamlining and auditing of activities by sources external to the organization. In the private sector, various kinds of certification have become major characteristics and 'must haves' for many companies. In a similar vein, in the public sector the wave of new public management or the accreditation movement in the field of higher education force organizations to adapt to the standards held by the respective certification agencies. The lack of such an approval threatens their role as a credible supplier, producer or player in the respective field. As a consequence, organizations commit themselves to certain standards, written documentations of processes, goals or strategies. In line with institutionalist arguments, both normative and mimetic pressures are at work here, that is, existing rules and regulations that have to be followed and the copying of arguably successful organizational role models.

Third, based on the premise that effective HRM can contribute to organizational profitability and overall organizational success, commentators have put forward the idea that the role of the HRM function in the organization will change. Specifically, it has been suggested that its strategic importance will increase (Gomez-Mejia, Balkin & Cardy, 2004). Among other things, such an increase should leave some structural and procedural traces. To that end, we might expect (4) *an increase in the representation of senior HRM specialists at the most senior, decision-making, level of the organization* and (5) *an increase in the strategic integration of HRM,* that is, the inclusion of HRM in early stages of strategic corporate decision-making. Such increases would signal that HRM issues are being considered at the highest level of decision-making in the organization and that HRM is seen as a function that could contribute to other strategic decisions.

Professionalization of HRM and profile of the top HR manager

An important factor that would enable the HRM department to take on a strategic role is the competency profile of the most senior HR manager (Truss et al., 2002). Truss (2003: 58) describes competency in this context as the 'HR director's personality, approach and focus'. In particular, the most senior HR manager's general business experience and orientation are essential for the HRM department's strategic integration (e.g. Buller, 1988; Golden & Ramanujam, 1985; Watson, 1988), and the department's people, particularly their top people, need to become more professional.

In its classical sense and based on organizational sociology, the concept of professionalization includes four dimensions: the knowledge required for fulfilling one's professional tasks; the incentives linked with individuals that are part of the profession; the ethical and normative code that supports practical action in one's profession; and the autonomy that is linked with profession with regard to other functions within the organization and competing bodies of knowledge (Altrichter & Gorbach, 1993). Attempts have been made to apply such principles to HRM (Farndale, 2005; Wächter & Metz, 1995). Drawing on institutional organizational theory, one would expect such changes because of pressures stemming from normative isomorphism. Fundamental to the concept of professionalization are the development of more highly qualified, and specifically qualified, senior people in the function and a degree of independence from employers created by a greater commitment to the norms of the profession (Farndale, 2005; Farndale & Brewster, 2005).

On the first point, the existence and importance of professional HRM associations such as SHRM in North America, CIPD in the UK, or DGfP in Germany (Farndale & Brewster, 2005), or the significance of standardized qualification certification such as, for example, various forms of ISO-certification processes, lead to a pressure for more homogeneous ('standardized') forms of practical HRM work, HRM tools, and also formal qualifications of HRM experts. The recent move to establish national, regional or even global HRM standards (see, for example, the process in Germany or the efforts to establish global HRM standards linked, among others, with SHRM) is a further indication that we see clear normative pressures. Furthermore, HRM has become part of the curricula that future managers in business schools have to follow. Again, considerable normative pressures emerge from such practice.

In line with such changes in HRM as a field, we expect changes in the profile of the HRM professionals themselves. For example, one can reason that (6) *senior HRM specialists will come increasingly from within the HRM function*, having developed an appropriate expertise and with a competency profile emphasizing (7) *formally certified higher education*, particularly education in *business or economics*. Finally, contradictory arguments have been advanced with respect to gender (Reichel, Brandl & Mayrhofer, 2010) (see also Chapter 2 in this book). On the one hand, given the general trend in most industrialized countries to promote equal employment rights, diversity and participation of women at all levels of employment, one can see a pressure on the HRM function to 'practise what it preaches' and be in the vanguard of the departments with an increased proportion of women reaching the top. Arguably, and less honourably, it may be seen by some as a function where women can be promoted to improve the averages of senior women in the organization who are female without having to change the sources of top executives in the more highly regarded financial or engineering functions. It has been suggested that as professions become more female they tend to lose influence. This would suggest that, in line with the top HRM role becoming more strategic, we would see a higher proportion of men being appointed to serve as top HR managers. Despite these conflicting views, we clearly expect a feminization of the top position within HRM. Overall, women – although slowly – increasingly fill top positions in different kinds of organizations, be it through legal regulations as with the required female quota for supervisory boards in Norway, or the favouring of women in the case of equally qualified candidates in the Austrian public service, or the normative pressure in many countries in the world. Therefore, we assume (8) *a decreasing proportion of men in top HRM positions.*

Given the focus of our chapter, we test each of these propositions against the competing notions that developments are the same (globalization) or are different (cultural or institutional embeddedness) in different regions within our sample. In other words, if there are differences between regions in the configuration of the HRM department are they reducing, so that, as either theorists or practitioners, we need not concern ourselves with them too much – or do they remain important such that we need to factor these geographical differences into our understanding of HRM.

Sample and method

We test our propositions using data from the Cranet project from four consecutive data rounds: 1995, 1999, 2004/2005 and 2008/2010 (data in the last three rounds were collected over several years, but in order to improve readability we only refer to the first year of each data collection round from this point forward). The basic set-up of Cranet is described in the introduction to this book (see also Brewster et al., 2004).

Country clusters

There have been many categorizations of countries. For example, the International Labour Office (ILO *Employment Development Report*, 2007) divides the world into eight clusters based on geographic location and level of economic development (for example, one cluster is 'Latin America and the Caribbean' and another is 'Developed Economies and European Union'). More theoretically grounded institutional explanations focus, for example, on various kinds of capitalism (Hall & Soskice, 2001) and open up a dichotomy between liberal and coordinated market economies. Other varieties of capitalism models are more nuanced (Amable, 2003; see also Hollingsworth & Boyer, 1997; Whitley, 1999). Countries have also been grouped based on national and regional cultures that reflect substantial differences in norms and values (Hofstede, 1980; House et al., 2004; Schwartz, 2004). Within comparative HRM (Brewster & Mayrhofer, 2012b), the core distinction is between the US version of HRM and its basic assumptions (Fombrun, Tichy & Devanna, 1984) and a European model of HRM (Brewster, 1995; Larsen & Mayrhofer, 2006). Further, focusing on Europe, several ways of clustering countries have been proposed (for a review, see Mayrhofer et al., 2011).

Overall, past research has not provided conclusive results regarding country clusters. Yet, it remains highly plausible that within Europe different patterns of HRM activities exist. In this chapter we use an amalgam of categories available from the cultural and the institutional literature to guide our research. This gave us categories of *Anglo-Saxon* (i.e. stock market-focused business systems, referred to as Liberal Market Economies in the comparative capitalisms literature); the *Germanic* states (largely corresponding to the Coordinated Market Economies where a stakeholder approach predominates and is enshrined in law); *South Western Europe* (the Latin cultures); the *Nordic* economies (where there are high levels of consensus and union membership); *Southern European* (the Mediterranean economies, characterized by a predominance of small firms, family ownership, even in larger firms, extensive legislation but common avoidance of it); and the transition economies (CEE) of *Central and Eastern Europe* (with their heritage of centrally planned economies during the communist era). We were limited by data availability as not all countries participated in all Cranet survey rounds. To that end, the country configuration for each cluster may vary across the years examined. Table 1.1 provides specific details of which countries were included in each survey round.

Results

Configuration of the HRM department

Proposition 1: The relative size of the HRM department

Following the suggestion in the literature that the size of HRM departments relative to total headcount is decreasing, we examined the ratio of employees working in the HRM department per 100 employees. Only data for 1999, 2005 and 2010 were available for this variable. We did not find support for the expected decrease in the relative size of the HRM department. More specifically, our analyses found *no discernible patterns* with regard to either an overall decrease or an overall increase (Figure 1.1).

Given previous research (Brewster et al., 2006), we did not expect to see the same relative size of the HRM department across countries. Rather, we set out to find out whether the relative size was changing in each cluster in a manner suggested by the strategic HRM literature, that is, do we see evidence for a decreasing ratio of the size of the HRM department in the various clusters? Although we find different patterns by cluster, we do not find consistent evidence for a decrease in HRM ratios in any specific cluster other than the Nordic one.

Specifically, in the time periods between 1999 and 2004 and between 2004 and 2008, there was an *overall decrease* in the Nordic, South Western European and the Anglo clusters. For the Nordic cluster the change between 1999 and 2004 was minimal, but this was followed by a sharp decrease in the subsequent time period. The opposite was true for the South Western cluster whereby a sharp decrease between 1999 and 2004 was followed by a minimal change between 2004 and 2008. For companies from the Anglo

19

Table 1.1 Clusters, countries and survey rounds

		1995	1999	2004	2008
Anglo-Saxon	Australia		X	X	X
	Canada			X	
	Ireland	X	X		
	New Zealand			X	
	Northern Ireland		X		
	UK	X	X	X	X
	USA			X	X
Germanic	Austria	X	X	X	X
	Germany	X	X	X	X
	Switzerland	X	X	X	X
South Western Europe	Belgium		X	X	X
	France		X	X	X
	Italy	X	X	X	
	Portugal		X		
	Spain	X	X	X	
Nordic	Denmark	X	X	X	X
	Finland	X	X	X	X
	Iceland			X	X
	Norway	X	X	X	X
	Netherlands	X	X	X	
	Sweden	X	X	X	X
Southern Europe	Greece		X	X	X
	Cyprus		X	X	X
	Turkey		X	X	
	Turkish Cypriot Community			X	X
Central and Eastern Europe (CEE)	Bulgaria		X	X	X
	Czech Republic		X	X	X
	Lithuania			X	X
	Estonia			X	X
	Hungary			X	X
	Russia			X	X
	Serbia				X
	Slovakia			X	X
	Slovenia			X	X
N across clusters		5909	6945	7290	5082
Average number of employees[a]		837	784	807	764
% private sector		74.4%	78.3%	72.4%	72%

Note: [a] 5% trimmed mean reported.

cluster a sharp decrease was followed by an equally sharp increase, but with overall lower ratio in 2008 compared to 1999. We found *no change* in the Germanic cluster and *an increase* in the Southern European cluster. For the CEE countries, we were only able to examine the change between 2004 and 2008, and the available data show an overall increase. Figure 1.1 shows the developments in the six clusters.

Proposition 2: Assignment to line management

To examine the assignment of HRM responsibilities to line managers we used the average of responses to a set of items asking respondents who had primary responsibility for five areas of HRM activities: pay and benefits, recruitment and selection, training and development, industrial relations and workforce expansion/reduction. The anchors of the scale were 0=HRM department primarily responsible, 1=HRM department responsible in consultation with line management, 2=line management responsible in consultation with HRM department, and 3=line management primarily responsible. Thus, the higher the number, the more responsibilities are assigned to line managers, or, to adopt another commonly used term that assumes that the responsibilities started in the HRM function, the more responsibilities were 'devolved' to line managers.

As shown in Figure 1.2, we see *relatively minimal change* in overall devolvement, with only a slight increase in four of the clusters: Nordic, Germanic, Anglo and South Western Europe. In CEE, we see an increase followed by a decrease.

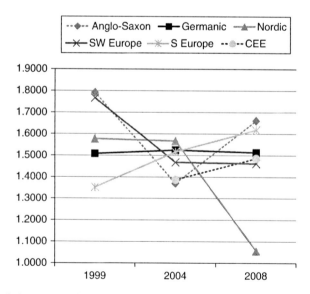

Figure 1.1   Relative size of the HRM department

To that end, we find limited support for the second change we expected, an increase in the assignment of HRM responsibilities to line managers.

Our results are generally consistent with the results reported by Larsen and Brewster (2003) about a decade ago. They too utilized the Cranet dataset but their study focused on data collected in 1995 and 1999. They concluded that while they uncovered evidence for increases in line management responsibility, the actual shift in responsibilities was generally small and did not reach statistical significance. Our results suggest a similar trend in the decade that followed the original study. One possible explanation for not seeing much increase in devolvement is that in most countries there is a high level of devolvement already (on average, it appears that for most organizations HRM activities are handled by line managers in consultation with the HRM department).

Proposition 3: Written personnel strategy

Given the increasing trend for accountability and responsibilities to be traceable, we expected to see an increasing demand for personnel policies to be formalized. We calculated the proportion of organizations that indicated that they had 'a written HRM/personnel strategy'. With the exception of the CEE countries, there appears to be *a steady increase* in the proportion of organizations that have a written personnel strategy (Figure 1.3).

The positive trend is most pronounced in the Nordic cluster (where the proportion of companies increased from 55 per cent in 1995 to 71 per cent in 2008). The trend was not completely universal (i.e. in some periods,

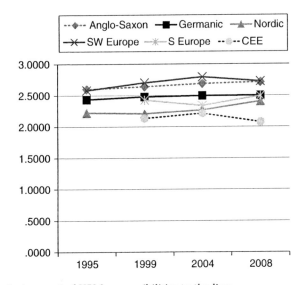

Figure 1.2   Assignment of HRM responsibilities to the line

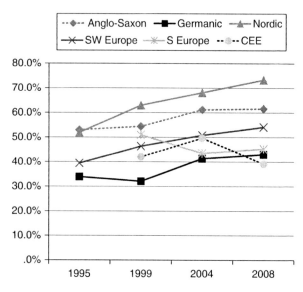

Figure 1.3   Existence of written personnel strategy

there was evidence for decreases in select countries), but even taking this into account, the overall percentage of companies with a written personnel strategy in the Nordic cluster exceeds that of organizations in all other clusters and has remained in that position throughout the decades. The lowest overall levels are observed in the Germanic cluster where, as of 2008, only 43 per cent of organizations had written personnel strategies. There is a marked within-cluster difference between countries, however, with fewer organizations in Austria and Germany with written personnel strategies compared to Switzerland. The Anglo-Saxon cluster as a whole also showed an increase, with 49 per cent and 61 per cent of organizations reporting having written personnel strategies in 1995 and 2008 respectively. Although there is an overall increase in the South Western European countries across the four time points, there are inconsistencies in the cluster, with Italy and Belgium showing increases, for the data periods available, and Spain and France showing increases followed by decreases. We found no consistent patterns in the Southern European and the CEE countries, although we only have data for two data points from the majority of the countries included in the clusters.

In summary, while there appears to be an overall increase of organizations with written HRM/personnel strategies, this overall trend masks important differences across and within clusters. The four clusters for which we have more consistent data appear to move in a parallel fashion of gradual – but by no means dramatic – increase.

Proposition 4: HRM representation on senior management level

Given the wide recognition of the role of HRM for increasing organizational performance, we also expected to see an increase in the extent to which HRM is represented at senior management level. We calculated the percentage of organizations in which the person responsible for HRM is a member of the board of directors (or the equivalent top executive body, for those countries and organizations that do not have a board of directors).

As illustrated by Figure 1.4, our expectation is largely supported. The data suggest an *overall increase* in the number of organizations reporting that HRM was being represented at board level across clusters and time periods. The pattern is not consistent across clusters, with some clusters showing a drop in the variable in select periods (e.g. a 10 per cent drop in Southern European countries between 1999 and 2004). But for all clusters the 2008 levels of representations are higher than the respective levels in 1995. In the latest wave of data collection, representation is highest in South Western European countries (at approximately 88 per cent of companies reporting HRM is represented on the board) and lowest in the Germanic cluster (54 per cent). Looking within clusters, there was most internal consistency in the Nordic cluster, with all countries showing a gradual increase in each time period. In contrast, countries from the Eastern European cluster exhibit the most inconsistency. Thus, in the last round of data collection, there was an increase of HRM representation in the Czech Republic, Hungary and

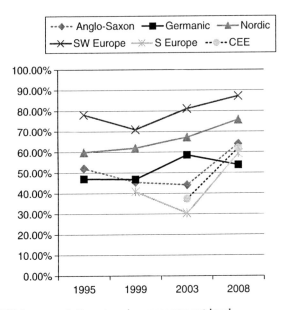

Figure 1.4   HRM representation at senior management level

Slovenia, no change in Estonia and a decrease in Bulgaria. Overall, however, the trend in the overall cluster is in the expected (upward) direction.

Proposition 5: Strategic integration of HRM

We also examined the extent to which HRM is involved in corporate decision-making, expecting to see a rise over time. The Cranet survey asks respondents at what stage the person responsible for HRM is involved in the development of the business strategy/strategic business planning of the organization. The possible answers are: (1) from the outset, (2) through subsequent consultation, (3) on implementation, and (4) not consulted. To capture strategic integration, we calculated the percentage of organizations that indicated that HRM was involved 'from the outset'.

While the data show more consistency among the clusters, there was no evidence for a rise in HRM strategic integration. With the exception of the Nordic countries, where there was a slight increase over time (about 5 percentage points between 1995 and 2008), there was an *overall decrease* in the relative portion of companies in which HRM is involved in the initial stages of strategy formulation (see Figure 1.5).

HRM department configuration summary

Overall, the five characteristics of the HRM configuration analysed here do not show a consistent and clear trend (see Table 1.2). Our key finding is that change has been limited and inconsistent. The only clear trends are towards an increase

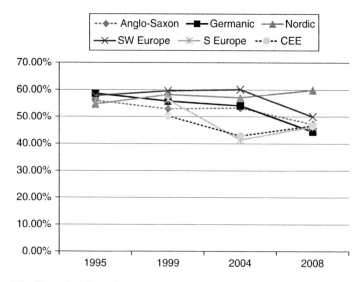

Figure 1.5   Strategic integration of HRM

in the formalization of written personnel strategies and the representation of HRM at the top decision-making body of the organization.

Profile of the top HR manager

We turn our attention from the configuration of the HRM department to the individuals who head it. As noted above, for the HRM department to be accepted as strategic the individual running it must have credibility and be seen as a professional contributor. Cranet data are largely collected from the most senior HRM specialist in the organization: in about two-thirds of organizations this is the case and the other third is mainly split between CEOs of smaller firms and Administrative Directors. As per our earlier discussion, we examined three key characteristics: whether they were hired for the top HRM job from the ranks of HRM specialists, their education and their gender.

Proposition 6: Recruitment of top HR managers

Organizations were asked from where they recruit the person responsible for HRM. We calculated the percentage of organizations indicating that the person comes from 'personnel/HRM specialists' either within or outside the organization. Generally speaking, the majority of organizations across clusters tend to staff their top HRM position with personnel/HRM specialists. Furthermore, the data suggest *an overall upward trend* (see Figure 1.6). Within this broad generalization, countries from the South Western European cluster

Table 1.2 Overview of cluster developments – HRM configuration[a]

	Ratio of HRM employees	Assignment to line	Written HRM strategy	HRM on board	HRM involved from the onset
Expected	↓	↑	↑	↑	↑
Anglo-Saxon	↓ ↑	→ → →	→ ↑ →	↓ → ↑	→ → ↓
Nordic	→ ↓	→ → →	↑ ↑ ↑	→ ↑ ↑	↑ → ↑
Germanic	→ →	→ → →	→ ↑ →	→ ↑ →	↓ ↓ ↓
SW Europe	↓ →	→ → →	↑ ↑ ↑	↓ ↑ ↑	→ → ↓
S Europe	↑ ↑	→ → →	↓ →	↓ ↑	↓ ↑
CEE[b]	↓	↑ ↓	↑ ↓	↓ ↑	↓ ↑
OVERALL	Inconsistent pattern	No change/ Minimal increase	Increase	Increase	Inconsistent pattern (but prevalent decrease)

Notes: [a] Each arrow represents change in a particular cluster for each time period studied (1995 to 1999, 1999 to 2004 and 2004 to 2008). Thus ↑ signifies an increase during a single period, ↓ signifies a decrease, and → signifies no change. For the CEE cluster, data were available for two periods only, 1999 to 2004 and 2004 to 2008.
[b] Only available time period is 2004 to 2008.

and the Anglo-Saxon cluster consistently reported high levels of staffing the top HRM positions with an HRM specialist, ranging from 68 per cent in 1995 to 74 per cent in 2008 for the Anglo cluster and from 70 per cent in 1995 to 77 per cent in 2008 in the South Western European cluster. Relative increases are seen in the Nordic and the Germanic clusters, albeit at lower absolute levels, with the percentage rising from 47 per cent in 1995 to 65 per cent in 2008 for the Germanic cluster and a rise from 53 per cent in 1995 to 65 per cent in 2008 in the Nordic cluster. The overall increase (18 percentage points) was highest in the Germanic cluster. There was only a marginal increase in recruiting HRM specialists as the top HR managers in the Southern European cluster (from 56 per cent in 2004 to 59 per cent in 2008) and an inconsistent pattern in organizations from the CEE countries (where current levels of recruitment from within the profession are 55 per cent, marginally up from 54 per cent in 1999 but down from 62 per cent in 2004).

In most clusters the data suggest a preference for hiring HRM specialists from outside the company. For example, in 2008 19 per cent of Nordic companies recruited their top HR manager from specialists within the organization and 46 per cent recruited from outside the organization. But this preference was not universal: in the Southern European and the CEE cluster, there appears to be an equal preference for hiring an HRM professional from within and from outside the company, reflecting perhaps the lower levels of trust between organizations in these rapidly changing and somewhat capricious societies.

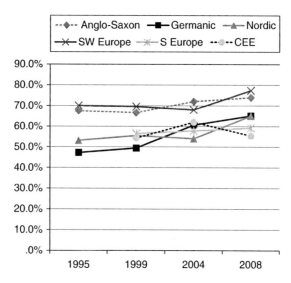

Figure 1.6   Recruitment of top HR managers

Proposition 7: Education of top HR managers

Data on the proportion of HR managers with university degrees were not collected in 1995, so we can only evaluate change since 1999 (data not shown here). The overall trend was *an increase* of top HR managers with higher education, and there were also signs of a decreasing gap between the country clusters (25 percentage points in 1999 versus 14 percentage points in 2008). We see increases of this indicator in the CEE cluster (from 80 per cent to 86 per cent), the Anglo-Saxon cluster (from 68 per cent to 80 per cent) and the Germanic cluster (from 64.6 per cent to 75.5 per cent). The Nordic and South European clusters both reported a drop in the proportion of top HR managers with university education between 1999 and 2004 followed by a rise. Compared to 1999, Nordic cluster organizations report an overall increase (from 66 per cent in 1999 to 82 per cent in 2008), whereas there is no change in companies from the South European cluster (90 per cent in 1999 and 89 per cent in 2008). South Western European organizations exhibit the opposite trend – a rise between 1999 and 2004 (from 81 per cent to 84 per cent) and a drop between 2004 and 2008 (down to 80 per cent), leaving their landscape relatively unchanged when both periods are considered.

Looking at the specific degrees of the top HR managers, we expected an increase in the proportion with business or economics training. However, *no consistent trend* is suggested by the data (see Figure 1.7). There was an increase of top HR managers with business or economics degrees in the Anglo cluster and a smaller increase in the CEE cluster. There was a decrease in the Nordic countries, and a smaller decrease in the Germanic countries. There was no change in the South and South Western European clusters. The picture is equally complicated within clusters – with different countries reporting different overall levels of top HR managers with business or economics degree and experiencing changes of a different kind.

The differences between clusters are fairly large, with close to 60 per cent of senior HRM specialists in the Southern European cluster having a business or economics degree, but less than 30 per cent of companies in the Nordic cluster reporting top HR manager with such degrees. This may indicate some differences in the concepts of HRM – is the primary purpose to serve the interests of the business or to serve a wider group of stakeholders? In the latter case, other degrees may be equally relevant. Furthermore, we must acknowledge the traditional differentiation in routes to management in, for example, Germany with its privileging of '*technisch*' training and the French '*grandes écoles*', which may encompass these business and economics degrees without them being selectively identified as such.

Proposition 8: Gender of top HR manager

A clear trend suggested by the Cranet data is that *more and more top HR managers are women*. Their numbers have been increasing steadily in all clusters, across the last four waves of data collection. There is only one

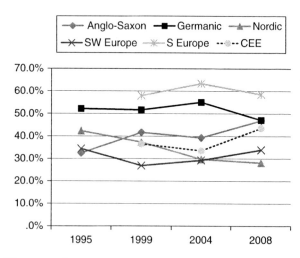

Figure 1.7   Education of top HR managers

exception, in the CEE cluster, where there is a small decrease between 2004 and 2008; notably, this was the cluster with the highest numbers of female top managers prior to that date (see Figure 1.8).

In 1995, 18 per cent of top HR managers in the South Western European cluster were women. The figure in 2008 was 53 per cent. The same trend is evident in the other clusters: in the Germanic cluster the share of companies with a top female HR manager increased from 16 per cent to 42 per cent, in the Nordic cluster the increase was from 25 per cent to 51 per cent, and in the Anglo-Saxon cluster the increase was from 28 per cent to 60 per cent. With data available only since 1999, a similar picture emerges for the Southern European cluster (increase from 21 per cent to 35 per cent) and the CEE cluster (increase from 38 per cent to 63 per cent). There appears to be a clear feminization of the senior reaches of the profession. There is evidence from previous research (Reichel, Brandl & Mayrhofer, 2009; Reichel et al., 2010) that has used the Cranet data that the growth of feminization among the top HRM specialists has been accompanied by a lower likelihood that HRM is strategically integrated, with a voice at the top table more likely to be found where the senior HRM specialist is male (see Chapter 2 of this book for a more in-depth discussion of this issue). In other words, the feminization of senior HRM positions may be, as it has been in other professions, less a reflection of success for women than a reflection of the declining credibility of the profession.

Profile of the HR manager summary

The following table gives an overview of developments in the profile of the organizational senior HRM specialists in the six clusters (Table 1.3).

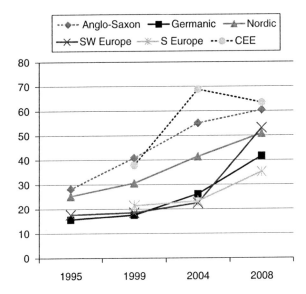

Figure 1.8 Female top HR managers

Again, changes in general seem to be quite limited with the exception of the growing feminization of the top of the profession. There is a consistent, if small, increase of top HRM persons recruited from within the profession. In other words, with the exception of the increase in the number of senior women, there is little, if any change and what change there is tends to be inconsistent.

Discussion and conclusions

In terms of the configuration of HRM the evidence seems to challenge the received wisdom. Although in some cases HRM does appear to be strategic (there is considerable assignment of responsibilities to the line, HRM strategies are being formalized in many organizations, senior HRM specialists are represented at the highest level and in about two-thirds of the organizations they are involved in strategy formalization from an early stage), there may be considerable differences in the meaning of these findings. Is the formalization of strategy necessarily strategic? Or may it represent rhetoric rather than reality? Is the relatively high level of HRM representation at the board, or board-equivalent, level evidence of strategic involvement or of a cultural requirement that the head of every department is represented at that level? In terms of the profile of the top HRM specialists, there is encouraging news. A large proportion is recruited from among the ranks of HRM professionals. Most of them are highly educated and have a degree, although the

Table 1.3   Overview of cluster developments – profile of top HR manager[a]

	Top HR person recruited from within the HR profession	Top manager with a business/ economic degree	Male top HR manager
Expected	↑	↑	↓
Anglo-Saxon	→ ↑ →	↑ → ↑	↓ ↓ ↓
Nordic	→ → ↑	↓ ↓ ↓	↓ ↓ ↓
Germanic	↑ ↑ ↑	→ → ↓	↓ ↓ ↓
SW Europe	→ → ↑	→ → →	→ → ↓
S Europe	→ →	→ →	→ ↓
CEE	↑ ↓	→ →	↓ ↑
OVERALL	Minimal increase	Inconsistent pattern	Decrease

Note: [a] Each arrow represents change in a particular cluster for each time period studied (1995 to 1999, 1999 to 2004 and 2004 to 2008). Thus ↑ signifies an increase during the respective period, ↓ signifies a decrease, and → signifies no change. For the CEE cluster, data were available for two periods only, 1999 to 2004 and 2004 to 2008.

subjects they have studied vary considerably by cluster. Apart from business and economics, in some societies law is considered to be a good way into the profession; in others it may be psychology or in yet others industrial sociology. Furthermore, a higher and higher proportion of the top HRM specialists are women. But what of our basic question about change?

Managerial and everyday rhetoric often claims that 'the present is always an exciting, challenging time to be contrasted with a stable past' (Collin, 1998: 412). Whole textbooks and indeed careers have been built on the notion of the world as one of increasing and dramatic change; of managers having to steer their way through never-ending 'white water', compared to the calm seas and occasional squalls of the past. To make such claims, these authorities have been obliged to select specific examples and generalize from broad principles back to assumed practices. In fact, at least in the case of human resource management (and we suspect more widely), empirical evidence for such rhetoric is not particularly strong. These may not be truly revolutionary times; they are shaped incrementally (Eccles & Nohria, 1992: 25) and, as we have shown, organizations seem to remain embedded in certain trajectories that they share with their immediate neighbours. This certainly applies to various aspects of HRM practice (Apospori et al., 2008; Goergen, Brewster & Wood, 2009; Pendleton et al., 2002; Tregaskis & Brewster, 2006). Indeed, looking at a considerable body of research on change over time in HRM seems to confirm the scepticism about pervasive change.

A similar argument could be made about convergence – despite the more or less convincing accounts of the inevitable effects of globalization and the consequent convergence towards the one-best-way of handling HRM, there appears to be more evidence of countries and clusters retaining their distinctive recipes for managing people than there is of convergence. For example, studies using Cranet data to empirically analyse the development of HRM in larger private sector firms in 13 European countries to find evidence of human resource management practices becoming more alike found considerable evidence of directional similarity – practices increasing or decreasing in the same way across the countries – but found no evidence whatsoever of final convergence, that is, countries becoming more alike in the way they manage people (Mayrhofer et al., 2011). That analysis is reflected in our evidence too.

We set out to see if we could uncover evidence for changes in the role of the HRM department and the profile of the most senior HR manager that have been implied or explicitly predicted by the growing body of literature on strategic HRM. Overall, the evidence presented here shows that the configuration of the HRM department and the people who lead it has changed little in the last fifteen years. Within that finding we can see some evidence of increased formalization of HRM strategies and of HRM being represented at the 'top table' but also some evidence of a reduced involvement in corporate strategy formulation. The people who are leading the departments at the end of the first decade of the twenty-first century are not very different from those that led it fifteen years before although they are considerably more likely to be female. While we found only very limited evidence of a development of more strategic approaches, there is considerable evidence of the embeddedness of HRM within the countries and clusters in which it is carried out.

References

Almond, P., Edwards, T. & Clark, I. 2003. 'Multinationals and changing national business systems in Europe: Towards the "shareholder value" model?' *Industrial Relations Journal*, 34(5): 430–45.

Altrichter, H. & Gorbach, S. 1993. 'Professionalität im Wandel: Konsequenzen für Begriffsbestimmung und professionelle Ausbildung diskutiert am Beispiel der Personalarbeit'. *Zeitschrift für Personalforschung*, (1): 77–95.

Amable, B. 2003. *The Diversity of Modern Capitalism*. Oxford: Oxford University Press.

Apospori, E., Nikandrou, I., Brewster, C. & Papalexandris, N. 2008. 'HRM and organizational performance in Northern and Southern Europe'. *International Journal of Human Resource Management*, 19(7): 1187–207.

Becker, B. & Gerhart, B. 1996. 'The impact of human resource management on organizational performance: Progress and prospects'. *Academy of Management Journal*, 39(4): 779–801.

Blyton, P. & Turnbull, P. 1992. *Reassessing Human Resource Management*. London: Sage.

Brewster, C. 1995. 'Towards an "European" model of human resource management'. *Journal of International Business Studies*, 26(1): 1–21.

Brewster, C. 1999. 'Different paradigms in strategic HRM: Questions raised by comparative research'. In P. Wright, L. Dyer, J.W. Boudreau & G.T. Milkovich (eds), *Research in Personnel and Human Resources Management*. Stamford, CT: JAI Press, 213–38.

Brewster, C. & Mayrhofer, W. 2012a. 'Comparative human resource management: An introduction'. In C. Brewster & W. Mayrhofer (eds), *Handbook of Research on Comparative Human Resource Management*. Cheltenham: Edward Elgar, 1–23.

Brewster, C. & Mayrhofer, W. (eds). 2012b. *Handbook of Research on Comparative Human Resource Management*. Cheltenham: Edward Elgar.

Brewster, C., Mayrhofer, W. & Morley, M. 2004. *Human Resource Management in Europe: Evidence of Convergence?* London: Butterworth-Heinemann.

Brewster, C., Wood, G., Brookes, M. & van Ommeren, J.V. 2006. 'What determines the size of the HR function? A cross-national analysis'. *Human Resource Management*, 45(1): 3–21.

Buller, P.F. 1988. 'Successful partnerships: HR and strategic planning at eight top firms'. *Organizational Dynamics*, 17: 27–43.

Chhokar, J.S., Brodbeck, F.C. & House, R.J. 2007. *Culture and Leadership Across the World: The GLOBE Book of In-Depth Studies of 25 Societies*. London: Routledge.

Collin, A. 1998. 'New challenges in the study of career'. *Personnel Review*, 27(5): 412–25.

Croucher, R., Brookes, M., Wood, G. & Brewster, C. 2010. 'Context, strategy and financial participation: A comparative analysis'. *Human Relations*, 63(6): 835–55.

Djelic, M.-L. & Quack, S. (eds). 2003. *Globalization and Institutions: Redefining the Rules of the Economic Game*. Cheltenham: Edward Elgar.

Drori, G.S., Meyer, J.W. & Hwang, H. (eds). 2006. *Globalization and Organization: World Society and Organizational Change*. Oxford: Oxford University Press.

Eccles, R.G. & Nohria, N. 1992. *Beyond the Hype: Rediscovering the Essence of Management*. Boston, MA: Harvard Business School Press.

Farndale, E. 2005. 'HR department professionalism: A comparison between the UK and other European countries'. *The International Journal of Human Resource Management*, 16(5): 660–75.

Farndale, E. & Brewster, C. 2005. 'In search of legitimacy: National professional associations and the professionalism of HR practitioners'. *Human Resource Management Journal*, 15(3): 33–48.

Fombrun, C.J., Tichy, N. & Devanna, M.A. 1984. *Strategic Human Resource Management*. New York: Wiley.

Friedman, T.L. 2007. *The World is Flat: The Globalized World in the Twenty-First Century*. London: Penguin.

Goergen, M., Brewster, C. & Wood, G. 2009. 'Corporate governance regimes and employment relations in Europe'. *Relations industrielles/Industrial Relations*, 64(4): 620–40.

Golden, K.A. & Ramanujam, V. 1985. 'Between a dream and a nightmare: On the integration of the human resource department and strategic business planning processes'. *Human Resource Management*, 24(2): 429–52.

Gomez-Mejia, L.R., Balkin, D.B. & Cardy, R.L. 2004. *Managing Human Resources*, 4th edn. Upper Saddle River, NJ: Pearson/Prentice Hall.

Greer, C.R. 2001. *Strategic Human Resource Management: A General Managerial Approach*, 2nd edn. Upper Saddle River, NJ: Prentice Hall.

Guest, D. 1987. 'HRM and industrial relations'. *Journal of Management Studies*, 24(5): 503–21.

Guest, D.E. 1990. 'Human resource management and the American dream'. *Journal of Management Studies*, 27(4): 377–97.

Hall, P. & Soskice, D. (eds). 2001. *Varieties of Capitalism: The Institutional Foundations of Comparative Advantage*. Oxford: Oxford University Press.

Hofstede, G. 1980. *Culture's Consequences: International Differences in Work-Related Values*. Beverly Hills, CA: Sage Publications.

Hofstede, G. 2001. *Culture's Consequences: Comparing Values, Behaviors, Institutions and Organizations across Nations.* Thousand Oaks, CA: Sage.

Hofstede, G. & Minkov, M. 2010. *Cultures and Organizations: Software of the Mind,* revised and expanded 3rd edn. New York: McGraw-Hill.

Holbeche, L. 2002. *Aligning Human Resources and Business Strategy.* Oxford: Butterworth-Heinemann.

Hollingsworth, J.R. & Boyer, R. 1997. *Contemporary Capitalism: The Embeddedness of Institutions.* Cambridge: Cambridge University Press.

House, R.J., Hanges, P.J., Javidan, M., Dorfman, P.W. & Gupta, V. (eds). 2004. *Culture, Leadership, and Organizations: The GLOBE Study of 62 Societies.* Thousand Oaks, CA.: Sage.

Larsen, H.H. & Brewster, C. 2003. 'Line management responsibility for HRM: What is happening in Europe?' *Employee Relations,* 25: 228–42.

Larsen, H.H. & Mayrhofer, W. (eds). 2006. *Managing Human Resources in Europe: A Thematic Approach.* London: Routledge.

Legge, K. 2005. *Human Resource Management: Rhetorics and Realities.* Basingstoke: Palgrave Macmillan.

Lengnick-Hall, C.A. & Lengnick-Hall, M.L. 1988. 'Strategic human resources management: A review of the literature and a proposed typology'. *Academy of Management Review,* 13: 454–70.

Mayrhofer, W., Brewster, C., Morley, M. & Ledolter, J. 2011. 'Hearing a different drummer? Evidence of convergence in European HRM'. *Human Resource Management Review,* 21(1): 50–67.

Pendleton, A., Poutsma, E., Brewster, C. & van Ommeren, J. 2002. 'Employee share ownership and profit sharing in the European Union: Incidence, company characteristics and union representation'. *Transfer,* 8(1): 47–62.

Pfeffer, J. 1998. *The Human Equation: Building Profits by Putting People First.* Boston, MA: Harvard Business School Press.

Price, A. 1997. *Human Resource Management in a Business Context.* London: Thomson.

Rasmussen, E. & Andersen, T. 2006. 'European employment relations: From collectivism to individualism?' In H.H. Larsen & W. Mayrhofer (eds), *Managing Human Resources in Europe: A Thematic Approach.* London: Routledge, 212–36.

Reichel, A., Brandl, J. & Mayrhofer, W. 2009. 'Departmental status in light of a growing proportion of female staff: The case of human resource management'. *European Journal of International Management,* 3(4): 457–77.

Reichel, A., Brandl, J. & Mayrhofer, W. 2010. 'The strongest link: Legitimacy of top management diversity, sex stereotypes and the rise of women in human resource management 1995–2004'. *Management Revue,* 21(3): 332–52.

Ricks, D., Toyne, B. & Martinez, Z. 1990. 'Recent developments in international management research'. *Journal of Management,* 16(2): 219–53.

Scholz, C. & Böhm, H. (eds), 2008. *Human Resource Management in Europe: Comparative Analysis and Contextual Understanding.* London: Routledge.

Schuler, R. & Jackson, S. 2007. *Strategic Human Resource Management.* Oxford: Blackwells.

Schwartz, S.H. 1992. 'Universals in the content and structure of values: Theoretical advances and empirical tests in 20 countries'. *Advances in Experimental Social Psychology,* 25: 1–65.

Schwartz, S.H. 1999. 'A theory of cultural values and some implications for work'. *Applied Psychology: An International Review,* 48(1): 23–47.

Schwartz, S.H. 2004. 'Mapping and interpreting cultural differences around the world'. In E. Vinken, J. Soeters & P. Ester (eds), *Comparing Cultures: Dimensions in Cultures. A Comparative Perspective.* Leiden: Brill.

Tregaskis, O. & Brewster, C. 2006. 'Converging or diverging? A comparative analysis of trends in contingent employment practice in Europe over a decade'. *Journal of International Business Studies*, 37(1): 111–26.

Truss, C. 2003. 'Strategic HRM: Enablers and constraints in the NHS'. *The International Journal of Public Sector Management*, 16(1): 48–60.

Truss, C., Gratton, L., Hope-Hailey, V., Stiles, P. & Zaleska, J. 2002. 'Paying the piper: Choice and constraint in changing HR functional roles'. *Human Resource Management Journal*, 12(2): 39–63.

Tsoukis, C., Agiomirgianakis, G.M. & Biswas, T. (eds), 2004. *Aspects of Globalization: Macroeconomic and Capital Market Linkage in the Integrated World Economy*. Boston, MA: Kluwer.

Ulrich, D. 1997. *Human Resource Champions: The Next Agenda for Adding Value and Delivering Results*. Boston, MA: Harvard Business School Press.

Ulrich, D. & Brockbank, W. 2005. *The HR Value Proposition*. Boston, MA: Harvard Business School Press.

Wächter, H. & Metz, T. (eds). 1995. *Professionalisierte Personalarbeit? Perspektiven der Professionalisierung des Personalwesens. Sonderband der Zeitschrift für Personalforschung*. München, Mering: Hampp.

Watson, D. 1988. *Managers of Discontent – Trade Union Officers and Industrial Relations Managers*. London: Routledge.

Welbourne, T.M. & Cyr, L.A. 1999. 'The human resource executive effect in initial public offering firms'. *Academy of Management Journal*, 6: 616–29.

Whitley, R. 1999. *Divergent Capitalisms: The Social Structuring and Change of Business Systems*. Oxford: Oxford University Press.

Wright, P.M., Gardner, T.M., Moynihan, L.M. & Allen, M.R. 2005. 'The relationship between HR practices and firm performance: Examining causal order'. *Personnel Psychology*, 58(2): 409–46.

2

New Captain but a Sinking Ship? The Influence of HR Director's Gender on the Status of the HR Department – A Longitudinal Study

Astrid Reichel, Julia Brandl and Wolfgang Mayrhofer

Introduction

The past decade has seen profound transformations within the HR profession, one of which is the dramatic increase in the number of women (Reichel, Brandl & Mayrhofer, 2010). Today, in numerous industrialized countries, women represent the majority of HR specialists, and increasingly occupy managerial HR positions (Brandl, Mayrhofer & Reichel, 2008a). Such a rise in the proportion of women working in an occupation is termed 'feminization' (e.g. Philipson, 1993; Reskin & Roos, 1990; Roos, 1997). This chapter examines the effect of feminization on the status of HRM.

Although feminization is a very visible trend, very little research has been conducted on its implications for the status of HR. Scholars who have paid attention to the situation of women in HR (e.g. Pichler, Simpson & Stroh, 2008) have started to look at conditions that facilitate employment of women in HR, but not at the implications of occupational feminization on the strategic role of HR. Previous studies on the effect of rising numbers of women entering a field in other occupations – such as scientists and college administrators – provide evidence that the inclusion of women affects salaries, employment conditions and work focus of the respective occupations (Lomperis, 1990; Pfeffer & Davis-Blake, 1987; Roos, 1997). Research on strategic integration and other status variables is especially important for the field of HRM, because an apparent gap exists between the rhetoric about the essential role of HRM for delivering 'resourceful' humans and the reality HR departments face (Morris & Burgoyne, 1973; Skinner, 1981). Despite the centrality rhetorically assigned to HRM, the function often experiences marginality in practice (Gowler & Legge, 1986). HR departments are incessantly struggling to achieve strategic integration but have been reported to be among the lowest-status departments holding the least power in organizations (Guest & King, 2004; Kelly & Gennard, 2001).

For the occupational field of HRM, the few empirical studies that have been conducted on feminization effects suggest that rises in the number of women are associated with a simultaneous decrease in the occupations' salaries (Hardin, 1991; Roos & Manley, 1996). HRM, however, is not only an occupational field but also a function within organizations and, while for the HR occupation salary is an important status indicator, we chose a status variable that stresses the organizational perspective. More precisely we use *strategic integration* as an intra-organizational status variable. Although operationalizations of this concept vary, authors agree that it is a variable that captures whether the most senior HR specialist is part of the top management team and involved in creating the business strategy (e.g. Brewster & Larsen, 1992; Budhwar & Sparrow, 1997; Lengnick-Hall & Lengnick-Hall, 1988). Holding such a powerful position reflects a high status of HRM in the organization.

This chapter on the effect of feminization on the status of HRM starts with summarizing theories and empirical results that previously linked feminization and status variables. Then the meaning and high relevance of strategic integration for HRM within the organization and beyond is described. Based on queuing theory, social exclusion mechanisms and previous findings, hypotheses are formulated. After describing the samples and measures used, these hypotheses are checked using a quasi-longitudinal and a longitudinal design.

Conceptual background

Feminization and status of HRM

A large number of studies in various countries and professions shows that feminization (i.e. a significant increase in the proportion of women working in an occupation) is generally accompanied by a status decrease of the occupation, mostly measured as a decrease in income for both men and women working in the occupation (Perales, 2010). Negative status effects have, for example, been shown for college administrators (Pfeffer & Davis-Blake, 1987), university teachers (Lomperis, 1990) and clerks (Roberts & Coutts, 1992).

HRM is an occupational field that has a history of female dominance. Since its emergence at the beginning of the twentieth century there have been long periods in which women by far outnumbered men in HRM. The strongest influx of women into HRM so far has occurred between 1970 and 1990. For example, the share of female HR professionals in the US increased from 27.3 per cent in 1970 to 53.3 per cent in 1990 (Blau, Simpson & Anderson, 1998). Similar trends can be observed in other countries, including the UK (Legge, 1987) and Australia (Trudinger, 2004). Accordingly, HRM has also been interpreted as an occupation that 'suits women well'. '[P]ersonnel as a function dedicated to the management of people would seem to be an "ideal" job for women' (Gooch & Ledwith, 1996: 99). Trying to find reasons for why HRM should be especially 'suited' for women is typical for periods in which women outnumber men in HRM. At the beginning of the twentieth century, for example, the function was seen as social or welfare work and clearly reflected stereotypically 'feminine' activities, tacitly assuming that women are more altruistic, nurturing, caring and moral than men (Legge, 1987; Roos & Manley, 1996).

Scholars examining historical developments of the HRM occupation have observed a co-evolution of changes in female representation and the status of HRM. In the past, the inclusion of women in HRM has accompanied status loss or hindered its ability to gain full status (Simpson & Simpson, 1969). On the other hand, a decrease in numbers of women has paralleled an improvement in the occupation's status. In trying to account for these developments, scholars emphasized that the representation of women within HRM depends on the attractiveness of the occupation to men (e.g. Legge, 1987; Roos & Manley, 1996). As long as HRM is not perceived as an important function within organizations, men are not interested and leave the positions to women. When the occupation's perceived importance increases, men become interested in entering the field and displace women. A core argument for why women get displaced is that employers tend to prefer men for HRM as long as they are available for a job (Reskin & Roos, 1990). For example, when the growth of scientific testing instruments shifted the image of HRM from a welfare to a professional function, the share of male HR specialists increased (Trudinger, 2004: 104). A close relationship between status decrease and rise of women's representation or vice versa was also observed from the early stages of HRM until the end of the 1980s (Roos & Manley, 1996).

From the 1990s and 2000s there are no statistics on the proportion of women in HRM or status variables, much less their relationship. Less recent studies either relied on anecdotal evidence (e.g. Legge, 1987) or used pay as their sole status variable (e.g. Hardin, 1991). Our research comprises a period from the mid-1990s to the mid-2000s and uses a status variable that is not only relevant for the occupation but also takes into account that HRM is a function within organizations. Strategic integration is a status variable that compasses factors that capture HRM's status within organizations. We will elaborate below.

Various theories try to explain feminization and status loss in occupations. Yet the processes behind these status loss effects are not well understood. Two of the most popular concepts for explaining feminization and status loss in occupations are queuing theory and mechanisms of social exclusion.

Queuing theory (Reskin & Roos, 1990) argues that the inclusion of women into positions results from two effects. First, employers rank groups of potential employees into labour queues according to their attractiveness.

The existence of gendered labour queues reflects employers' preference of men for managerial jobs relative to their preference for women in such jobs. Second, employees rank potential jobs in job queues according to their attractiveness. Employees choose the most attractive job first, followed in line by those jobs lower in desirability. This implies that men occupy jobs within HRM, but also that they leave HRM jobs for other alternatives if they find HRM jobs unattractive. Of course, many factors account for the attractiveness of HRM positions. Men are more likely to leave HR in settings where they perceive that HR jobs do not correspond with the image of male employment and where men have opportunities. This opens up opportunities for women to access HRM positions. Empirical research in the US context (Roos & Manley, 1996) indicates that female HR professionals are more likely to reach managerial positions in HR when HRM as an occupation is less attractive for men. This implies that, in queuing theory, status loss leads to feminization of an occupational field.

Social exclusion mechanisms (Murphy, 1988; Reskin, 1993) analyse how powerful groups in organizations seek to maintain their position in the organizational hierarchy by excluding members from other groups with different characteristics from high authority positions. Exclusion implies that in the course of assignment of a female HR director, the HR department turns into a more administrative and less strategic function. Women are excluded from more powerful positions for many reasons: employers see women as better qualified for administrative work than for strategically integrated positions and provide them with less support for fulfilling their strategic role. In line with this explanation, Gooch (1994: 18) found that female HR managers in the UK felt excluded from organizational power networks. Supporting these subjective perceptions, a recent comparison of networking activities among male and female HR managers in Germany (Blickle & Boujataoui, 2005) revealed that female HR managers showed a tendency to network with less influential parties such as individuals from the same or lower hierarchical level or other women. Social exclusion mechanisms thus suggest that status loss is a consequence of feminization. This is also in line with devaluation theories. Their central proposition is that 'cultural processes of valuation are gendered' (Kilbourne et al., 1994: 694). Women, social roles and skills that are associated with women are culturally devalued compared to those associated with men (Kilbourne et al., 1994).

Strategic integration

In order to capture the status of HRM we will use *strategic integration*. While operationalizations of the concept vary, the key variables consistently used are top management team representation of the HR director and integration into the formulation of the business strategy (Brandl, Mayrhofer & Reichel, 2008b; Brewster & Larsen, 1992; Budhwar & Sparrow, 1997). Most authors concentrate on how strategic integration can help shape the quality of HRM in organizations (e.g. Lengnick-Hall & Lengnick-Hall, 1988). It is argued that a high degree of strategic integration allows the HR director and the HR representatives to have a long-term focus, linking business and HR strategic objectives and forward planning (Golden & Ramanujam, 1985; Sheehan, 2005) and to build an HR strategy and coherent HR systems consistent with organizational goals and strategies (Novicevic & Harvey, 2001). In contrast, lack of strategic integration involves the HR director primarily focusing on the implementation of HRM programmes or even on completing merely administrative and routine tasks (e.g. payroll administration, training coordination). There is a greater likelihood of emerging personnel problems requiring reactive problem-solving, with high costs to the company (Legge, 1978).

Some authors have realized that strategic integration has meanings beyond the possibility to create coherent HR systems (e.g. Reichel, Brandl & Mayrhofer, 2009). In this chapter we acknowledge the high importance of strategic integration for implementing and practising strategic HRM in organizations but argue that it also conveys information about the status of HRM in organizations.

Status in sociology is regularly defined as a position, condition or standing in a social structure that carries with varying degrees of responsibility, prestige and esteem (e.g. Andersen & Taylor, 2006; Brym & Lie, 2007). For HRM strategic integration arguably captures the position and standing of HRM in the social structure of an organization. A strategically integrated HR director is part of the organization's top management team and is integrated into business strategy development from the outset. Thus, the HR director has an influential position with access to strategic processes within the organization, which allows the position holder to participate in the strategic planning process right from the beginning by identifying relevant issues and by developing solutions for them (e.g. by formulating HRM programmes) (Purcell, 2001). Strategic integration also captures important aspects of power (Galang & Ferris, 1997; Provan, 1980). And while power and status are distinct concepts, still some bases of power confer status. Among them is recognition that someone is an expert, informed, legitimate or admired (Fiske, 2010). Formally being a member of the top management team confers power through legitimacy. Taking part in top management meetings and especially in strategy formulation leaves the HR director better informed than being excluded from these conversations.

Hypotheses

Continuing the trend of feminization starting in the 1970s in the US and the UK we suggest that the proportion of women working in HRM (on the staff as well as the director level) continued to increase between the mid-1990s and mid-2000s.

> *Hypothesis 1:   The degree of feminization in HRM has increased between the mid-1990s and mid-2000s.*

Summarizing the relationships suggested by queuing theory, social exclusion and devaluation mechanisms and taking into account evidence from various professional fields, we expect an increase in the proportion of women to be accompanied with a status decrease. To formulate the following hypotheses we use the argumentation put forth by social exclusion mechanisms because they take into account processes within organizations. Queuing theory in contrast focuses on the labour market level. Social exclusion mechanisms argue that when women get into HR director positions, the strategic integration level does not necessarily remain stable. Due to the tendency to exclude women from power in organizations, their inclusion into HR director positions in many cases may be associated with the decrease of the strategic integration of HR departments. Thus, on the aggregate level, feminization in a country will lead to a decrease in strategic integration.

> *Hypothesis 2:   Over time, an increasing degree of feminization of the HR department leads to less strategic integration.*

On the level of single organizations, social exclusion mechanisms suggest that when there is a change in the HR director position and a new female HR director follows a male one, strategic integration in this organization should go down because women will be excluded from powerful high-status groups (top management team) and decisions (strategy formulation).

> *Hypothesis 3:   In an organization, when there is a change from male HR director to female HR director strategic integration decreases.*

Method

Sample

The data for our analysis has been generated within Cranet (see the Introduction to this book), a research network dedicated to analysing developments in HRM in public and private organizations with more than 200 employees in a national, cross-national and quasi-longitudinal way since 1989 (Brewster & Hegewisch, 1994; Brewster, Mayrhofer & Morley, 2000, 2004).

At the outset, the two most important objectives of this international comparative survey were: (1) to research whether a pattern of convergence of HRM practices in the included countries can be found over time, and (2) to identify whether changes in personnel policies towards a more strategic human resource management approach occur (Brewster et al., 1996). Currently, more than 40 countries are part of the network. Each member country is

Table 2.1 Sample size

	1995	2004
Belgium	249	172
Denmark	534	405
Finland	175	209
France	353	94
Germany	274	196
Italy	67	84
Netherlands	211	241
Sweden	292	307
Spain	175	123
Switzerland	193	243
UK	968	839
Total	3491	2913

responsible for creating a sample representative of the respective company population. Postal and online surveys are filled out by HRM specialists, most often the HR director. Every four to five years survey rounds are conducted.

We will use two types of analyses: one takes a macro perspective and uses longitudinal trend-data; one focuses on changes within single organizations and uses panel data. The trend sample includes data from the Cranet survey rounds in 1995 and 2004 from 11 Western European countries. The choice of countries within Western Europe was guided by availability. Independent cross-sectional data collected in each year is seen as especially suitable when general developments at a higher level such as feminization of an occupation are analysed (Mayrhofer & Reichel, 2005). After excluding surveys *not* filled out by the HR director the total sample sizes were 3491 for 1995 and 2913 for 2004. Table 2.1 displays the numbers of companies included from each country.

Cranet from the outset was intended to gather trend data. Tracing specific organizations was not a primary goal. Accordingly member countries did not put any effort into creating panels. However, a limited number of countries used an empirical design that allowed them to identify organizations that have filled in the questionnaire in both rounds (and have not changed substantially between survey rounds). A number of such organizations could be identified between the two consecutive survey rounds in 1999 and 2004. So, part of the time span covered by the trend data could also be covered by the panel. A total of 212 organizations from the UK, Germany, Austria and Greece are part of this panel. According to hypothesis 3, those organizations that have changed their HR director during this time period are of special interest. Tracing the development in strategic integration when an HR director of one sex is succeeded by a new director of the other sex will give us more insight into effects of feminization and status.

In almost half of the organizations in the sample such a change took place. The respective sample size is 101 (UK 36, Germany 37, Greece 18, Austria 10).

Measures

The dependent variable is strategic integration of the HR director. The measure for *strategic integration* includes both potential ('formal') and enacted ('informal') forms of strategic integration (Galang & Ferris, 1997). Formal strategic integration is measured as representation of the HR director on the board (1 = yes, 0 = no) and informal integration as the degree of involvement in strategy formulation (3 = from outset, 2 = through consultation, 1 = on integration, 0 = not consulted). A composite measure with both items equally weighted ranges from 0 to 2.

We mainly use descriptive statistics to illustrate developments over time. However, previous research (Brandl et al., 2008b; Simpson & Lenoir, 2003) suggests that characteristics of the HR director, of the company and the country are likely to have an impact on the status of HRM. So, in order to be able to include control variables we will also use general linear models with year as the independent variable, thus testing for significant differences between points in time. We control for country. Controls on the organizational level are organizational size (log number of employees) and relative size of the HR department (percentage of employees that work in HR department compared to all employees of the organization). As individual characteristics of the HR director we measure education (academic degree yes/no), experience in HRM (number of years) and sex.

Findings

Table 2.2 shows that the trend of occupational feminization of HRM starting in the 1970s continued between 1995 and 2004. The mean percentage of female employees increased in all but one of the 11 countries (i.e. Denmark). T-tests reveal that the rise was significant in eight countries as well as in the combined sample. It also shows that the majority in HR departments in all the countries over all years is female. In total, an average Western European HR department consists of almost three-quarters women and a little more than one quarter male employees. This constitutes a significant increase compared to 69 per cent female employees in 1995. The column 'relative change' highlights the change in percentage based on the numbers of 1995. The highest relative increase is found in Switzerland, with more than 20 per cent points. For the total sample the mean percentage of women working in HRM increased by almost 7 per cent.

In contrast to the staff level, the director level is not female-dominated (Table 2.3). In 1995 the highest percentage of female HR directors was 31.5 per cent in the UK. The average percentage across all 11 countries in 1995

Table 2.2 Mean percentage of female employees in HR departments (staff level)

	1995	2004	Absolute change	Relative change in %
Belgium	57.05	65.45	8.40***	14.72
Denmark	78.69	77.92	–.77	–0.98
Finland	74.76	80.81	6.05*	8.09
France	72.18	74.85	2.67	3.70
Germany	62.39	66.87	4.48***	7.18
Italy	59.62	62.62	3.00	5.03
Netherlands	60.58	68.09	7.51*	12.40
Spain	50.58	54.39	3.81+	7.53
Sweden	68.58	71.85	3.27*	4.77
Switzerland	59.27	71.19	11.92***	20.11
UK	71.57	79.82	8.25***	11.53
Total	68.61	73.40	4.79***	6.98

Note: *** $p < .001$, ** $p < .01$, * $p < .05$, + $p < .10$.

Table 2.3 Percentage of female HR directors based on all HR directors

	1995	2004	Absolute change	Relative change in %
Belgium	14.1	25.0	10.9**	77.30
Denmark	30.9	42.2	11.3**	36.57
Finland	25.1	44.0	18.9***	75.30
France	22.4	31.9	9.5	42.41
Germany	6.2	21.4	15.2***	245.16
Italy	14.9	14.3	–0.6	–4.03
Netherlands	17.1	35.7	18.6***	108.77
Spain	9.7	15.4	5.7	58.76
Sweden	23.6	42.7	19.1***	80.93
Switzerland	14.0	32.9	18.9***	135.00
UK	31.5	58.9	27.4***	86.98
Total	23.0	41.2	18.2***	79.13

Note: *** $p < .001$, ** $p < .01$, * $p < .05$, + $p < .10$.

was 23 per cent. However, a massive rise in the number of women-led HR departments has been taking place. Chi^2 tests show a (highly) significant increase in the percentage of female HR directors in eight of the 11 countries between 1995 and 2004. As the relative change indicates, the percentage in Switzerland has more than doubled: 135 per cent based on 1995. In Germany, the proportion of female HR directors has more than tripled from 6 per cent to 21.4 per cent. Also countries such as the UK and Denmark that already showed relatively high numbers in 1995 experienced a significant increase over the years. On average we find a highly significant rise from 23 per cent to over 40 per cent (an almost 80 per cent increase). Hypothesis 1 is therefore fully supported: between 1995 and 2004 significant feminization of the HR function has taken place in Western Europe.

In order to see whether this clear feminization has the proposed negative effect on status we describe the development of strategic integration of HR directors between 1995 and 2004.

In contrast to the status effects known from the past, our data show a different picture. Despite strong feminization of the occupation at both the staff (Table 2.2) and director level (Table 2.3) the expected status effect (i.e. a decrease) was not found between 1995 and 2004. Table 2.4 displays the percentage of highly integrated HR directors as a percentage of all HR directors. Comparing the two columns displaying the numbers for all HR directors, we find an increase in the percentage of highly integrated HR directors in all but two countries. The rise in the proportion of highly integrated HR directors turned out to be significant in France, the Netherlands and Sweden significantly increased. Only in the UK and Finland does a decrease occur, which is in line with previous explanations of occupational feminization.

Using the change in mean strategic integration (Table 2.5) as a measure for status development, the picture is a similar one. In all but three countries total mean strategic integration increased between 1995 and 2004; in five cases this increase is significant. Only in the UK do we find a significant decrease in mean status. Note, though, that almost in all cases the mean strategic integration of male HR directors is higher than the mean strategic integration for women.

Table 2.4   Percentage of highly integrated HR directors from all HR directors

	1995			2004			Change Total
	Total	Women	Men	Total	Women	Men	
Belgium	41.6	28.1	44.0	47.9	41.0	49.2	6.3
Denmark	29.5	21.3	32.8	35.3	32.9	36.8	5.8
Finland	61.4	67.6	59.1	50.9	52.3	50.0	− 10.5**
France	53.3	44.3	55.5	72.3	59.3	79.6	19**
Germany	31.6	18.8	32.1	33.9	31.6	34.3	2.3
Italy	45.5	50.0	44.7	53.3	62.5	51.9	7.8
Netherlands	31.2	30.0	30.6	38.8	35.4	40.7	7.6**
Spain	56.7	46.7	57.9	56.0	43.8	58.1	−0.7
Sweden	53.3	58.7	51.4	65.4	62.8	66.2	12.1**
Switzerland	39.5	23.8	42.1	46.7	41.1	49.3	7.2+
UK	37.3	27.7	41.1	30.7	27.0	36.0	−6.6*
Total	41.0			42.5			1.5

Note: *** p < .001, ** p < .01, * p < .05, + p < .10.

Table 2.5   Mean strategic integration of HR directors

	1995			2004			Change Total
	Total	Women	Men	Total	Women	Men	
Belgium	1.35	1.02	1.40	1.56	1.36	1.62	.21***
Denmark	1.19	1.05	1.24	1.26	1.19	1.32	.07
Finland	1.61	1.64	1.60	1.48	1.47	1.49	−.13
France	1.63	1.51	1.66	1.85	1.75	1.90	.22***
Germany	1.18	1.17	1.25	1.25	1.16	1.27	.07
Italy	1.37	1.29	1.38	1.62	.62	1.64	.27**
Netherlands	1.19	1.18	1.19	1.35	1.29	1.38	.14**
Spain	1.65	1.53	1.66	1.51	1.48	1.52	−.14
Sweden	1.61	1.59	1.62	1.74	1.68	1.78	.13**
Switzerland	1.29	1.05	1.33	1.38	1.43	1.26	.09
UK	1.26	1.03	1.36	1.15	1.06	1.26	−.11**
Total	1.35			1.37			.02

Note: *** p < .001, ** p < .01, * p < .05, + p < .10.

Combining the descriptive results of the trend data on HR department feminization and status, we clearly find a strong feminization of the occupation between 1995 and 2004 for the staff as well as for the director level, and a concurrent increase of strategic integration. This provides initial evidence that feminization of HRM does not involve status deprivation through decreasing strategic integration. Although more and more women work in HR and HR directors' positions, the status of the profession has not declined in the decade between 1995 and 2004. Hypothesis 2 is therefore not supported by the data.

Of course these descriptions do not take into account other variables that potentially influence strategic integration of HR directors. Thus, in the next step we create a general linear model with strategic integration as the dependent variable. The main independent variable is year. Since we have seen that over the years the percentage of female HR directors and professionals has increased significantly, we use year as a proxy[1] for feminization and compare if strategic integration differs between the two points in time (1995 and 2004) while controlling for other probable influencing factors.

The model (see Table 2.6) confirms the descriptive results in producing a significant result for year. There is a significant difference between the strategic integration of HR directors in 1995 and 2004. Despite feminization of HRM, strategic integration significantly increases over the years. The level of strategic integration HR director's reach, however, is dependent on their sex, experience and education. Strategic integration also differs – as we have seen from the descriptive statistics – between countries.

To gain a better understanding of what happens to the status of the HR department when the HR director changes we use our panel data set and

Table 2.6   General linear model – strategic integration between years

	Mean sum of squares	f-value
Constant	2304.04	5859.28***
Year	1.52	3.86*
Education	27.89	70.91***
Experience	9.30	23.64***
Sex of HR director	29.09	73.99***
Relative size of HR department	.41	1.03
Size of company	1.17	2.98+
Country	17.96	45.67***
Error	.39	

Note: *** p < .001, ** p < .01, * p < .05, + p < .10.

Table 2.7   Mean strategic integration when HR director has changed (panel)

	1999	2004	t-test
HR director's sex	male	female	
Strategic integration	1.48	1.36	1.06
HR director's sex	female	male	
Strategic integration	1.29	.93	1.88+
HR director's sex	female	female	
Strategic integration	1.24	1.52	−2.39*
HR director's sex	male	male	
Strategic integration	1.45	1.39	.47

Note: *** p < .001, ** p < .01, * p < .05, + p < .10.

follow organizations over time. In Table 2.7 we describe strategic integration of the HR director for those organizations in which the HR director changed between 1999 and 2004. From a comparison of combined personal information about the HR director (i.e. sex, experience, education) we concluded that more than 70 per cent of the changes happened between same-sex HR directors; almost 50 per cent were male to male. There were 23 per cent between two women, 18 per cent from male to female and 10 per cent from female to male.

In almost all countries male HR directors play a more strategic role than female ones (see Tables 2.4 and 2.5). Likewise, the model in Table 2.6 displays a significant influence of sex on strategic integration. The picture does not change when looking at the panel data (Table 2.7), where we find that in 1999 male HR directors reach a higher level of strategic integration. Those HR directors entering (new) organizations, however, seem to find a different situation. When women start as HR directors – no matter if they succeed another women or a man – they are assigned higher strategic integration than their predecessor. Men, in contrast, are endowed with less strategic integration than their predecessor – male or female. Thus, we do not find evidence for Hypothesis 3.

Discussion

Our study takes a longitudinal and country-comparative angle and relies on two complementary perspectives, queuing theory and social exclusion mechanisms, which have turned out to be useful for explaining differences in the access to desirable organizational positions. In this way, we are able to take a fresh look at the effects of feminization on the status of HRM and, as our results show, question some of the prevailing notions, which assume universal and uniform effects linked with feminization in general and related to the status of HRM in particular. As a starting point, we expect that the feminization of HRM, that is, an increasing proportion of women working in HRM and a growing number of women in top HR positions, will negatively influence the status of HRM within the organization. From our point of view it is important to consider feminization at different hierarchical levels since previous research emphasizes that feminization at lower levels does not necessarily lead to equal feminization at the managerial level (Baron & Bielby, 1985; Goodman, Fields & Blum, 2003) because gender stereotypes still hinder the entry of qualified women into senior managerial positions.

Our results partly reinforce existing knowledge. We confirm that women are concentrated in lower-level HR jobs compared to men, that in general HRM departments are female and that in nearly all the countries analysed the proportion of women has increased since 1995. Our findings also show that, by and large, this is not only true for members of HRM departments in general, but also for the top HRM position. Overall, the number of women in HR director positions has nearly doubled, with some countries such as Germany, though starting from a low level, tripling this proportion. In addition, our panel data confirm the persistence of a gap in the status of jobs that men and women hold. Comparing strategic integration of female and male HR directors shows lower levels for women. Much of this is in line with a plethora of studies about the sex-related differences regarding power, influence and pay (e.g. Özbilgin, 2009; Zahidi & Ibarra, 2010).

Prima facie, part of this seems to be good news in the context of diversity and equality considerations. However, reasoning along the lines of queuing theory and social exclusion mechanisms provides some warning signals. A growing proportion of women in a profession or an organizational function definitely shows better access of women to the profession. Yet it may also indicate that men are increasingly leaving this profession or function because new alternatives are becoming more attractive and/or the current position loses status and is less appealing. Overall, we have comparatively little theoretical and empirical evidence about effects of variations in the gender structure within the HR departments and the consequences of the top HR person being either female or male. In particular, it is unclear whether jobs in the HR profession have lower status *because* HR jobs are held by women. Hence, it is necessary to take a closer look and also analyse the developments related to the status of HRM within the organization. Indeed, our data are only partially consistent with the traditional theoretical reasoning.

In the great majority of European countries analysed, we do not find any evidence for a negative effect of feminization on status. This finding is empirically quite robust when looking at this issue from different angles. The analysis of a panel subsample in four countries (Austria, Germany, Greece and the UK) strengthens the results of the trend study. An analysis of different job incumbent/successor combinations in terms of gender not only shows that the great majority of succession happens along the line of same-sex HR directors. It also reveals that there is no support for Hypothesis 3, stating a decrease of strategic integration in case of a change from male to female HR director.

Overall, our findings are not in line with the theoretical arguments used in this chapter. Social exclusion theory predicts that when women are hired for HR jobs, these jobs lose status because women face difficulties to defend a high-status position against pressures from powerful male groups in organizations. Yet, our study shows such an effect in only two of the countries. In essence, then, the data challenge the assumption of a universal negative effect of feminization on the status of an occupation – here: HRM. This raises the question why this is the case. Are the results HRM-specific or has the relationship between feminization and status generally changed over time? In any case the explanations and predictions from both queuing theory and social exclusion seem to be insufficient for our empirical evidence. The increase of HRM department status in some (but not all) countries in the wake of feminization and the parallel lack of a universal decrease point to different and more varied mechanisms at work. The demographic group power approach (Pfeffer, 1983; Pfeffer & Davis-Blake, 1987) can help us to account for the positive effect of feminization on HR department status. Proposing that different groups struggle over the allocation of resources (e.g., status, reputation), demographic group power research argues that the power of groups is determined by the relative number of its members. When the share of women increases, women can exercise more pressure and are more likely to maintain or expand influence in organizations. Our evidence supports this line of reasoning.

However, group power arguments alone cannot explain the negative status effect in those countries that have a high proportion of women. Drawing on an institutionalization perspective can be useful here. Institutionalization approaches explain differences in the nature of effects on status – negative or positive – by differences in the level of feminization of a profession. The proportion of women in HRM signals whether a particular profession (or job category) is 'women's work' (Pfeffer & Davis-Blake, 1987: 7). With increasing employment of women, jobs tend to get stereotyped as 'women's work'. Assuming that women's work has less status than men's work, labelling jobs as women's work leads to devaluation and status loss for job holders – irrespective from whether the actual job holder is male or female. Importantly, to be labelled as 'women's work', a profession must have been feminized to a considerable extent already. Our results that the two countries with the highest levels of feminization – UK and Finland – display negative effects on HR status while other countries show positive effects support such reasoning.

Limitations

Before turning to practical and scientific implications we would like to point towards some limitations of our research. The survey addresses top HR persons who should have the relevant information. Yet, for some of the data used here this might be questionable, for example, exact gender ratio in larger organizations. The sampling procedures when conducting the Cranet survey vary to some degree in the countries involved. Likewise, a slight variation in terms of the representativeness in the countries involved exists. However, neither issue has raised major concerns over the years of the survey when publishing the results. In addition, the operationalization of strategic integration as a core theoretical construct remains limited. While we are confident that in the light of the available data we have covered its major theoretical dimensions, it remains limited. For example, from a more process-oriented view of strategic integration, both informal and formal access to key decision-makers, beyond being represented at the top decision-making body, are missing. While these limitations caution us against too far-reaching conclusions from our results, we are confident that we can address a number of issues.

Practical implications

In practical terms, the study emphasizes the importance of gender demography within organizations. Changes in the gender composition of the workforce do have a number of effects – although not always in the immediately assumed directions (e.g., 'more women in HR departments will lead to more female top HR directors, which is a good thing when promoting gender and diversity issues'). The existing differences between HR departments led by women and men also emphasize the necessity of improving gender equality in today's organizations. This seems to indicate the need for institutionalizing such programmes.

Consequences for research

Our results raise a number of issues in terms of existing research. At a more fundamental level, the findings support a more contextual and multi-level concept of HRM in general and in comparative HRM in particular (see, e.g., Brewster & Mayrhofer, 2012). The data illustrate the role of various layers of internal and external context such as gender demography within the organization, national approaches towards the participation of women in various segments of the workforce for crucial HRM and management-related issues such as the strategic importance of HRM and its status. Mono-dimensional concepts of HRM without an adequate reference to these contextual layers are not able to grasp the full array of important influencing factors.

Along the same line of reasoning, the study also shows the importance of a comparative approach to HRM. Without any doubt, single-country studies do have their value when looking at a phenomenon, especially if they allow an in-depth view. Yet, it is through the systematic comparison of the same phenomenon and its explanations across a broad set of countries that we gain insight into both universal mechanisms and explanatory power of contextual factors. While this makes the resulting models and research more complicated, it also allows some progress to capture reality more deeply.

Regarding future research, we would like to highlight two important aspects. At a theoretical level, the study shows the urgent need for broader conceptual frameworks, which can enable researchers to combine several lines of reasoning coming from different theoretical sources. When we started this study, we expected, building on queuing theory and social inclusion, that feminization would have negative effects on the status of HR because of exclusion mechanisms at the organizational level. The results of our study and our interpretation, however, lead us to conclude that there are different mechanisms at work and that an institutionalization angle helps us to make sense of the findings. Yet, currently there is no existing framework that allows us to integrate these different theoretical viewpoints.

At the empirical level, more efforts are needed to gain additional insight into the more complicated mechanisms linking feminization and HRM status. To examine the group power arguments, for example, studies need to take into account changes in the gender demographic structure of organizations. The institutionalization perspective is appealing for explaining differences in effect directions between countries. When examining this argument, one important issue is what Pfeffer and Davis-Blake (1987) name the 'tipping point': the level of feminization at which HR becomes labelled 'women's work'. Identifying the tipping point is important to define when status loss tends to occur and why it affects both, male and female HR professionals. Here, we need studies that allow an in-depth look into the development path of organizations, requiring not only macro-trend studies but also panel-studies at the organizational level.

Note

1. We are aware that also other macro factors possibly influencing strategic integration such as new best practice models of HRM might have changed over time.

References

Andersen, M.L. & Taylor, H.F. 2006. *Sociology: Understanding a Diverse Society*, 4th edn. Belmont, CA: Thomson.

Baron, J.N. & Bielby, W.T. 1985. 'Organizational barriers to gender equality: Sex segregation of jobs and opportunities'. In A. Rossi (ed.), *Gender and the Life Course*. New York: Aldine, 233–51.

Blau, F., Simpson, P.A. & Anderson, D. 1998. 'Trends in occupational segregation in the United States over the 1970s and 1980s'. *Feminist Economics*, 4(Fall): 29–71.

Blickle, G. & Boujataoui, M. 2005. 'Mentoren, karriere und geschlecht: Eine feldstudie mit führungskräften aus dem personalbereich'. *Zeitschrift für Arbeits- und Organisationspsychologie*, 49(1): 1–11.

Brandl, J., Mayrhofer, W. & Reichel, A. 2008a. 'Equal, but different? The impact of gender egalitarianism on the integration of female/male HR directors'. *Gender in Management*, 23(1): 67–80.

Brandl, J., Mayrhofer, W. & Reichel, A. 2008b. 'The influence of social policy practices and gender egalitarianism on strategic integration of female HR directors'. *International Journal of Human Resource Management*, 19(11): 2113–31.

Brewster, C. & Hegewisch, A. (eds), 1994. *Policy and Practice in European Human Resource Management: The Price Waterhouse Cranfield Survey*. London & New York: Routledge.

Brewster, C. & Larsen, H.H. 1992. 'Human Resource Management in Europe: Evidence from ten countries'. *International Journal of Human Resource Management*, 3(3): 409–34.

Brewster, C. & Mayrhofer, W. 2012. 'Comparative human resource management: An introduction'. In C. Brewster & W. Mayrhofer (eds), *Handbook of Research on Comparative Human Resource Management*. Cheltenham: Edward Elgar, 1–23.

Brewster, C., Mayrhofer, W. & Morley, M. (eds), 2000. *New Challenges in European Human Resource Management*. London: Macmillan.

Brewster, C., Mayrhofer, W. & Morley, M. (eds), 2004. *Human Resource Management in Europe: Evidence of Convergence?* Oxford: Elsevier/Butterworth-Heinemann.

Brewster, C., Tregaskis, O., Hegewisch, A. & Mayne, L. 1996. 'Comparative research in human resource management: A review and an example'. *International Journal of Human Resource Management*, 7: 585–604.

Brym, R.J. & Lie, J. 2007. *Sociology: Your Compass to a New World*, 3rd edn. Belmont, CA: Thomson.

Budhwar, P.S. & Sparrow, P.R. 1997. 'Evaluating levels of strategic integration and devolvement of human resource management in India'. *International Journal of Human Resource Management*, 8: 476–94.

Fiske, S.T. 2010. 'Interpersonal stratification. Status, power and subordination'. In S. T. Fiske, D.T. Gilbert & G. Lindzey (eds), *Handbook of Social Psychology*, 5th edn, Vol. 2. Hoboken, NJ: Wiley, 941–82.

Galang, M.C. & Ferris, G.R. 1997. 'Human resource department power and influence through symbolic action'. *Human Relations*, 50(11): 1403–26.

Golden, K.A. & Ramanujam, V. 1985. 'Between a dream and a nightmare: On the integration of the human resource department and strategic business planning processes'. *Human Resource Management*, 24(2): 429–52.

Gooch, L. 1994. 'The career experiences of women in personnel'. *Women in Management Review*, 9(1): 17–20.

Gooch, L. & Ledwith, S. 1996. 'Women in personnel management – Re-visioning of a handmaiden's role?' In S. Ledwith & F. Colgan (eds), *Women in Organizations: Challenging Gender Politics*. Basingstoke: Macmillan Business, 99–124.

Goodman, J., Fields, D. & Blum, T. 2003. 'Cracks in the glass ceiling: In what kinds of organizations do women make it to the top?' *Group & Organization Management*, 28: 475–501.

Gowler, D. & Legge, K. 1986. 'Personnel and paradigms: Four perspectives on the future'. *Industrial Relations Journal*, 17(3): 225–35.

Guest, D. & King, Z. 2004. 'Power, innovation and problem-solving: The personnel managers' three steps to heaven?' *Journal of Management Studies*, 41(3): 401–23.

Hardin, E. 1991. 'The integration of women into professional personnel and labour relations work'. *Industrial and Labor Relations Review*, 44(2): 229–40.

Kelly, J. & Gennard, J. 2001. *Power and Influence in the Boardroom: The Role of the Personnel/HR Director*. New York: Routledge.

Kilbourne, B.S., Farkas, G., Beron, K., Weir, D. & England, P. 1994. 'Returns to skill, compensating differentials, and gender bias: Effects of occupational characteristics on the wages of white women and men'. *American Journal of Sociology*, 100(3): 689–719.

Legge, K. (ed.), 1978. *Power, Innovation and Problem-Solving in Personnel Management*. London: McGraw-Hill.

Legge, K. 1987. 'Women in personnel management: Uphill climb or downhill slide?'. In A. Spencer & D. Podmore (eds), *In a Man's World: Essays on Women in Male-Dominated Professions*. London: Tavistock Publications, 33–60.

Lengnick-Hall, C.A. & Lengnick-Hall, L.M. 1988. 'Strategic human resource management: A review of literature and a proposed typology'. *Academy of Management Journal*, 13: 454–70.

Lomperis, A.M. 1990. 'Are women changing the nature of the academic profession?' *Journal of Higher Education*, 61(6): 643–77.

Mayrhofer, W. & Reichel, A. 2005. 'Looking for the Holy Grail? Tracking human resource management developments over time – reflections on theoretical and methodological issues'. Paper presented at the 21st Strategic HRM Workshop, Aston Business School, UK, 30–1 March 2006.

Morris, J. & Burgoyne, J.G. 1973. *Developing Resourceful Managers*. London: Institute of Personnel Management.

Murphy, R. 1988. *Social Closure: The Theory of Monopolization and Exclusion*. Oxford: Clarendon Press.

Novicevic, M. & Harvey, M. 2001. 'The changing role of the corporate HR function in global organizations of the twenty-first century'. *International Journal of Human Resource Management*, 12: 1251–68.

Özbilgin, M. (ed.), 2009. *Equality, Diversity, and Inclusion at Work: Theory and Scholarship*. Cheltenham, UK & Northampton, US: Edward Elgar.

Perales, F. 2010. *Occupational Feminization, Specialized Human Capital and Wages: Evidence from the British Labour Market*. ISER Working Paper Series. University of Essex: Institute for Social and Economic Research.

Pfeffer, J. 1983. 'Organizational demography'. In L.L. Cummings & B.M. Staw (eds), *Research in Organizational Behavior*, Vol. 5. Greenwich, CT: JAI Press, 299–357.

Pfeffer, J. & Davis-Blake, A. 1987. 'The effect of the proportion of women on salaries: The case of college administrators'. *Administrative Science Quarterly*, 32: 1–27.

Philipson, I.J. 1993. *On the Shoulders of Women*. New York: Guilford Press.

Pichler, S., Simpson, P.A. & Stroh, L.K. 2008. 'The glass ceiling in human resources: Exploring the link between women's representation in management and the practices of strategic human resource management and employee involvement'. *Human Resource Management*, 47(3): 463–79.

Provan, K.G. 1980. 'Recognizing, measuring, and interpreting potential/enacted power distinction in organizational research'. *Academy of Management Review*, 5: 549–59.

Purcell, J. 2001. 'Personnel and human resource managers: Power, prestige and potential'. *Human Resource Management Journal*, 11(3): 3–4.

Reichel, A., Brandl, J. & Mayrhofer, W. 2009. 'Departmental status in light of a growing proportion of female staff: The case of human resource management'. *European Journal of International Management*, 3(4): 457–77.

Reichel, A., Brandl, J. & Mayrhofer, W. 2010. 'The strongest link: Legitimacy of top management diversity, sex stereotypes and the rise of women in human resource management 1995–2004'. *Management Revue*, 21(3): 332–52.

Reskin, B. 1993. 'Sex segregation in the workplace'. *Annual Review of Sociology*, 19: 241–70.

Reskin, B.F. & Roos, P.A. 1990. *Job Queues, Gender Queues: Explaining Women's Inroads into Male Occupations*. Philadelphia, PA: Temple University Press.

Roberts, J. & Coutts, J.A. 1992. 'Feminization and professionalization: A review of an emerging literature on the development of accounting in the United Kingdom'. *Accounting, Organizations and Society*, 17(3/4): 379–95.

Roos, P.A. 1997. 'Occupational feminization, occupational decline? Sociology's changing sex composition'. *The American Sociologist*, 28(1): 75–88.

Roos, P.A. & Manley, J.E. 1996. 'Staffing personnel: Feminization and change in human resource management'. *Sociological Focus*, 39(3): 245–61.

Sheehan, C. 2005. 'A model for HRM strategic integration'. *Personnel Review*, 34(2): 192–209.

Simpson, P. & Lenoir, D. 2003. 'Win some, lose some: Women's status in the field of human resources in the 1990s'. *Women in Management Review*, 18(4): 191–8.

Simpson, R.L. & Simpson, I.H. 1969. 'Women and bureaucracy in the semi-professions'. In A. Etzioni (ed.), *The Semi-Professions and their Organization*. New York: Free Press.

Skinner, W. 1981. 'Big hat, no cattle: Managing human resources'. *Harvard Business Review*, September–October: 106–14.

Trudinger, D. 2004. 'The Comfort of Men: A Critical History of Managerial and Professional Men in Post-war Modernisation, Australia 1945–1965'. Sydney: University of Sydney. Unpublished Doctoral Dissertation.

Zahidi, S. & Ibarra, H. 2010. *The Corporate Gender Gap Report 2010*. Geneva: World Economic Forum.

3
CSR and Responsible HRM in the CEE and the Nordic Countries

*Rūta Kazlauskaitė, Paul E.M. Ligthart, Ilona Bučiūnienė
and Sinikka Vanhala*

Introduction

The purpose of this chapter is to shed light on the debate about the congruence between the corporate discourse on corporate social responsibility (CSR) and the implementation of respective policies, and the contextual influences on this. This chapter will be based on Cranet data from Nordic and Central and Eastern European (CEE) countries.

Corporate social responsibility is becoming a mainstream issue and a global trend. The growing interest in CSR can be accounted for by the fact that, being intertwined with local communities and society at large, organizations have to perform the role of a social actor in order to stay in business (Schoemaker, Nijhof & Jonker, 2006). Additionally, organizations face pressures from multiple stakeholder groups to devote their resources to CSR-related activities (McWilliams & Siegel, 2001). Prior research on CSR has mainly focused on external stakeholders and organizational benefits, such as the enhancement of corporate reputation, customer attraction and retention, higher consumer receptiveness to new products and customer satisfaction (Branco & Rodrigues, 2009; Drews, 2010). In this chapter we address the issue of CSR from an internal stakeholder (current and potential employees) perspective, which has received a lesser conceptual and empirical attention so far. Specifically, we will study the adoption of HRM action programmes aimed at the integration of disadvantaged groups of society into the workforce.

Along with the pressure to engage in CSR activities, organizations are also expected to disseminate information about their CSR commitment on respective activities. Demands for greater CSR formalization, however, have evoked a debate among business practitioners and academics. It is unclear whether CSR discourse, or its formalization and communication, translate into more responsible corporate behaviour, or whether CSR is merely a public relations tool used to enhance corporate image. Empirical research on CSR formalization and actual engagement in CSR is still lacking.

Therefore, this chapter aims to test the linkage between CSR-related policy formalization and communication, and the actual corporate engagement in CSR-related activities, namely responsible HRM action programmes.

CSR is argued to be context-specific, that is, affected by various firm-level and country-level factors (Wanderlay et al., 2008), and the relations between the organization and its environment (Nielsen & Thomsen, 2007). This therefore requires taking into account the different interests of organizations that come from divergent organizational and national contexts. However, the impact of the context on CSR has been widely ignored in prior research, and only recently have comparative studies started emerging (Gjølberg, 2009). In this chapter we aim to compare and contrast the CSR formalization–implementation linkage between Nordic and CEE countries, which differ in their institutional and cultural contexts, and historical developments, and which according to prior studies show varying degrees of corporate engagement in CSR activities (Elms, 2006; Gjølberg, 2009).

CSR practice: Responsible HRM action programmes

Despite the great popularity of the CSR concept, CSR practice measurement still constitutes a major problem. This can be accounted for by a number of factors. First, no universally accepted definition of the CSR concept exists. Second, organizational engagement in CSR may be driven by different motives (which will be discussed in the following section) and may address different stakeholder groups.

We will not go more deeply into the debate over the meaning of the CSR concept and will refer to it broadly as 'beyond law', that is, voluntary actions pertaining to multiple fields of activities (World Business Council for Sustainable Development, 1999). In a broad sense, CSR practices may be categorized into five areas: corporate governance, natural environment, employees, local communities and business environment. Here we limit the scope of CSR practice analysis to one of the above five areas, employees, and study it through organizational engagement into responsible HRM action programmes.

What does responsibility mean in the HRM context? The CSR–HRM linkage is still largely under-researched. However, following prior works in the field, responsible HRM can be defined as a set of HRM policies and practices aimed at guaranteeing current and potential employee wellbeing, following the principles of equal opportunity, perceived fairness and business ethics (Bučiūnienė & Kazlauskaitė, 2010).

How does responsible HRM translate into actual HRM practices? In the Green Paper promoting the European framework for CSR (2001), speaking of the internal dimension of CSR and HRM, the European Commission refers to responsible recruitment practices, in particular non-discriminatory practices, which are expected to facilitate the recruitment of people representing ethnic minorities, older workers, women, long-term unemployed and people at a disadvantage. In a special appeal to CSR, among other priorities, the European Council (2000) emphasized the improvement of employability and furthering of all aspects of equal opportunities. Similarly, the World Business Council for Sustainable Development (WBCSD, 1999) referred to the involvement of and respect for diverse cultures and disadvantaged people.

The above listed CSR-related HRM practices make a clear reference to a critical need for better integration of the disadvantaged groups of society into the workforce. Integration in this case refers to recruitment, adoption of special training programmes to reduce their skill gaps and concern about their future, which involves career planning. Thus in this study we refer to responsible HRM as special action programmes aimed at recruitment, training and career development of disadvantaged groups of society.

CSR discourse: Communication and formalization

Recently organizations have been facing considerable pressures not only to engage in socially responsible activities, but to disseminate information about them too. Therefore, it is becoming increasingly important for organizations to communicate their CSR-related policies and activities. As a result, organizations develop formal CSR policies or informal agendas on CSR and choose different forms and means to report on their CSR activities.

CSR communication is generally aimed at providing information to legitimize one's actions (Birth & Illia, 2008). Organizations use a wide range of channels and forms of CSR communication (social reports, codes of conduct, codes of ethics, websites, advertising, packaging, etc.) and reporting (sustainability report, CSR report, social and environment report, health and safety report, etc.). The choice of communication channels to a large extent depends on the objectives of CSR communication, which vary from one stakeholder group to another. For instance, with respect to shareholders, such objectives rest on the development and maintenance of a favourable climate for the financial situation. With respect to customers, objectives include reputation, product differentiation and customer loyalty. Employee-related CSR communication is aimed at reputation building through word-of-mouth, enhancement of employee satisfaction and commitment, employer attractiveness and turnover reduction.

Demands for greater CSR formalization have evoked a discussion among both practitioners and academics. As regards the world of business, it is noteworthy that claims for transparency and accountability have pushed a lot of multinationals and larger companies to include their social and environmental activities in their annual reports or produce special CSR reports (Perrini, 2006). Small and medium-sized organizations, however, are rather sceptical about CSR communication and reporting and are more reluctant to follow such demands (Fassin, 2008). With regard to the public opinion, empirical findings show that, although there is an expectation among consumers and society at large that organizations engage in CSR, they do not appreciate excessive communication about such activities (Morsing, Schultz & Nielsen, 2008).

The academic approach towards CSR formalization, communication and reporting is also divided. Proponents argue that it is essential to report CSR actions. Not only does it make organizational actions more visible and measurable; it also leads to a more active engagement in CSR (Fassin, 2008). Critics of formalization, however, propose that possession of a formal CSR policy does not necessarily imply that it is actually being implemented (Welford, 2005). CSR has become a popular concept, and following this trend organizations are tempted to offer public declarations on their engagement in responsible activities in order to enhance their corporate image in the community. Therefore it cannot be argued that organizations that develop formal CSR policies and communicate them act more socially responsibly than organizations that do not possess such policies and do not engage in CSR-related activity communication.

As seen from the above debate, prior research has not come up with a clear answer to the question of the relationship between CSR discourse and practice. In this chapter, referring to the meaning of the CSR concept, where the main emphasis is on the principle of voluntarism, we propose that CSR formalization and its implementation through various responsible HRM programmes are interrelated (i.e. that the higher CSR formalization the more active is organizational engagement in various CSR-related actions). Respectively we raise the following proposition:

Proposition 1:   *CSR policy formalization is positively associated with organizational engagement in responsible HRM action programmes.*

CSR discourse and practice: Organizational and national context

CSR initiatives may be dependent on contextual factors (Werther & Chandler, 2006; Wanderlay et al., 2008); therefore, to understand the relationship between the corporate discourse and practice of CSR, it is necessary to recognize the specifics of the organizational and national contexts behind corporate engagement in CSR practices and their communication and formalization.

Speaking of the organizational context, it can be argued that CSR formalization and practice depend on the organizational size and industry. Larger organizations are more likely to invest more heavily both in CSR formalization and implementation in comparison to smaller ones. This has been supported by some prior research in the field. For instance,

Brammer and Millington (2006) found a positive relationship between firm size and philanthropic expenditure. As regards to industry specifics, CSR formalization may be higher in the banking and finance sector, chemical industry and manufacturing with high emission levels, as consumers and society at large look at them with higher levels of distrust. Thus corporate visibility is positively associated with engagement in CSR. For instance, findings of an empirical study on organizational participation in Responsible Care (a global voluntary initiative in the chemical industry) revealed that larger companies, those with better-known corporate names, dirtier companies (with higher average pollution levels), and companies from dirtier sectors would be more often found among the initiative membership (King & Lenox, 2000).

Sector can also be argued to have a significant impact on CSR discourse and practice, as traditionally the public sector is perceived as a model employer, specifically in terms of fair treatment of employees, guarantee of job security, equal opportunities, individual development and working conditions, clear career progression and strong internal labour markets (MacKenzie, 2002; Brown, 2008). Public sector organizations can therefore be expected to be more heavily engaged in various CSR-related activities and programmes.

The levels of CSR formalization and communication may also vary across different national contexts. For instance, governments may promote CSR policies to enhance international competitiveness, to encourage integration of the economically marginalized into the mainstream or to develop a better society (Aguilera et al., 2007). Empirical evidence also shows that country of origin has a significant impact on CSR (Wanderlay et al., 2008). In regard to CSR reporting, it is voluntary in most countries worldwide. In the past decade, however, growing numbers of governments within and outside Europe (e.g. Denmark) have launched regulations on sustainability reporting. Respectively it can be argued that firm and country-level variables have to be taken into consideration in studies on the relationship between CSR discourse and practice.

CSR in the CEE and Nordic country context

As mentioned above, CSR is considered to be context specific; therefore, to study the linkage between CSR policy formalization and implementation and to contrast it against different national contexts, two distinct clusters of European countries – Nordic and CEE – were selected. The two clusters differ in their institutional and cultural contexts, historical developments and degrees of corporate engagement in CSR activities (Elms, 2006; Gjølberg, 2009), which allows exploring country- (region) level effects on CSR policy formalization and implementation.

The Nordic countries are characterized by geographic and cultural proximity, for they share strong historical, linguistic, religious and ethnic binds, thus fulfilling the definition of a country cluster according to Clark and Mallory (1996). The Nordic countries are welfare states with generous social benefits, which are funded by high taxes and available for all. Another typical feature of Nordic countries is the egalitarian image of gender relations and a close cooperation between the social partners in the labour market: employee unions, employer organizations and the state (the so-called corporatist industrial relations system) (Byrkjeflot, 2001; Andersen, 2008).

What mainly justifies putting CEE countries in one cluster is their socialist heritage. During the socialist period the institutional context of the CEE countries was relatively uniform. After the fall of the Berlin wall, the CEE countries may have taken different developmental paths in their transition from a planned to free market economy; nevertheless, this heritage and current transition distinguish the CEE countries from the rest of Europe.

The two country clusters also differ in their CSR and HRM practices. According to several international comparisons, the Nordic countries rank highly in CSR activities. Applying an index of CSR practices in a study of companies in 20 advanced industrialized countries worldwide, Gjølberg (2009) found out that the leading CSR nations were Switzerland and the Nordic countries. In another study published by Accountability (2007), the Nordic countries were the most advanced in responsible business practices – all five Nordic countries among the top six, alongside the UK.

In contrast, in the CEE countries, the role and practice of corporate social responsibility is considerably weaker. CSR is commonly understood as corporate philanthropy (charity), or public relations/marketing instead of being viewed from a balanced stakeholder perspective. Among the probable causes is weak stakeholder activism in CSR in the region, mainly resulting from the socialist history of these countries (Elms, 2006). Until recently stakeholders could not make any demands on organizations and faced restrictions in consumerism, which has affected the attitudes and behaviour of citizens of these countries. Besides memories of the socialist indoctrination, to work for the good of the socialist country made people distrust the CSR rhetoric of 'common good' (Lewick-Strzalecka, 2006). Recently, however, CSR activities started gaining increasing support and popularity in the region (Elms, 2006).

The Nordic and CEE countries also differ in HRM. According to European-level comparative studies, Nordic HRM is more strategic, more formalized and more employee-oriented than HRM in other European countries (Vanhala, 2008). Ignjatovic & Svetlik (2003) have identified four European HRM clusters: Western, Nordic, Central Southern and Peripheral. The Nordic countries fall into the unique Nordic cluster, while the CEE countries are distributed between the Central Southern and Peripheral clusters. In the Nordic cluster, employees' involvement in HRM is higher, and flexibility and training policies are more common than in Central Southern and Peripheral country clusters, which focus more highly on managers and centralization of HR policy-making.

As depicted above, the Nordic and CEE clusters differ in multiple aspects – national contexts, historical developments, CSR perceptions and practice, and the HRM role. Countries within the two clusters may also be expected to differ in the levels of CSR formalization and implementation, where organizations in the Nordic countries are likely to demonstrate higher levels of both CSR formalization and offers of responsible HRM programmes. Taking into account the above regional CSR and HRM differences, we make the following proposition:

Proposition 2a: *The level of CSR formalization is higher in organizations in the Nordic countries in comparison to the CEE region.*
Proposition 2b: *The level of engagement in responsible HRM action programmes is higher in organizations in the Nordic countries in comparison to the CEE region.*

Research methodology

Sampling and data collection

The research is built on the 2008–10 Cranet survey data from 1719 companies from 13 European countries, comprising 5 Nordic and 8 CEE countries (Table 3.1). The respondents of the survey were HR directors/managers or employees with HRM responsibility. A total of 61.7 per cent of the respondents were from private companies and 38.3 per cent from public, non-profit or mixed (public and private). According to the company size (number of employees), the median organization has 350 employees. Most organizations operate in services (49.8 per cent) or manufacturing (25.0 per cent).

Measures

The Cranet questionnaire was used to measure whether companies had a CSR-related policy and what type of CSR-related practices they engaged in. CSR formalization was measured on the basis of the presence of a CSR statement, corporate values statement, diversity statement and code of ethics (see Table 3.2 for variables under study) on a three-point scale, where 0 = No, 1 = Yes (unwritten), and 2 = Yes (written) (see Table 3.2 for variables under study). A high level of CSR formalization means that a respondent organization has the above policies in writing, whereas the absence of the policies refers to a low CSR formalization.

Responsible HRM (RHRM) action programmes were studied through organizational engagement in the integration of disadvantageous groups into the labour force. Namely they referred to such action programmes as recruitment, training and career progression of the following groups of people: ethnic minorities, older workers, people with disabilities, women,

Table 3.1   Descriptive statistics of the respondent (company) characteristics

Determinants	Overall sample		Nordic cluster		CEE cluster	
Country						
Sweden (Sw)	16.2%		30.8%			
Denmark (DK)	19.0%		35.9%			
Norway (Nor)	5.2%		9.9%			
Finland (Fin)	7.4%		14.1%			
Iceland (Ice)	4.8%		9.2%			
Czech Republic (Cz)	3.1%				6.8%	
Bulgaria (Bul)	7.6%				14.7%	
Hungary (H)	4.2%				9.1%	
Estonia (Est)	2.8%				6.1%	
Slovenia (Slve)	11.6%				25.4%	
Slovakia (Slvk)	9.8%				21.2%	
Lithuania (Lith)	6.1%				12.4%	
Serbia (Serb)	2.2%				4.3%	
	100.0%		100.0%		100.0%	
European Region						
Nordic: Sw, DK, Fin, Nor, Ice	52.6%					
CEE: Cz, Bul, H, Est, Slve, Slvk, Lith, Serb	47.4%					
Industry						
Construction	4.0%		2.9%		5.2%	
Transportation/ Communication	6.7%		5.8%		7.7%	
Banking and Finance	7.8%		9.5%		6.0%	
Chemicals (energy; non-energy)	6.7%		5.0%		8.4%	
Other industries (e.g., services)	49.8%		57.9%		41.6%	
Manufacturing	25.0%		18.9%		31.0%	
Type of organization						
Public (or mixed) organizations	38.3%		41.0%		35.4%	
Private organizations	61.7%		59.0%		64.6%	
	mean	sd	mean	sd	mean	sd
lnSize	6.12	1.13	6.34	1.21	5.90	1.00
Size p50	350		430		284	
N = 100%	1719		898		783	

women returners, low skilled labour and younger workers (under 25) (see Table 3.2 for the variables under study). This comprised 21 RHRM practices (three practices applied to nine groups of people). A dummy indicator was used to measure the adoption of the above programmes, where 0 = No, and 1 = Yes.

Table 3.2   Percentage of companies having responsible HRM Action Programmes (AP) and CSR policies

Descriptions	Labels	Proportions of action programmes used			
Responsible HRM		Any action programme*** (dAP)	Recruitment (dAPR)	Training (dAPT)	Career (dAPC)
Minority ethnics	*minet	.14	.13	.08	.04
Older workers (aged >50)	*oldw	.16	.10	.09	.07
People with disabilities	*disab	.13	.09	.07	.04
Women	*women	.16	.14	.09	.11
Women returners	*woret	.10	.06	.07	.06
Low skilled labour	*lowsk	.17	.07	.14	.05
Younger workers (aged <25)	*young	.22	.14	.17	.12
CSR policies		**Written**	**Unwritten**		
Corporate values statement	CorpVal**	.65	.19		
Diversity statement	DivStat**	.36	.20		
Code of ethics	CoE**	.48	.24		
CSR statement	CSR**	.30	.24		

Notes:
* dAP, APR, APT or APC
** wr or un
*** any (one or more) action programme, irrespective of the activity (recruitment, training, and/or career).

Control variables

Prior research (e.g. Lindgreen, Swaen & Johnston, 2009; Wanderlay et al., 2008; Werther & Chandler, 2006) showed that such variables as organizational size, sector and industry may have an impact on CSR formalization and implementation. Therefore they were included in the study as statistical controls.

Data analysis

Data analysis comprised four stages. First, a hierarchical cluster analysis was performed to combine RHRM practices applied to different types of the disadvantaged into larger groups. Next, a correlation analysis was conducted to study the relationship between CSR policy formalization and engagement in responsible HRM action programmes. In the third stage, a multi-level logistic analysis was conducted to determine the regional impact, that is, CEE versus the Nordic region on the implementation of these practices and the existence of a formal policy when controlling for the initial country, organizational size and industry differences. Finally, a multi-dimensional analysis was performed to investigate the clustering of the RHRM action programmes and the CSR polices within the CEE and Nordic regions.

Research findings

As already mentioned, 21 RHRM action programmes were analysed in the study. Therefore first of all hierarchical clustering was performed to combine them into larger groups. The hierarchical cluster analysis (Figure 3.1) led to the identification of seven bundles of RHRM action programmes (indicated by a dashed vertical line). Namely, those are responsible HRM action programmes (each bundle including recruitment, training and career progression practices) adopted in respect to seven groups of disadvantaged employees: ethnic minorities, older workers, people with disabilities, women, women returners, low skilled labour and younger workers (under 25). Thus apparently the main focus of responsible HRM appears to be the group of disadvantaged employees and not a specific HRM practice.

Proposition testing

Following proposition 1, CSR policy formalization is positively associated with organizational engagement in responsible HRM action programmes. To study the relationship between CSR policy formalization and engagement in responsible HRM action programmes, a correlation analysis was performed. The results (Table 3.3) show that overall written CSR policies are positively correlated with responsible HRM action programmes. The unwritten CSR policies are mostly not significantly or negatively associated with responsible HRM action programmes. An exception is a weak but positive correlation between the unwritten CSR statement and responsible HRM action programme for low-skilled employees (rho = .0419). It is noteworthy, however, that the correlation between this programme and the formalized (written) CSR statement is higher (rho = .101). These findings support proposition 1 that expected a positive association between CSR policy formalization and organizational engagement into responsible HRM action programmes.

The second proposition was related to the regional (country) impact on CSR policy formalization and engagement in responsible HRM action programmes. To investigate the regional (country) effect on the RHRM action programmes and CSR policies, a multi-level analysis[1] was conducted, controlling for the country variation (level 2) and initial differences

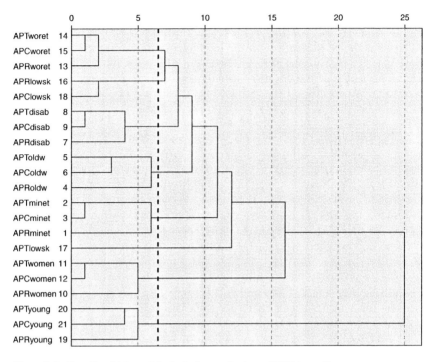

Figure 3.1   Results of hierarchical cluster analysis on RHRM practices

concerning organizational size, industry and sector (private or [semi-] public). Findings are summarized in Table 3.4 for every CSR policy being formalized or less formalized and in Table 3.5 for RHRM programmes. The significant odds-ratios reported in the tables indicate a positive effect if larger than 1 and a negative effect if smaller than 1.

Proposition 2a stated that Nordic organizations have more formalized CSR policies than organizations in the CEE region. The odds-ratios (OR) presented in Table 3.4 show that this is the case for two CSR policies. That is, the CEE region effect appears to be negative (i.e. the odds-ratio is below 1) for the formalized corporate value statement (CorpVal, OR: .162, p < .01) and the formalized diversity statement (DivStat, OR: .382, p < .05). In other words, CSR formalization is more likely among the Nordic organizations than among organizations in the CEE region. On the other hand, no regional effects are found in respect to the formalized code of ethics (CoE) and corporate social responsibility statement (CSR). With respect to the less formalized CSR policies, our findings show no significant differences between CEE and Nordic countries. These findings thus partially support our proposition 2a that expected a higher level of CSR policy formalization in organizations in the Nordic cluster.

Table 3.3 Spearman's correlation coefficients among the CSR policies (unwritten/written) and the responsible HRM programmes

	CSR formalized (written)				CSR unwritten				Responsible HRM action programmes						
	CorpVal wr	DivStat wr	CoE wr	CSR wr	CorpVal un	DivStat un	CoE un	CSR un	dAP minet	dAP oldw	dAP disab	dAP women	dAP woret	dAP lowsk	dAP young
CorpValwr	1														
DivStatwr	0.357*	1													
CoEwr	0.378*	0.426*	1												
CSRwr	0.322*	0.368*	0.389*	1											
CorpValun	-0.563*	-0.17*	-0.185*	-0.155*	1										
DivStatun	-0.036*	-0.364*	-0.084*	-0.066*	0.204*	1									
CoEun	-0.132*	-0.15*	-0.532*	-0.174*	0.258*	0.315*	1								
CSRun	-0.062*	-0.094*	-0.093*	-0.386*	0.209*	0.283*	0.304*	1							
dAPminet	0.151*	0.285*	0.180*	0.120*	-0.088*	-0.039*	-0.059*	-0.008	1						
dAPoldw	0.065*	0.066*	0.011	0.088*	-0.022	0.026	0.024	0.031	0.333*	1					
dAPdisab	0.032	0.125*	0.072*	0.099*	-0.027	-0.009	-0.011	-0.005	0.405*	0.421*	1				
dAPwomen	0.074*	0.186*	0.108*	0.133*	-0.042*	-0.034*	-0.023	-0.010	0.451*	0.415*	0.401*	1			
dAPworet	0.018	0.068*	0.018	0.096*	-0.008	0.001	0.018	0.028	0.244*	0.399*	0.322*	0.491*	1		
dAPlowsk	0.014	0.040*	0.041*	0.101*	0.019	0.018	0.002	0.042*	0.265*	0.350*	0.319*	0.289*	0.3282*	1	
dAPyoung	0.005	0.034*	0.040*	0.096*	0.002	0.023	0.011	0.021	0.229*	0.336*	0.317*	0.342*	0.3648*	0.430*	1

Notes: * p-value < .05.
Labels of CSR policies and RHRM action programmes: CorpValwr (written corporate value statement), DivStatwr (written diversity statement), CoEwr (written code of ethics), CSRwr (written CSR statement), CorpValun (unwritten corporate value statement), DivStatun (unwritten diversity statement), CoEun (unwritten code of ethics), CSRun (unwritten CSR statement), dAPminet (action programme for minorities), dAPoldw (action programme for older workers), dAPdisab (action programme for people with disabilities), dAPwomen (action programme for women), dAPworet (action programme for women returners), dAPlowsk (action programme for low skilled labour), dAPyoung (action programme for young workers).

Table 3.4 Odds-ratios for the determinants affecting the adaptation of the formalized and less formalized CSR policies by organizations

	CorpVal		DivStat		CoE		CSR	
	Unwritten	Written	Unwritten	Written	Unwritten	Written	Unwritten	Written
Region (refcat: Nordic region)								
CEE region	0.855 [0.433]	0.162** [0.0822]	0.621 [0.313]	0.382* [0.183]	0.945 [0.375]	0.573 [0.321]	0.869 [0.377]	0.577 [0.314]
Industry (refcat: Manufacturing)								
Construction	1.085 [0.275]	0.876 [0.283]	1.125 [0.482]	1.067 [0.373]	0.866 [0.450]	0.945 [0.250]	0.981 [0.325]	0.874 [0.264]
Transportation	0.853 [0.379]	1.231 [0.587]	1.197 [0.459]	1.728 [0.496]	1.146 [0.333]	1.268 [0.479]	1.498 [0.450]	1.048 [0.330]
Banking_Financials	1.196 [0.657]	2.366** [0.761]	1.488 [0.365]	1.233 [0.242]	2.123* [0.721]	2.274* [0.950]	1.832 [0.630]	1.796* [0.428]
Chemicals	0.550* [0.155]	0.906 [0.252]	0.789 [0.185]	1.415* [0.211]	0.84 [0.270]	1.173 [0.285]	1.615* [0.331]	1.383 [0.296]
OtherInd_services	0.654 [0.260]	1.326 [0.419]	1.353 [0.295]	1.646** [0.289]	0.986 [0.229]	1.271 [0.338]	1.128 [0.240]	1.035 [0.186]
Size of company (log)	1.184* [0.0847]	1.385** [0.109]	1.077 [0.0620]	1.338** [0.0575]	1.025 [0.0820]	1.298** [0.121]	1.144 [0.110]	1.310** [0.0774]

Private company (refcat: Public)	1.155	2.389**	1.482*	1.321	0.811	1.471	1.496	1.356
	[0.358]	[0.431]	[0.290]	[0.234]	[0.287]	[0.404]	[0.309]	[0.331]
Constant (L1)	0.669	0.741	0.253**	0.136**	0.953	0.301	0.179**	0.134*
	[0.383]	[0.576]	[0.121]	[0.0735]	[0.657]	[0.284]	[0.114]	[0.107]
Country (L2)	2.085**		1.891*		1.636		1.990**	
	[0.393]		[0.472]		[0.455]		[0.456]	
Model statistics								
Observations	1653		1590		1662		1581	
Log-likelihood (df = 19)	−1329**		−1580**		−1717**		−1611**	

Notes: Standard errors in brackets; ** p < 0.01, * p < 0.05; *Labels*: CorpVal (corporate value statement), DivStat (diversity statement), CoE (code of ethics), CSR (corporate social responsibility statement).

Table 3.5 Odds-ratios for the determinants affecting the adaptation of the action programmes for specific groups by organizations

	dAPminet Implemented	dAPoldw Implemented	dAPdisab Implemented	dAPwomen Implemented	dAPworet Implemented	dAPlowsk Implemented	dAPyoung Implemented
Region (refcat: Nordic region)							
CEE region	0.360* [0.161]	0.592 [0.310]	1.055 [0.444]	0.599 [0.163]	2.097* [0.668]	1.108 [0.361]	2.848** [1.031]
Industry (refcat: Manufacturing)							
Construction	1.431 [0.919]	0.598 [0.180]	0.862 [0.471]	0.909 [0.360]	0.945 [0.583]	1.565 [0.557]	1.756* [0.400]
Transportation	1.002 [0.332]	0.582 [0.161]	0.944 [0.256]	0.812 [0.194]	0.865 [0.327]	0.638 [0.166]	1.078 [0.286]
Banking_Financials	0.895 [0.207]	0.687 [0.153]	0.573* [0.126]	1.202 [0.271]	1.484 [0.400]	0.575 [0.232]	1.114 [0.213]
Chemicals	1.299 [0.524]	1.027 [0.282]	1.108 [0.345]	1.371 [0.438]	1.478 [0.456]	0.73 [0.148]	0.975 [0.257]
OtherInd_services	1.22 [0.254]	0.763* [0.0961]	1.105 [0.193]	0.963 [0.154]	0.981 [0.136]	0.804 [0.215]	0.839 [0.151]
Size of company (log)	1.397**	1.157*	1.250**	1.268**	1.215**	1.249**	1.121

	(1)	(2)	(3)	(4)	(5)	(6)	(7)
	[0.0976]	[0.0832]	[0.0611]	[0.0959]	[0.0876]	[0.0616]	[0.0684]
Private company (refcat: Public)	0.729	0.779	0.815	0.949	1.111	1.254	1.286
	[0.188]	[0.104]	[0.213]	[0.117]	[0.210]	[0.306]	[0.262]
Constant (L1)	0.0261**	0.119**	0.0353**	0.0605**	0.0211**	0.0509**	0.0729**
	[0.0182]	[0.0727]	[0.0150]	[0.0380]	[0.0113]	[0.0259]	[0.0294]
Country (L2)	1.823**	2.174**	1.987**	1.425**	1.530*	1.610**	1.682**
	[0.263]	[0.299]	[0.371]	[0.0973]	[0.285]	[0.206]	[0.138]
Model statistics							
Observations	1577	1576	1570	1569	1569	1567	1575
Ll	−604.3**	−674.4 n.s.	−597.1*	−713.8**	−534.1*	−712.9**	−790*

Notes: Standard errors in brackets; ** $p < 0.01$, * $p < 0.05$; *Labels*: dAPminet (action programme for minorities), dAPoldw (action programme for older workers), dAPdisab (action programme for people with disabilities), dAPwomen (action programme for women), dAPworet (action programme for women returners), dAPlowsk (action programme for low skilled labour), dAPyoung (action programme for young workers).

Organizational size, industry, sector and country-level effects on CSR policy formalization

The results show that larger organizations in general adopt more formalized CSR policies than smaller organizations (Table 3.4). The incidence of all four formalized CSR policies – corporate value, diversity and CSR statements and code of ethics – is higher among larger organizations. With regard to less formalized policies, a positive impact can be observed only in respect to corporate value statement.

Some significant differences in CSR policy incidences have been also revealed industry-wise. Importantly, organizations operating in the field of banking and finance appear to have more – mostly formalized – CSR policies implemented than their counterparts in manufacturing industry (reference category). Specifically, the latter organizations are more commonly in possession of formalized code of ethics and corporate value and CSR statements. Organizations in the chemical industry also scored more highly on a more formalized diversity statement and less formalized CSR statement than those in manufacturing. When controlled for the sector (private versus [semi-] public organizations), the data analysis did not reveal any significant differences with the exception of one more formalized CSR policy – diversity statement – and one less formalized policy – corporate value statement – which are higher among private sector organizations. Three of the four CSR policies were affected by the country component. Specifically there were significant differences between countries with respect to less formalized corporate value, diversity and CSR statements. However, country had no effect on the possession of a less formalized code of ethics or any of the four written CSR-related policies.

Organizational size, industry, sector and country-level effects on engagement in responsible HRM action programmes

Table 3.5 shows the effects of the determinants on the action programmes. In common with CSR policies, we also find a positive effect of the organizational size on the incidence rates of six out of seven RHRM action programmes, that is, all disadvantaged groups except for younger people. Industry barely affects the incidence rate of the RHRM action programmes. Organizations in the construction field appear to have more action programmes focusing on young people (dAPyoung) than manufacturers, whereas financial organizations offer fewer programmes for people with disabilities and service organizations for older workers. Sector has no effect at all on RHRM action programmes incidence rates. All RHRM practices appear to have a sizeable country effect, as shown by the significant level-2 country parameter.

Next, we conducted a multi-dimensional scaling (MDS) analysis to explore the observed similarities between the RHRM action programmes and

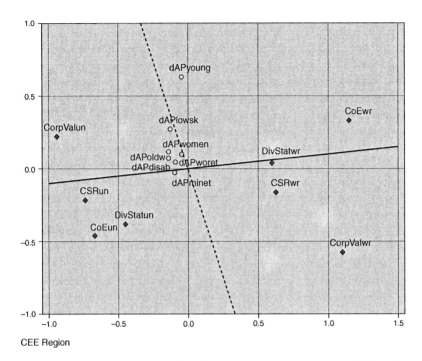

CEE Region

Figure 3.2 Multi-dimensional analysis of RHRM action programmes and CSR policies for the CEE region

Note: Distance for the common space is based on the binary Euclidian distance; Normalized raw stress level is 0.0167 and Tucker's Coefficient of Congruence is .992, N = 682.

the CSR policies. The MDS was conducted for the CEE and Nordic region separately in order to assess the regional differences (Figures 3.2 and 3.3).

The CEE findings (Figure 3.2) indicate a two-dimensional common space containing one clear dimension capturing the formalization of the CSR policies (solid line). The second, less distinctive dimension describes RHRM programmes for the specified groups (dashed line). The cluster of the action programmes is located more or less in between the less formal (unwritten) programmes on the left and the more formalized (written) programmes on the right of the common space.

The Nordic common space (Figure 3.3) also indicates one clear dimension for the formalization of the four CSR policies (solid line). The second dimension (dashed line), which is less distinctive, captures the cluster of the RHRM practices. Compared to the CEE's location of the RHRM practices, the RHRM practices in the Nordic common space are located closer to the less formalized (unwritten) CSR policies.

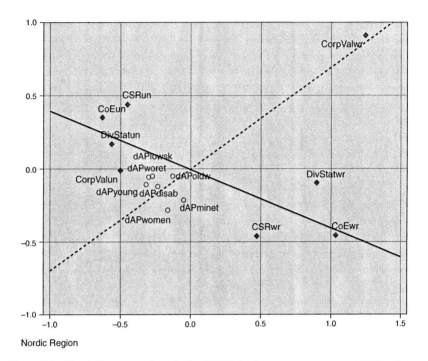

Figure 3.3   Multi-dimensional analysis of RHRM action programmes and CSR policies for the Nordic region

Note: Distance for the common space is based on the binary Euclidian distance; Normalized raw stress level is .0102 and Tucker's Coefficient of Congruence is .995, N = 921.

Both regions show distinct dimensions for CSR policies and RHRM practices, that is, one distinctive dimension for the extent of the formalized CSR practices and one indicating the cluster of the RHRM practices.

Discussion, limitations and conclusions

The overall aim of this chapter was to study the relationship between CSR discourse and practice and to look into contextual influences on them based on the comparison of the CEE and Nordic regions. Specifically, we looked into CSR policy adoption and its level of formalization, and organizational engagement into CSR-related activities, namely the adoption of responsible HRM action programmes. The first included such CSR-related policies as a corporate value statement, diversity statement, code of ethics and CSR statement. The CSR-related practice group embraced responsible HRM action programmes aimed at recruitment, training and career programmes for disadvantaged groups of people.

Overall our findings show a positive association between CSR policy formalization and engagement in responsible HRM action programmes. Possession of written CSR policies was found to be positively correlated with the adoption of all responsible HRM programmes, which implies that CSR discourse and practice are congruent, that is, organizations that have written CSR policies tend to be more engaged in the adoption of responsible HRM action programmes. These findings show that CSR is taken seriously by organizations and that it is not just a public relations tool.

Our research findings also revealed some region-specific differences in CSR formalization and involvement in responsible HRM. As proposed our findings revealed higher incidence rates of CSR policy formalization in the Nordic cluster, where more organizations possess formal diversity and corporate value statements than their CEE counterparts. These findings to some extent can be explained through the Nordic legislation on equality. For instance, in Finland organizations with 30-plus employees have to produce equality plans stating specific measures foreseen to guarantee equality between men and women and sexual minorities. Many organizations include other disadvantaged groups too.

As regards the adoption of responsible HRM programmes, our findings revealed significant differences between the two clusters only with respect to three out of seven practices: that is, CEE organizations seem to be investing more in the integration of women returners and younger people, while Nordic organizations are more concerned about minorities. On the one hand, these findings are surprising, as they do not support prior research findings that placed Nordic countries in the CSR leader group (Gjølberg, 2009; Accountability, 2007). On the other hand, current findings can be explained through the above-mentioned legislation on equal rights. Equality plans being a must, not surprisingly Nordic organizations score higher on addressing ethnic minority-responsible HRM programmes. As regards higher engagement of CEE organizations in women-returners action programmes, it can be to some extent explained by legislation in the region. In most CEE countries, women have entitlement to a maternity leave for up to three years after a birth of a child, and they usually return to work full-time. In most Nordic countries the leave is shorter and women are more likely to return to work part-time, as for instance in Sweden both parents may receive some compensation for lost working hours (Grimshaw, Rubery & Almond, 2011).

Lower than expected incidence rates of CSR formalization and responsible HRM adoption in the Nordic countries can be explained by a long Nordic tradition in social and ethical legislation, which can be traced back to the building of the Nordic welfare society (Nordic Council, 2012). Nordic welfare states, earlier than many other countries, were strongly fostered by legislation related to labour relations, social security, reconciliation between work and family, position of women and minorities, as well as environmental and CSR-related issues (Gjølberg, 2010). Owing to the legislation, organizations there face less pressure to adopt the above RHRM action programmes, as they are taken care of by the state.

Our findings also revealed that CSR formalization and engagement in responsible HRM action programmes are context-specific. To be precise, significant differences were determined between the Nordic and CEE region when organizational size, industry and country were controlled for. Larger organizations in general adopt more formalized CSR policies and responsible HRM action programmes than smaller organizations. In respect to industry, we found that organizations operating in the field of banking and finance tend to have more (and more formalized) CSR policies than those in the manufacturing industry; while organizations in the construction field appear to have more responsible HRM action programmes focusing on young people than manufacturers. Financial organizations offer fewer programmes for people with disabilities, and service organizations focus less on older workers. Sector has no significant effect on the responsible HRM action programmes and CSR policies with the exception of one more formalized CSR policy – diversity statement – and one less formalized policy – corporate value statement – which are higher among private sector organizations. Country has a significant effect in respect to less formalized corporate value, diversity and CSR statements, and all responsible HRM action programmes. These findings are to some extent in line with prior research in the field, which determined firm-level (Moura-Leite, Padgett & Galan, 2012), industry-level (O'Connor & Shumate, 2010), and country-level (Wanderlay et al., 2008) effects on CSR initiatives and policies.

Limitations

The chapter has certain limitations that should be noted here. First, the study of CSR implementation was limited only to organizational engagement in providing action programmes relating to recruitment, training and career progression of disadvantaged people. Therefore further research into CSR formalization and actual engagement should look at other responsible HRM practices, such as work–life balance, flexible work arrangements, fair performance appraisal and pay and work non-related skills development.

Secondly, corporate responsibility embraces a wider scope of responsibilities than the inclusion of disadvantaged people into the workforce. CSR policies may refer to stakeholder groups other than those listed above and fields of actions other than employees. Future studies could address such areas as corporate governance, the natural environment, local communities or business environment.

This chapter looked into the usage of responsible HRM action programmes in 13 European countries. However, the institutional and cultural contexts of the countries were not analysed in great detail and the analysis was limited to generalized regional context differences. Therefore to account for differences in CSR formalization and engagement in responsible HRM across Europe needs further contextual analysis. Future research could also look closer into the CEE country specific, for though commonly conceived as a uniform cluster the CEE countries are rather heterogeneous.

Future studies on the subject could try to address these limitations and contribute towards advancing research addressing the relationship between CSR and HRM. Our study provides some initial understanding that despite differences between Nordic and CEE countries, CSR is not just a public relations tool but is taken seriously by organizations in the countries of our study. Such understanding can inform not only research, but also practice, even national policy on how CSR can be more widely applied.

Note

1. STATA v12.1, gllamm (v2.3.20); Rabe-Hesketh & Skrondal (2005).

References

Accountability, 2007. *The State of Responsible Competitiveness 2007*. London: Accountability.

Aguilera, R.V., Rupp, D.E., Williams, C.A. & Ganapathi, J. 2007. 'Putting the s back in corporate social responsibility: A multilevel theory of social change in organisations'. *Academy of Management Review*, 32: 836–63.

Andersen, T.M. 2008. 'The Scandinavian model – Prospects and challenges'. *International Tax and Public Finance*, 15: 45–66.

Birth, G. & Illia, L. 2008. 'Communicating CSR: Practices among Switzerland's top 300 companies'. *Corporate Communications: An International Journal*, 13: 182–96.

Brammer, S. & Millington, A. 2006. 'Firm size, organisational visibility and corporate philanthropy: An empirical analysis'. *Business Ethics: A European Review*, 15: 6–18.

Branco, M.C. & Rodrigues, L.L. 2009. 'Exploring the importance of social responsibility disclosure for human resources'. *Journal of Human Resource Costing & Accounting*, 13: 186–205.

Brown, K. 2008. 'Human resource management in the public sector'. In R.S. Beattie & S.P. Osborne (eds), *Human Resource Management in the Public Sector*. London: Routledge, 1–8.

Bučiūnienė, I. & Kazlauskaitė, R. 2010. 'Disclosing the meaning of responsible human resource management'. *Proceedings of the 18th Annual Conference on Marketing and Business Strategies for Central and Eastern Europe*. Vienna: Vienna University of Economics and Business and DePaul University Chicago, 51–8.

Byrkjeflot, H. 2001. 'The Nordic model of democracy and management'. In H. Byrkjeflot, S. Myklebust, C. Myrvang & F. Sejersted (eds), *The Democratic Challenge to Capitalism: Management and Democracy in the Nordic Countries*. Bergen: Fagbokforlaget.

Clark, T. & Mallory, G. 1996. 'The cultural relativity of human resource management: Is there a universal model?' In T. Clark (ed.), *European Human Resource Management: An Introduction to Comparative Theory and Practice*. Oxford: Blackwell, 1–33.

Drews, M. 2010. 'Measuring the business and societal benefits of corporate responsibility'. *Corporate Governance*, 10: 421–31.

EC Commission. 2001. *Promoting a European Framework for Corporate Social Responsibilities*. Brussels: COM.

Elms, H. 2006. 'Corporate (and stakeholder) responsibility in Central and Eastern Europe'. *International Journal of Emerging Markets*, 1: 203–11.

European Council. 2000. *Lisbon European Council 23rd and 24th March: Presidency Conclusions*. Lisbon: European Council.

Fassin, Y. 2008. 'SMEs and the fallacy of formalising CSR'. *Business Ethics: A European Review*, 17: 364–78.

Gjølberg, M. 2009. 'Measuring the immeasurable? Constructing an index of CSR practices and CSR performance in 20 countries'. *Scandinavian Journal of Management*, 25: 10–22.

Gjølberg, M. 2010. 'Varieties of corporate social responsibility (CSR): CSR meets the "Nordic model"'. *Regulation & Governance*, 4: 203–29.

Grimshaw, D., Rubery, J. & Almond, P. 2011. 'Multinational companies and the host country environment'. In A.-W. Harzing & A.H. Pinnington (eds), *International Human Resource Management*. Los Angeles: Sage, 227–66.

Ignjatovic, M. & Svetlik, I. 2003. 'European HRM clusters'. *EBS Review*, Autumn: 25–39.

King, A.A. & Lenox, M.J. 2000. 'Industry self-regulation without sanctions: The chemical industry's responsible care program'. *Academy of Management Journal*, 43: 698–716.

Lewick-Strzalecka, A. 2006 'Opportunities and limitations of CSR in the postcommunist countries: Polish case'. *Corporate Governance*, 6: 440–8.

Lindgreen, A., Swaen, V. & Johnston, W.J. 2009. 'Corporate social responsibility: An empirical investigation of U.S. organisations'. *Journal of Business Ethics*, 85: 303–23.

MacKenzie, R. 2002. 'The migration of bureaucracy: Contracting and the regulation of labour in the telecommunication industry'. *Work, Employment and Safety*, 16: 599–616.

McWilliams, A. & Siegel, D. 2001. 'Corporate social responsibility: A theory of the firm perspective'. *Academy of Management Review*, 26: 117–27.

Morsing, M., Schultz, M. & Nielsen, K.U. 2008. 'The "Catch 22" of communicating CSR: Findings from a Danish study'. *Journal of Marketing Communications*, 14: 97–111.

Moura-Leite, R.C., Padgett, R.C. & Galan, J.I. 2012. 'Is social responsibility driven by industry or firm-specific factors?' *Management Decisions*, 50: 1200–21.

Nielsen, A.E. & Thomsen, C. 2007. 'Reporting CSR – what and how to say it?' *Corporate Communications: An International Journal*, 12: 25–40.

Nordic Council. 2012. Nordic legislative cooperation: http://www.norden.org/en/about-nordic-co-operation/areas-of-co-operation/justice-co-operation/nordic-legislative-co-operation [accessed 12 March 2012].

O'Connor A. & Shumate, M. 2010. 'An economic industry and institutional level of analysis of corporate social responsibility communication'. *Management Communication Quarterly*, 24: 529–51.

Perrini, F. 2006. 'The practitioner's perspective on non-financial reporting'. *California Management Review*, 48: 73–103.

Schoemaker, M., Nijhof, A. & Jonker, J. 2006. 'Human value management: The influence of the contemporary developments of corporate social responsibility and social capital on HRM'. *Management Revue*, 17: 448–65.

Vanhala, S. 2008. 'Nordic model of HRM? HR practices in the Nordic and other European countries'. In *HRM Global 2008, Sustainable HRM in the Global Economy. Conference Proceedings*. Turku: Turku School of Economics, 348–56.

Wanderlay, L.S.O., Lucian, R., Farache, F. & Sousa Filho, J.M. 2008. 'CSR information disclosure on the web: A context-based approach analysing the influence of country of origin and industry sector'. *Journal of Business Ethics*, 82: 369–78.

WBCSD (World Business Council for Sustainable Development), 1999. *Meeting Changing Expectations. Corporate Social Responsibility*. New York: WBCSD.

Welford, R. 2005. 'Corporate social responsibility in Europe, North America and Asia'. *Journal of Corporate Citizenship*, 17: 33–52.

Werther, W.B. & Chandler, D. 2006. *Strategic Corporate Social Responsibility*. Thousand Oaks, CA: Sage Publications.

4

HRM Policies and Firm Performance: The Role of the Synergy of Policies

Erik Poutsma, Paul E.M Ligthart and Bart Dietz

Introduction

For both academics and practitioners, an insight into the relationship between Human Resource Management (HRM) and performance is essential. In exploring this link, HRM scholars have arrived at a point where the universalistic approach of the performance effects of best *HRM practices* are criticized. In an effort to move beyond a best-practice mode of theorizing, scholars have proposed different bundles of HRM practices that relate to better performance (Huselid, 1995). An emerging stream of literature proposes that *systems* of HRM practices have synergic performance effects (e.g. Delery & Doty, 1996). Scholars from the latter research stream argue that systems of HRM practices in so called 'High Performance Work Systems' (HRM Systems) lead to significant effects on firm performance, and hence propose that 'ideal' systems of HRM practices (i.e. best-systems) lead to superior firm performance (Becker & Huselid, 1998). Against this backdrop, Delery and Doty (1996) called upon scholars to adopt a 'configurational mode of theorizing' and indeed sparked a plethora of research in search of ideal-type HRM systems (Becker & Huselid, 1998; Lepak et al., 2006). Taking stock of this field today, its theoretical and empirical advancement is still hindered by 'deficient empirical support', in part because researchers have focused on bundles of large numbers of practices. For instance, Guest et al. (2003) identified 48 HRM practices and grouped them into nine HRM domains, but concluded that these formed no coherent factors. Also, measuring and examining the interactions between large numbers of practices is empirically very complex (Martín-Alcázar, Romero-Fernández & Sánches-Gardey, 2005: 645). Individual practices' interactions with many variables are not as easily empirically testable. Some 20 years after the emergence of the perspective of HRM configurations, this perspective has yet to deliver on its promise.

In order to advance the debate concerning configurations of HRM, we propose to focus on the interaction of policies instead of interactions of large number of practices. We define policies as a coherent set or bundles of practices, which we further elaborate below. We argue for the need to investigate the interaction of policies. We follow the call of Collins and Smith (2006) and Cappelli and Neumark (2001) to look for interaction effects of policies and provide a theoretical rationale for these.

The present study aims to advance the debate on configuration of HRM systems and firm performance by empirically exploring the direct and synergistic performance implications of three specific HRM policies: (a) calculative policy (i.e. efficiency-focused), (b) collaborative policy and (c) collective sharing policy. As will be detailed, these HRM policies are theoretical extensions of the work of Gooderham, Nordhaug and Ringdal (1999), which delineate 'calculative' and 'collaborative' HRM policies. Drawing from the literature on profit sharing and employee ownership, we further distinguish a collective sharing policy consisting of collective rewards such as profit sharing and share ownership (e.g. Poutsma, Ligthart & Veersma, 2006; Rousseau & Shperling, 2003). The results show that the three HRM policies are positively related to firm performance. In addition, we demonstrate that an HRM configuration of *calculative* and *collaborative* HRM policies has a positive relationship with firm performance.

In search of HRM systems

In the mid-1990s, several HRM scholars argued that HRM practices are more likely to influence firm performance when conceptualized as a 'system', 'bundle' or 'configuration' (e.g. Arthur, 1994; MacDuffie, 1995). Building on configuration theory, which indicates that a pattern of multiple independent variables may relate to a dependent variable, Delery and Doty (1996) outlined the 'configurational perspective of theorizing' in HRM, which suggests that we should look for configurations of practices or policies. As a consequence, authors have since been developing numerous HRM configurations, and the extant body of literature on HRM configurations has grown rapidly (e.g. Kintana, Alonso & Olaverri, 2006; Evans & Davis, 2005). A common theme in the HRM configurations literature is the exploration of performance effects of 'ideal type' HRM configurations. In their quest for empirical evidence for the impact on firm performance of these configurations, a broad variety of ideal designs have emerged, such as: 'Traditional', 'Innovative', 'Calculative', 'Collaborative', 'Internal' or 'Market Type' HRM configurations (Ichniowski, Shaw & Prennushi, 1997; Gooderham, Nordhaug & Ringdal, 1999; Delery & Doty, 1996). However, the broad stream of HRM configurations literature has yielded mixed and conflicting results (Delaney & Huselid, 1996; Delery & Doty, 1996).

Scholars have been proposing several arguments for these unsatisfactory outcomes, such as the level of analysis (i.e. which parts of the workforce) (Lepak & Snell, 2002) or the measurement methods in operationalizing HRM systems of practices (Delery, 1998) and the limited rationale for the fit between practices (Kaarsemaker & Poutsma, 2006). After reviewing this literature (see also Lepak et al., 2006; Kaarsemaker & Poutsma, 2006), we conclude that one of the most prevalent debates in the field is about the theoretical underpinnings and the significance and strength of the HRM system–firm performance relationship. While the idea behind the systems notion has widespread appeal, the same cannot be said about agreement on the specific make up of HRM systems. Moreover, empirical evidence for synergistic relationships has been lacking, in part because researchers have focused on a single system of large numbers of practices. In this case, individual practice interactions are not as easily empirically testable. As argued by Lepak et al. (2006: 222), HRM policies can be described as programmes of employee-focused HRM practices that are grouped together based on an organizing theoretical logic. These policies aim to have an impact on performance by focusing on one or more HRM policy domains. HRM policies are implemented with specific HRM practices, yet a particular policy might be implemented by one practice in one firm and another in a different firm. If HRM practices are substitutable, in that one or more practices would be equally effective in the implementation of a particular policy, focusing solely on the practice level may limit our ability to find meaningful generalizing results. Studying a particular practice may mask the true relationship between the policy and any specific outcome. Therefore, we concentrate on policy-level HRM.

HRM policies

While authors have used many different labels for HRM ideal designs, a closer look at their meaning shows two general foci of HRM systems. Essentially, HR systems are either oriented towards high performance through investment in employees or towards a more administrative or controlling approach to managing employees (Arthur, 1992, 1994; Delery & Doty, 1996, Guthrie, 2001). Guthrie (2001), for instance, created a continuum HR system index with high scores reflecting high involvement and low scores reflecting a more control-oriented HR system. In a similar vein Gooderham et al. (1999) distinguished between calculative and collaborative HRM policies. Most of these ideal types have been presented as independent or opposing strategies. Given the complexity of most systems and the lack of agreement on the practices that make up these systems, we have chosen instead to focus on a smaller number of policies consistent with the two overriding foci of HRM systems described by Gooderham et al. (1999).

Calculative and collaborative perspectives

First, the *calculative* perspective emphasizes designing HRM systems to ensure that employees act in the best interest of the principal through such policies as closely monitoring performance and tying employee pay with employee performance. These policies would then be implemented with specific HRM practices that fit the individual firm's context. Second, the *collaborative* perspective emphasizes treating employees as active partners in the organization by sharing greater information with them and ensuring that they understood how they contributed to the success of the organization. In addition to calculative and collaborative policies we propose a third policy: a collective sharing policy. While the calculative policy focuses on monitoring the right abilities and efforts, and the collaborative policy develops a shared understanding of the goals, a third policy is needed to ensure that employees will disclose their tacit knowledge to raise labour productivity and innovation. Following Rizov and Croucher (2009), we argue that a policy that creates high trust in the exchange relationship between employee and employer develops this willingness on the part of the employee.

The calculative–collaborative distinction is useful but should be supplemented in order to capture high trust relations. Collectively sharing company-level benefits through profit sharing and employee share ownership is a policy that develops these trust relations since it signals to employees that owners and managers do not reap all the benefits that accrue from the increased efforts of the employees (Ferrante & Rousseau, 2001). Whereas the collaborative policy focuses on achieving partnership through employee communications and information sharing, the *collective sharing policy* aims to do so through giving employees a feeling of ownership, or, in the words of Rousseau and Shperling (2003: 553), a 'piece of the action'.

Whereas others have looked at the potential complementarity between practices, we are investigating: (1) the performance effects of HRM policies (i.e. direct effects), and (2) potential complementary performance effects between HRM policies (i.e. interaction effects). In the following section, we develop hypotheses for these performance implications. Our basic model is shown in Figure 4.1. We suggest direct effects on relative firm performance

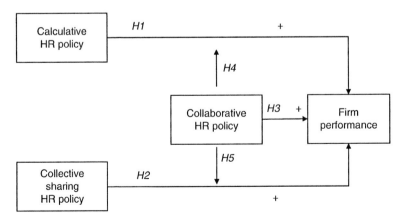

Figure 4.1   Conceptual model: HRM policies and business performance

from the HRM policies and two indirect (or moderator) effects: the effect of a calculative policy as well as the effect of a collective sharing policy on firm performance is moderated by a collaborative HRM policy. We now proceed first with an elaboration of the relationship of each policy with performance.

Calculative HRM policy

Gooderham et al. (1999: 510) argued that calculative HRM policies are 'efficiency seeking' and aim to supply the production activities with the necessary input of human resources. More recently, scholars have explored the performance consequences of 'HRM Control' strategies (Liao, 2005). We argue that one of the HRM policies is the 'Calculative HRM policy'. This policy coordinates HRM practices such as individual performance-related pay and performance appraisal in order to boost performance. From this perspective (individual) human behaviours are monitored and controlled. Through this control perspective potential deviations from efficient behaviours are relatively transparent and can be easily acted upon by management. Thus, a calculative HRM policy is likely to funnel workforce efforts into efficient behaviours, while at the same time behaviours that are undesirable (e.g. free riding) for firm performance are a transparent target for management intervention. Gooderham, Parry and Ringdal (2008) found support for a calculative policy effect. Therefore, we forward the following hypothesis:

Hypothesis 1:   The calculative HRM policy is positively related to firm performance.

Collective sharing policy

Empirical evidence in the financial participation literature shows positive impacts on performance from collective sharing HRM practices, such as profit sharing and employee share ownership. Sharing the surplus signals trust between employees and managers. When organizations have a collective sharing HRM policy, it is likely that individuals and groups inside organizations will be more inclined to engage in more cooperative efforts and align their interests with business outcomes. In an extensive study Kruse, Freeman and Blasi (2010) showed that these cooperative efforts indeed occur under these sharing and trust conditions and have a positive impact on performance. Conte and Svejnar (1990), Kruse and Blasi (1995), Sesil, Kruse and Blasi (2001) and Poutsma and Braam (forthcoming) found support for the positive relationship between collective sharing and performance. Our second hypothesis is:

Hypothesis 2:   The collective sharing HRM policy is positively related to firm performance.

Collaborative HRM policy

From the perspective of the collaborative HRM policy, it is argued that employees are viewed as active partners and core assets. And 'ideally, they are viewed as participants in a project premised on commitment, communication and collaboration' (Gooderham et al., 1999: 511). A collaborative HRM policy is based on an emphasis on management–workforce communication and cooperation. Consequently, individuals and groups are better informed on the goals of the organization. This is likely to increase commitment to these goals, as well as motivate alignment between organizational, team and individual goals. Guest (1997) and Rizov and Croucher (2009) found support for the positive relationship between collaborative policy and performance. We therefore formulate our third hypothesis:

Hypothesis 3: The collaborative HRM policy is positively related to firm performance.

Synergy between policies

Gooderham et al. (1999) argued that: although the calculative and collaborative approaches constitute two distinct sets of HRM practices consisting of dissimilar activities and techniques, they should not be conceived of as representing two different ends of a continuum; rather, they are separate (orthogonal) concepts (512). Others also emphasize the possibility of co-existence of HRM policies. Lepak and Snell (2002) suggested that certain policies are linked to different employment modes in the company, that is, differences in employment relationships targeted to different groups representing differences in human capital, for example, knowledge workers or workers in operations. Different employee groups may be treated differently. In a later study (Lepak et al., 2006), the authors indeed found different employment modes accompanied with variations in the HR configurations used to manage employees.

In addition, a theoretical rationale for the interaction of calculative and commitment policies comes from agency theory. It indicates that calculative behaviour of employees in line with incentives is more likely to lead to performance when employees are better informed about the incentives and how to obtain them (Eisenhardt, 1989). In view of this, we therefore posit that a collaborative policy increases the returns of a calculative policy. In terms of agency theory: an outcome-oriented contract becomes more efficient in combination with information about the outcomes that are expected. An additional argument for the existence of interaction effects is the 'disciplined worker thesis' as suggested by Edwards, Collinson and Rees (1998). These authors argue that workers have an interest in orderly and disciplined working environments with ultimately positive outcomes.

They contend that an HRM system that includes collaboration in combination with output control contributes to this orderly and disciplined working environment. A variety of information-sharing and consultative mechanisms ensure that employees are fully aware of workplace issues and have input to decisions. These features of the HRM system could be expected to increase the extent to which employees enjoy orderly and predictable working environments, because they are likely to increase control of work processes, development of detailed knowledge of production processes and access to information on outcomes of work processes. Because calculative policy generally involves measurement of performance against targets, and links performance to rewards, it should provide employees with a clear set of expectations as well as with feedback on performance, thereby increasing predictability and order.

A further argument for the interaction effect may come from organizational climate literature where organizational climate is seen as a moderator or mediator of the relationship between HRM and performance (Bowen & Ostroff, 2004). Organizational climate, defined as shared perception of what the organization is in terms of practices and policies, may be developed through collaborative policy, through communicating with and informing employees about the strategy and targets. Therefore, we forward the following hypothesis:

Hypothesis 4:　*The positive relationship of a calculative HRM policy with firm performance is stronger for organizations that have a high collaborative HRM policy than for organizations that have a low collaborative HRM policy.*

In the financial participation literature, the issue of complementarity between collective sharing and forms of collaboration has received much attention (e.g. Poutsma, Kalmi & Pendleton, 2006). Several reasons have been forwarded why HRM policies that are highly based on collective sharing can be complementary to a collaborative policy. In themselves, collective sharing plans are vulnerable to a free-rider effect: each employee may rely on other workers to deliver the enhanced output and performance necessary to bring about the incentive of profit sharing or share ownership. This is likely to be a significant limitation of these plans in all but the smallest work environment (e.g. Oyer, 2004). Collaboration may mitigate the free-rider problem by encouraging a co-operative corporate culture (Weitzman & Kruse, 1990) and/or mutual monitoring (Kandel & Lazear, 1992). At the same time, collective sharing signals trust relationships that can provide an incentive for employees to share information, thereby contributing to the collective performance (e.g. Ben-Ner & Jones, 1995; MacDuffie, 1995). As argued above with regard to the outcomes of the interaction of calculative and collaborative policies, here again a collaborative policy may provide for the proper organizational climate. We therefore formulate the following hypothesis:

> Hypothesis 5: *The positive relationship of a collective sharing HRM policy with firm performance is stronger for organizations that have a high collaborative HRM policy than for organizations that have a low collaborative HRM policy.*

The role of country

Differences among countries exist in the adoption and use of different HRM policies by companies (Gooderham & Brewster, 2003; Poutsma et al., 2006; Schuler & Rogovsky, 1998). Cultural and institutional theory provide explanations for these differences, where cultural approaches tend to use national cultural value dimensions (mostly Hofstede's dimensions) for their explanations (Schuler & Rogovsky, 1998), and institutional approaches tend to focus on regulatory frameworks such as labour law and industrial relations institutions (Hall & Soskice, 2001; Whitley, 1999). Gospel and Pendleton (2005) used the institutional approach and argued that the calculative HRM approach fits with liberal market economies since this approach emphasizes the 'market' to secure employee commitment. The collaborative approach emphasizes a more relational approach to secure employee commitment and tends to be found in coordinated market economies such as the Nordic countries. Schuler and Rogovsky (1998) used the cultural approach and found that the cultural dimensions of Individualism and Uncertainty Avoidance were related to calculative and participative HRM approaches. Participative approaches had a better fit with lower levels of individualism and higher levels of uncertainty avoidance, as found in Nordic countries. In addition, institutional factors may develop further and shape a legal regulatory framework that may be very specific to a country. For instance, higher scores for the collective incentive policy are found in the UK and France due to the fact that in those countries important tax benefits are gained when introducing profit sharing and share ownership schemes. In France a form of profit sharing is even mandatory for companies with more than 50 employees (Pendleton et al., 2003). An interesting question is to what extent we see country-specific interactions between policies that enhance performance (Boxall & Purcell, 2008). These possible country-specific configurations of policies are in line with research on the role of institutional fit where research is focused on the optimal level of conforming to institutional pressures while maintaining differentiation from competitors (Stavrou, Brewster & Charalambos, 2010). In this chapter we are not focused on this question but would like to see if main and interaction effects of policies on performance can be found beyond the different patterns in countries in order to discover the overall performance effect of the interaction of policies. Using country as an important control factor provides us with a robust test of the relationship.

Methodology

The sample of the present study has been derived from the Cranfield survey on Human Resource Management (i.e. Cranet), in 1999–2000. For the purposes of this study, firms were excluded from further analyses that were: (a) public or semi-public, and (b) employed less than 100 employees. While response rates for the individual countries were relatively low and generally varied between 12 and 35 per cent, analyses indicate no non-response bias. Table 4.1 in the Appendix presents an overview of the number of firms for the main explanatory factors and their categories within the data set.

Operationalization of HRM policies

Table 4.2 in the Appendix contains a list of variables included in each policy. *Calculative HRM policy* consisted of the following attributes: (1) performance appraisal, (2) formal evaluation of training and (3) individual performance related rewards. *Collective sharing HRM policy* consisted of: (1) employee share options, (2) group bonus and (3) profit sharing. *Collaborative HRM policy* consisted of (1) strategy briefings, (2) written mission statements and (3) written communication policies.

Based on the survey, we constructed scales for each HRM policy, based on multiple indicators using Kruder-Richardson KR20 (for reliability) and the more restrictive scaling procedure of Mokken's nonparametric latent trait model (Mokken & Lewis, 1982; Molenaar & Sijtsma, 2000). For this study, we used our database to analyse the items of Gooderham's (1999) calculative and participative HRM policy scales, as well as our collective incentive HRM policy scale, using the 'Mokken Scaling Program' (MSP; Molenaar & Sijtsma, 2000). Mokken's scaling approach is a probabalistic version of the deterministic Guttman model, which allows for the possibility that a subject responds positively to an item and negatively to another, 'easier' item.

Table 4.1   Descriptive statistics of the three HR bundles and business performance

	Labels	Mean	Stdev.	Calc*	Share	Coll	BP
Calculative HR	CALC	5.49	2.93	1			
Collective sharing HR	SHARE	1.95	2.29	0.21	1		
Collaborative HR	COLL	6.27	2.53	0.29	0.19	1	
Business performance	BP	5.04	1.69	0.16	0.17	0.15	1

Note: * All Pearson's correlation coefficients have p< .001.

Table 4.2 Regression coefficients of the three multi-level models (controls, generic, synergic) predicting firm performance

	Model 2 with control variables only		Model 3 with control variables, and generic HRM policy effects			Model 4 with control variables and interactions HRM policies effects		
	Control	SE	Main	SE		Full	SE	
Industry								
Construction	−0.548***	[0.161]	−0.450***	[0.156]		−0.468***	[0.156]	
Transportation	−0.148	[0.174]	−0.0668	[0.169]		−0.0801	[0.169]	
Banking, Finance	−0.0126	[0.146]	−0.109	[0.142]		−0.104	[0.142]	
Chemicals	−0.248*	[0.128]	−0.294**	[0.125]		−0.297**	[0.124]	
Other (e.g., services)	−0.284***	[0.091]	−0.264***	[0.089]		−0.268***	[0.088]	
Manufacturing *(reference)*								
Firm Size (log.)	0.226***	[0.032]	0.148***	[0.032]		0.147***	[0.032]	
Unionization								
Union_0 (reference)								
Union_6	0.0532	[0.147]	0.0364	[0.145]		0.0497	[0.144]	
Union_18	−0.129	[0.160]	−0.0808	[0.157]		−0.0713	[0.157]	
Union_38	−0.277*	[0.158]	−0.235	[0.155]		−0.235	[0.155]	
Union_63	−0.127	[0.158]	−0.105	[0.156]		−0.0891	[0.156]	
Union_88	−0.469***	[0.158]	−0.452***	[0.159]		−0.449***	[0.159]	
Union_mv	−0.126	[0.150]	−0.103	[0.148]		−0.0937	[0.148]	
HRM policies								
Calculative HRM policy (CALC)			0.0589***	[0.0148]		0.0628***	[0.014]	
Collaborative HRM policy (COLL)			0.0581***	[0.016]		0.0598***	[0.016]	

(continued)

Table 4.2 Continued

	Model 2 with control variables only		Model 3 with control variables, and generic HRM policy effects		Model 4 with control variables and interactions HRM policies effects	
	Control	SE	Main	SE	Full	SE
Collective sharing HRM policy (SHARE)			0.134***	[0.017]	0.137***	[0.017]
Interaction effects						
CALC x COLL					0.0137***	[0.005]
COLL x SHARE					−0.00633	[0.007]
CALC x SHARE					−0.00432	[0.006]
Constant	3.822***	[0.228]	4.460***	[0.250]	4.451***	[0.250]
Model statistics						
Variance firm level	0.002	0.001	0.189	0.078	0.190	0.078
Variance countries level	2.673	0.082	2.506	0.077	2.496	0.076
−2 log likelihood [a]	8260		8124		8114	
R-square [b]	0.051		0.110		0.114	
R-square change [b]	0.051		0.059		0.004	
Improvement LR test chi^2	110.3*** (df: 13)		135.99*** (df: 3)		8.76*** (df: 3)	

Notes: * p < .05, ** p < .01, *** p < .001.
[a] (Null-model (L1): −2 LL = 8369.3, N = 2153).
[b] Pseudo R-square (Cragg-Uhler).

In contrast to reliability analysis that assumes unidimensionality, Mokken's approach calculates an internal scaling criterion, or so-called 'Loevinger's H-coefficient', to evaluate the unidimensionality of a pair of items and the scale directly. The Loevinger's H-coefficient (H) signifies the deviation of the observed data structure of the scale from the perfect scalogram structure as incorporated in Guttman's approach. Following Mokken (1971), Molenaar and Sijtsma (2000) considered a set of items as a 'weak' scale if $0.3 <= H < 0.4$, whereas 'reasonable' scalability is reached if $0.4 <= H < 0.5$, and 'strong' scalability is considered if $0.5 <= H < 1.0$. A set of items with $H < 0.3$ is considered to be unscalable.

Overall, the three HRM policy scales demonstrated encouraging high levels of reliability (KR20 respectively: 0.81, 0.84 and 0.79), besides the satisfying scalability (based on the Loevinger's H-coefficient) of the scales (see Appendix, Table 4.2). Note that the HRM scales included a *coverage* dimension: the higher the score, the more categories of personnel are covered by the system of practices. This makes the scales very useful for our analysis of variations in the degree of use of HRM policies. Within each scheme, practices appeared to be most commonly adopted at higher hierarchical levels than at lower ones. Firms implemented – on average – mostly calculative HRM practices, followed by collaborative practices. Relative to the scale maximum, firms generally appeared to be most active concerning the collaborative HRM practices. In both absolute and relative terms, the number of firms that implemented the collective sharing schemes was small.

Firm performance

Following Laursen and Foss (2003), we adopted a multi-dimensional definition of firm performance covering seven performance indicators. We included the following perceptual financial indicators: (1) gross revenue, (2) stock market performance and (3) profitability, as well as non-financial indicators: (4) innovation rate, (5) productivity, (6) service quality and (7) market-time relative to other organizations in the company's sector. The use of perceptual measures of firm performance is consistent with prior research in Strategic HRM (e.g. Delaney & Huselid, 1996; Stavrou, 2005).[1] The reliability analyses showed satisfying R-squares indicating a common variance between the items and the remaining items with each scale. The Loevinger's H-coefficient of this scale shows satisfactory high levels of reliability (See Appendix, Table 4.3).

Since the Cranet data set includes firm-level data (N = 2153) nested in 18 countries, we conducted a multi-level random-intercept regression model using STATA's (v12.1) program GLLAMM (v2.3.20; Rabe-Hesketh & Skrondal, 2004, 2005). A traditional analysis of these data using only OLS-regression would violate the independency assumption and would result in unreliable standard deviations and hypothesis testing (Snijders & Bosker, 1999).

Results

Table 4.1 presents the descriptive statistics of the main variables. The results in Table 4.1 demonstrate that all three HRM policies were, on a *bivariate* level, positively related to firm performance.

The results of the regression analyses for firm performance of the three HRM policies are summarized in Table 4.2.

The first three hypotheses predicted a positive main effect on the firm performance for each HRM policy. Testing only these main effects (Table 4.2, model 3), the results confirmed the positive main performance effects of calculative HRM policy (i.e. CALC), collaborative HRM policy (i.e. COLL) and of the collective sharing HRM policy (i.e. SHARE). Based on their relative importance (i.e. Beta coefficient), collective sharing policy affected the firm performance most. Introducing the interaction effect of the collaborative policy on the performance relationship of the calculative and collective sharing policies, the main effects of all three policies remained supporting hypotheses 1, 2 and 3. The two interaction effects of *Collaborative HRM ⋆ Calculative HRM* and *Collaborative HRM ⋆ Collective sharing HRM* show support for hypothesis 4 and not for hypothesis 5. Results confirmed the predicted complementarity effect of a collaborative HRM policy on the performance effects of a calculative HRM policy. The performance effects of calculative HRM policy increased if combined with collaborative practices. The results of this interaction are presented in Figure 4.2. Although predicted by hypothesis 5, the collaborative HRM policy did not result in complementary effects on firm performance by a *collective sharing* HRM policy. Apparently, a collaborative HRM policy does not generate additional information for the workforce to increase the effectiveness of a collective

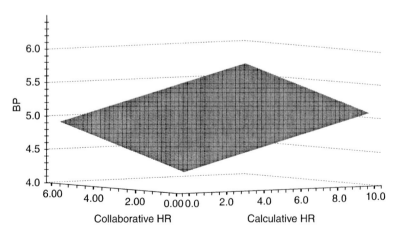

Figure 4.2   Synergic effects of calculative HR and collaborative HR on business performance (BP)

sharing HRM policy. Although not hypothesized, the interaction effect of calculative and collective sharing HRM policies appeared to be insignificant. It must be noted that the magnitude of the relationships is relatively small. Discussing the magnitudes of the relationship of policies with performance, Gooderham et al. (2008) suggested that country may be an important mediator for the policies and suggest future research to cover this.

Discussion

The present study presents two major findings. It provides empirical evidence for the configurational perspective on HRM (Delery & Doty, 1996). In sum, while many scholars have found non-relationships between HRM systems and firm performance (Delaney & Huselid, 1996; Delery & Doty, 1996; Ahmad & Schroeder, 2003), and authors have concluded that HRM systems may be 'unwarranted' (Godard, 2004), our study invigorates the field by a focus on the policy level in designing HRM systems. The calculative collaborative and collective sharing HRM policies have a positive relationship with firm performance.

Second, our study shows that HRM policies can reinforce each other's performance effects. More specifically, our findings indicate that HRM directors who have designed their HRM strategy around a calculative HRM policy may benefit more from this HRM policy, if it is complemented by a collaborative HRM policy.

From a theoretical perspective, these findings should guide researchers seeking to look for optimal HRM systems leading to superior performance. Whereas the search for these systems appears logical from the configurational practices perspective, we call upon researchers to move *beyond* the practices level and further explore potential interaction effects between HRM policies in their relationship with firm performance.

The finding that calculative and collaborative policies are complementary strikes a balance between the two different perspectives in HRM, between the 'hard' and the 'soft' approach. This resembles the notion of *ambidexterity* in the strategic management literature (Jansen, Volberda & Van Den Bosch, 2005). Implementing a calculative *and* collaborative HRM policy in chorus challenges managers to engage in simultaneous 'exploitation' and – in addition – 'exploration' of the workforce.

This ambidextrous HRM could be interpreted as an HRM principle (Colbert, 2004), and could be a fruitful avenue for future research. Researchers could, for instance, investigate the implications of our findings for the relational (i.e. collaborative) and transactional (i.e. calculative) employment relationship and the implications for the functioning of the 'psychological contract' (e.g. Robinson, 1996). Recent insights in the leadership literature have also pointed in this direction, by suggesting interaction effects between transactional and transformational leadership. Also, research in strategic management has pointed in this direction by showing that relational governance and formal contracting are complementary (Poppo & Zenger, 2002). Thus, whereas researchers in High Performance Work Systems (HPWS) have argued that practitioners should strategically align HRM practices to form HPWS that are collaborative, we advocate further research on how different policies can comprise an internal fit with each other and reinforce one another.

Among others, a fruitful venue would be to take up the disciplined worker thesis of Edwards, Collinson & Rees (1998), which suggests that employees have an interest in both policies since it contributes to a predictable and orderly work environment. Limited research has found support for this thesis (Harley, Sargent & Allen, 2010).

Another focus of research on the possible positive association between policies is a follow up to the HR architecture model (Lepak & Snell, 2002) in dealing with the issue of different employee groups. This is based on the configurational view, which argues that it is unlikely that a company will use a single approach for all its employees. The positive interaction effect of calculative and collaborative policy may have to do with the fact that each policy is targeted to different employee workforce categories where each group reacts to their target policies with improved performance levels simultaneously. Research results find indications of this.

This finding calls for more empirical research on the *multi-level* implications of collective sharing schemes. For HRM systems research, this could imply that study designs exploring 'cross-level interactions' could yield valuable insights. Scholars could, for instance, investigate the effects of HRM policies from a *within*-group (e.g. between individual employees), as well as a *between*-group (e.g. between different segments of the workforce) perspective.

In addition, our study analysed HRM systems beyond the two policies of Gooderham et al. (1999) and conceptualized a third HRM policy: a *collective sharing* HRM policy. While this HRM policy had a significant relationship with firm performance, it did not predict performance in combination with an HRM policy of collaboration (Hypothesis 3).

Another line of research would be to explore the role of country. The descriptive analysis showed country-specific HRM policy profiles, yet no country-specific differences in firm performance. These results imply an important venue for further research. Cultural and institutional conceptualizations explain country-specific differences in the use of policies. One possible research perspective would be to investigate specific interactions of policies in countries and the impact on performance. Rizov and Croucher (2009) performed such an analysis and showed, for instance, that a collaborative policy is related to firm performance where national institutions support this policy.

In the tradition of the Strategic HRM literature, we have investigated the relationships of HRM variables with firm performance. In the present study, we operationalized firm performance as a composite of multiple underlying facets, such as: *productivity*, *service quality* and *innovation rate*. We like to call upon researchers to investigate differential effects of HRM policies, on different aspects of firm performance. This could yield a more fine-grained insight in the link between HRM systems and performance, allowing managers to better craft, and subsequently pinpoint their HRM policies. In addition, although there is evidence that self-report measures of firm performance show convergent construct validity with objective measures (Wall et al., 2004), we suggest that future research include objective measures.

One limitation of this study is that it is based on cross-sectional data, which limits our ability to infer strong causal claims. We call upon future researchers to design studies that adhere to the requirements of inferring causal HRM–performance relationships: covariation between cause and effect, time precedence and the possibility of controlling for, or ruling out, alternative explanations for a relationship (Paauwe, 2009).

Finally, our study focused on the HRM–performance relationship from the configurational perspective. Hence, we conceptually and empirically designed our study to test direct and moderating relationships of HRM policies with firm performance. However, in addition to these relationships, mediators could play a substantive role. Scholars have, for instance, proposed that variables such as 'strength of the HRM system' (Bowen & Ostroff, 2004), employee perceptions of HRM (Nishii & Wright, 2008) or 'involvement of the HRM function' (Buyens & Vos, 2001) could mediate between HRM and performance. Future research testing these mediating effects could enrich the field.

Appendix Table 4.1   Descriptive statistics of the determinants

EU country	Relative frequency	Mean	Stdev.
UK	22%		
France	8%		
Germany	17%		
Sweden	6%		
Spain	6%		
Denmark	8%		
The Netherlands	3%		
Italy	2%		
Switzerland	3%		
Portugal	4%		
Finland	5%		
Greece	2%		
Czech	3%		
Austria	5%		
Belgium	7%		
Slovenia	1%		

(continued)

Appendix Table 4.1 Continued

EU country	Relative frequency	Mean	Stdev.
Industry			
Construction	5%		
Transportation	5%		
Banking	7%		
Chemicals	9%		
Other	24%		
Manufacturing	49%		
Unionization			
0%	10%		
1–10%	17%		
11–25%	12%		
26–50%	13%		
51–75%	14%		
75–100%	19%		
Missings	15%		
LNsize (log)		6.33	1.14
Size (median)		460	

Note: 100% N = 2153.

Appendix Table 4.2 Means, scalability and reliability coefficients of the three HR bundles

Items	MSP*		Reliability analysis**	
	Score	Loevinger's H coeff	R^2	Reliability
Calculative HR				
Individual rewards: manual	0.36	0.35	0.13	
Individual rewards: clerk	0.39	0.46	0.28	
Individual rewards: professional	0.48	0.43	0.31	
Individual rewards: manager	0.50	0.30	0.14	
Formal evaluation training: some	0.51	0.36	0.21	
Performance appraisals: manual	0.57	0.36	0.22	
Formal evaluation training: immediate	0.61	0.33	0.17	
Performance appraisals: clerk	0.66	0.47	0.34	
Performance appraisals: professional	0.71	0.54	0.38	
Performance appraisals: manager	0.72	0.47	0.28	
Scale		0.40		
KR20				0.81

(*continued*)

Appendix Table 4.2 Continued

Items	MSP*		Reliability analysis**	
	Score	Loevinger's H coeff	R^2	Reliability
Collective sharing HR				
Profit sharing: professional	0.31	0.59	0.43	
Profit sharing: manager	0.43	0.55	0.23	
Stock options: manual	0.13	0.57	0.30	
Profit sharing: manual	0.24	0.55	0.40	
Stock options: clerk	0.14	0.55	0.30	
Stock options: professional	0.16	0.55	0.32	
Profit sharing: clerk	0.26	0.57	0.44	
Stock options: manager	0.27	0.42	0.23	
Scale		0.54		
KR20				0.84
Collaborative HR				
Strategy briefing: manual	0.32	0.62	0.35	
Written communication policy	0.38	0.26	*0.07*	
Strategy briefing: clerk	0.39	0.58	0.38	
Performance briefing: manual	0.55	0.52	0.35	
Strategy briefing: professional	0.57	0.47	0.28	
Performance briefing: clerk	0.65	0.54	0.35	
Written mission statement	0.73	0.35	0.11	
Performance briefing: professional	0.77	0.54	0.25	
Performance briefing: manager	0.95	0.46	0.05	
Strategy briefing: manager	0.96	0.57	0.07	
Scale		0.49		
KR20				0.79

Notes: * Loevinger's coefficient of homogeneity, weighted. All H-coefficients are significantly different from zero at the 0.001 level, n = 2153.
** Kruger-Richardson is the reliability coefficient of the scale.

Appendix Table 4.3 Means, scalability and reliability coefficients of business performance

Items	MSP*		Reliability analysis**	
	Score	Loevinger's H	R^2	Reliability
Business performance				
Time to market	0.67	0.40	0.17	
Stock market performance	0.32	0.55	0.31	
Profitability	0.74	0.46	0.27	
Gross revenue	0.81	0.34	0.12	
Productivity	0.86	0.42	0.14	

(*continued*)

Appendix Table 4.3   Continued

Items	MSP*		Reliability analysis**	
	Score	Loevinger's H	R^2	Reliability
Service	0.94	0.46	0.08	
Innovation	0.70	0.39	0.18	
Scale		0.42		
KR20				0.74

Notes: * Loevinger's coefficient of homogeneity, weighted. All H-coefficients are significantly different from zero at the 0.001 level, n = 2153.
** Kruger-Richardson is the reliability coefficient of the scale.

Note

1. For a detailed argumentation for the use of perceptual measures of firm performance in international HRM research, see Stavrou (2005).

References

Ahmad, O. & Schroeder, R.G. 2003. 'The impact of human resource management practices on operational performance: Recognizing country and industry differences'. *Journal of Operations Management*, 21(1): 19–43.

Arthur, J.B. 1992. 'The link between business strategy and industrial relations systems in American steel mini mills'. *Industrial and Labor Relations Review*, 45: 488–506.

Arthur, J.B. 1994. 'Effects of human resource systems on manufacturing performance and turnover'. *Academy of Management Journal*, 37(3): 670–87.

Becker, B.E. & Huselid, M.A. 1998. 'High performance work systems and business performance: A synthesis of research and managerial implications'. In G.R. Ferris (ed.), *Research in Personnel and Human Resources Management*, Vol. 16. Amsterdam: JAI, 53–101.

Ben-Ner, A. & Jones, D.C. 1995. 'Employee participation, ownership, and productivity: A theoretical framework'. *Industrial Relations*, 34(4): 532–54.

Bowen, D.E. & Ostroff, C. 2004. 'Understanding HR–firm performance linkages: The role of the "strength" of the HRM system'. *Academy of Management Review*, 29: 203–21.

Boxall, P. & Purcell, J. 2008. *Strategy and Human Resource Management*, 2nd edn. New York: Palgrave Macmillan.

Buyens, D. & De Vos, A. 2001. 'Perceptions of the value of the HR function'. *Human Resource Management Journal*, 11(3): 70–89.

Cappelli, P. & Neumark, D. 2001. 'Do "high-performance" work practices improve establishment-level outcomes?' *Industrial and Labor Relations Review*, 54(4): 737–75.

Colbert, B.A. 2004. 'The complex resource-based view: Implications for theory and practice in strategic human resource management'. *Academy of Management Review*, 29(3): 341–58.

Collins, C.J. & Smith, K.G. 2006. 'Knowledge exchange and combination: The role of human resource practices in the performance of high-technology firms'. *Academy of Management Journal*, 46(6): 740–51.

Conte, M. & Svejnar, J. 1990. 'The effects of worker participation in management, profits, and ownership of assets on enterprise performance'. In K. Abraham & R. McKersie (eds), *New Developments in the Labor Market*. Cambridge, MA: MIT Press, 59–84.

Delaney, J.T. & Huselid, M.A. 1996. 'The impact of human resource management practices on perceptions of organizational performance'. *Academy of Management Journal*, 39(4): 949–69.

Delery, J.E. 1998. 'Issues of fit in strategic human resource management: Implications for research'. *Human Resource Management Review*, 8(3): 289–310.

Delery, J.E. & Doty, D.H. 1996. 'Modes of theorizing in strategic human resource management: Tests of universalistic, contingency and configurational performance predictions'. *Academy of Management Journal*, 39(4): 802–35.

Edwards, P., Collinson, M. & Rees, C. 1998. 'The determinants of employee responses to total quality management: Six case studies'. *Organization Studies*, 19(3): 449–75.

Eisenhardt, K.M. 1989. 'Agency theory: An assessment and review'. *Academy of Management Review*, 14(1): 57–74.

Evans, W.R. & Davis, W.D. 2005. 'High-performance work systems and organizational performance: The mediating role of internal social structure'. *Journal of Management*, 31(5): 758–75.

Ferrante, C. & Rousseau, D.M. 2001. 'Bringing open book management into the academic line of sight: Sharing the firm's financial information with workers'. In C.L. Cooper & D.M. Rousseau (eds), *Trends in Organizational Behavior*. New York: Wiley, 8, 97–116.

Godard, J. 2004. 'A critical assessment of the high-performance paradigm'. *British Journal of Industrial Relations*, 42(2): 349–78.

Gooderham, P.N. & Brewster, C. 2003. 'Convergence, stasis or divergence? Personnel management in Europe'. *Scandinavian Journal of Business Research*, 17: 7–18.

Gooderham, P.N., Nordhaug, O. & Ringdal, K. 1999. 'Institutional and rational determinants of organizational practices: Human resource management in European firms'. *Administrative Science Quarterly*, 44(3): 507–31.

Gooderham, P., Parry, E. & Ringdal, K. 2008. 'The impact of bundles of strategic human resource management practices on the performance of European firms'. *International Journal of Human Resource Management*, 19: 2024–40.

Gospel, H.F. & Pendleton, A. 2005. 'Corporate governance and labour management: An international comparison'. In H.F. Gospel & A. Pendleton (eds), *Corporate Governance and Labour Management: An International Comparison*. Oxford: Oxford University Press.

Guest, D.E. 1997. 'Human resource management and performance: A review and research agenda'. *International Journal of Human Resource Management*, 8: 263–76.

Guest, D.E., Michie, J., Conway, N. & Sheehan, M. 2003. 'Human resource management and corporate performance in the UK'. *British Journal of Industrial Relations*, 41: 291–314.

Guthrie, J.P. 2001. 'High-involvement work practices, turnover and productivity: Evidence from New Zealand'. *Academy of Management Journal*, 44: 180–90.

Hall, P. & Soskice, D. (eds), 2001. *Varieties of Capitalism: The Institutional Basis of Competitive Advantage*. Oxford: Oxford University Press.

Harley, B., Sargent, L. & Allen, B. 2010. 'Employee responses to "high performance work system" practices: An empirical test of the disciplined worker thesis'. *Work, Employment & Society*, December, 24: 740–60.

Huselid, M.A. 1995. 'The impact of human resource management practices on turnover, productivity, and corporate financial performance'. *Academy of Management Journal*, 38: 635–72.

Ichniowski, C., Shaw, K. & Prennushi, G. 1997. 'The effects of human resource management practices on productivity: A study of steel finishing lines'. *American Economic Review*, 87(3): 291–313.

Jansen, J., Volberda, H. & van den Bosch, F. 2005. 'Managing potential and realized absorptive capacity: How do organizational antecedents matter?' *Academy of Management Journal*, 46(6): 999–1015.

Kaarsemaker, E.C.A. & Poutsma, E. 2006. 'The fit of employee ownership with other human resource management practices: Theoretical and empirical suggestions regarding the existence of an ownership high-performance work system, or Theory O'. *Economic and Industrial Democracy*, 27(2): 669–85.

Kandel, E. & Lazear, E. 1992. 'Peer pressure in partnerships'. *Journal of Political Economy*, 100: 801–17.

Kintana, M.L., Alonso, A.A. & Olaverri, C.G. 2006. 'High-performance work systems and firms' operational performance: The moderating role of technology'. *International Journal of Human Resource Management*, 17(1): 70–85.

Kruse, D. & Blasi, J. 1995. *Employee Ownership, Employee Attitudes, and Business Performance*. Cambridge, MA: National Bureau of Economic Research.

Kruse, D., Freeman, R. & Blasi, J. (eds), 2010. *Shared Capitalism at Work: Employee Stock Ownership, Profit and Gain Sharing, and Broad-based Stock Options*. Chicago: University of Chicago Press.

Laursen, K. & Foss, N.J. 2003. 'New human resource management practices, complementarities and the impact on innovation performance'. *Cambridge Journal of Economics*, 27(2): 243–63.

Lepak, D.P. & Snell, S.A. 2002. 'Examining the human resource architecture: The relationships among human capital, employment, and human resource configurations'. *Journal of Management*, 28(4): 517–43.

Lepak, D.P., Liao, H., Chung, Y. & Harden, E.E. 2006. 'A conceptual review of human resource management systems in strategic human resource management research'. *Research in Personnel and Human Resources Management*, 25: 217–72.

Liao, Y-S. 2005. 'Business strategy and performance: The role of human resource management control'. *Personnel Review*, 34(3): 294–309.

MacDuffie, J.P. 1995. 'Human resource bundles and manufacturing performance: Organizational logic and flexible production systems in the world auto industry'. *Industrial and Labor Relations Review*, 48: 197–221.

Martín-Alcázar, F., Romero-Fernández, P.M. & Sánchez-Gardey, G. 2005. 'Strategic human resource management: Integrating the universalistic, contingent, configurational and contextual perspectives'. *International Journal of Human Resource Management*, 16(5): 633–59.

Mokken, R.J. 1971. *A Theory and Procedure of Scale Analysis*. The Hague: Mouton.

Mokken, R.J. & Lewis, C. 1982. 'A nonparametric approach to the analysis of dichotomous item responses'. *Applied Psychological Measurement*, 6: 417–30.

Molenaar, I.W. & Sijtsma, K. 2000. *Manual for MSP, a Program for Mokken Scale Analysis for Polytomous Items Version 5.0*. Groningen: IEC ProGramma.

Nishii, L. & Wright, P. 2008. 'Variability within organizations: Implications for strategic human resource management'. In D.B. Smith (ed.), *The People Make the Place*. Mahwah, NJ: Lawrence Erlbaum.

Oyer, P. 2004. 'Why do firms use incentives that have no incentive effects?' *Journal of Finance*, 59(4): 1619–49.

Paauwe, J. 2009. 'HRM and performance: Achievements, methodological issues and prospects'. *Journal of Management Studies*, 46: 129–42.

Pendleton, A., Poutsma, E., Van Ommeren, J. & Brewster, C. 2003. 'The incidence and determinants of employee share ownership and profit sharing in Europe'. In T. Kato & J. Pliskin (eds), *The Determinants of the Incidence and the Effects of Participatory Organizations*. Amsterdam: JAI Press.

Poppo, L & Zenger, T. 2002. 'Do formal contracts and relational governance function as substitutes or complements?' *Strategic Management Journal*, 23(8): 707–25.

Poutsma, E. & Braam, G. (forthcoming). The Relationship between Financial Participation Plans and Company Financial Performance Evidence from a Dutch Longitudinal Panel.

Poutsma, E., Kalmi, P. & Pendleton, A. 2006. 'The relationship between financial participation and other forms of employee participation: New survey evidence from Europe'. *Economic and Industrial Democracy*. 27(2): 637–68.

Poutsma, E., Ligthart, Paul, E.M. & Veersma, U. 2006. 'The diffusion of calculative and participative HRM practices in European firms'. *Industrial Relations*, 45(2): 513–46.

Rabe-Hesketh, S. & Skrondal, A. 2005. *Multilevel and Longitudinal Modelling Using Stata*. College Station: Stata Press.

Rabe-Hesketh, S., Skrondal, A. & Pickles, A. 2004. *GLLAMM Manual*. Working Paper Series, 160. Berkeley: UC Berkeley Division of Biostatistics.

Rizov, M. & Croucher, R. 2009. 'Human resource management and performance in European firms'. *Cambridge Journal of Economics*, 33: 253–72.

Robinson, S.L. 1996. 'Trust and breach of the psychological contract'. *Administrative Science Quarterly*, 41(4): 574–99.

Rousseau, D.M. & Shperling, Z. 2003. 'Pieces of the action: Ownership and the changing employment relation'. *Academy of Management Review*, 28: 553–70.

Schuler, R.S. & Rogovsky, N. 1998. 'Understanding compensation practice variations across firms: The impact of national culture'. *Journal of International Business Studies*, 29(1): 159–177.

Sesil, J., Kruse, D.L. & Blasi, J.R. 2001. *Sharing Ownership via Employee Stock Ownership*. Helsinki: UBU/WIDER.

Snijder, T. & Bosker, R. 1999. *Multilevel Analysis: An Introduction to Basic and Advanced Multilevel Modelling*. London: Sage Publications.

Stavrou, E.T. 2005. 'Flexible work bundles and organizational competitiveness: A cross-national study of the European work context'. *Journal of Organizational Behaviour*, 26(8): 923–48.

Stavrou, E., Brewster, C. & Charalambos, C. 2010. 'Human resource management and firm performance in Europe through the lens of business systems: Best fit, best practice or both?'*International Journal of Human Resource Management*, 21: 50–67.

Wall, T.D., Michie, J., Patterson, M., Wood, S.J., Sheehan, M., Clegg, C.W. & West, M. 2004. 'On the validity of subjective measures of company performance'. *Personnel Psychology: A Journal of Applied Research*, 57: 95–118.

Weitzman, M.L. & Kruse, D.L. 1990. 'Profit sharing and productivity'. In A.S. Blinder (ed.), *Paying for Productivity: A Look at the Evidence*. Washington, DC: Brookings Institution, 95–141.

Whitley, R. 1999. *Divergent Capitalisms: The Social Structuring and Change of Business Systems*. Oxford: Oxford University Press.

Section Two
Regional Trends in HRM

5

Human Resource Management in the Central and Eastern European Region

Rūta Kazlauskaitė, Ilona Bučiūnienė, József Poór, Zsuzsanna Karoliny, Ruth Alas, Andrej Kohont and Ágnes Szlávicz

Introduction

The aim of this chapter is to examine recent developments of human resource management (HRM) practices in the Central and Eastern European (CEE) region and to compare these against the similarities and differences of their national contexts.

With an increasingly growing organizational dependency on international operations, the understanding of management practices across different countries has become of critical relevance not only to large multinationals (MNC), but also to small domestic firms. Human resource management, a potential source of competitive advantage in this context, constitutes one of the most complex challenges. Specifically, there has been an ongoing debate over the transferability of HRM practices across different national boundaries. Drawing on the contextual paradigm, which argues that HRM practices are context-specific rather than universal, a distinction has been made between the US model and European HRM models (Brewster, 2007). What makes HRM across the world dissimilar is the role of the state, national culture differences, varying patterns of consultation, and different patterns of ownership.

European HRM is not only different from the standpoint of respective practices in other continents, but it is also unique in terms of the diversity of HR practices across countries within its continental boundaries. Interestingly, on the one hand, the formation of the European Union has had important implications on the member state legislation, economy, market forces, etc., which in turn have developed a dynamic towards convergence (Nikandrou, Apospori & Papalexandris, 2005). On the other hand, despite the unified context provided by the EU, national cultural and institutional contexts still allow for differences at the country and/or organizational level.

The HRM convergence–divergence debate has received a lot of research attention in the past two decades, as there is no agreement on the effect of globalization on HRM practices. Supporters of the convergence approach believe that HRM is becoming more alike across the world, while followers of the divergence approach argue that management practices continue to be country-specific. Some regional HRM similarities and traces of directional convergence have been determined (Mayrhofer & Brewster, 2005); however, they are insufficient to treat HRM in different European countries as a homogeneous bundle (Apospori et al., 2008). Rather, Europe can be argued to consist of a set of distinctive HRM regimes (Gooderham & Nordhaug, 2011), which in turn necessitates analysis of national antecedents of HRM developments.

Following the contextual paradigm and arguments on multiple HRM patterns across Europe, this chapter aims to look into HRM practices in Central and Eastern European countries. A comparative study of HRM patterns in the CEE region is relevant and necessary from both a national and international perspective, as it can be used as a benchmark for domestic companies in an attempt to enhance their performance, and a relevant source of information for MNCs that operate in or consider entering the CEE region. However, specialized and systematic research dedicated to HRM in the CEE region is still rather limited (Michailova, Heraty & Morley, 2009). Most of the prior research in the field is based on a single or two–three country analysis (Poór et al., 2011; Szerb, Richbell & Vitai, 2010; Kazlauskaitė & Bučiūnienė, 2010), which underlines a need for a more comprehensive study of HRM in the region. Further, although commonly conceived as a uniform cluster owing to the common socialist heritage and subsequent transition to the free market economy, the CEE countries are actually heterogeneous in respect to their HRM.

To examine HRM in the CEE region, in this chapter we first draw on some secondary data to reveal contextual differences between the countries. Next, we look into HRM practice specifics in eight CEE countries on the basis of 2008/10 Cranet survey data.

CEE country context and HRM developments

Cultural and institutional theories are two dominant perspectives in comparative HRM studies. The first maintains that national culture is the decisive factor in shaping HRM in a country (Sparrow, Schuler & Jackson 1994), while the latter emphasizes the impact of national institutions such as the state, legal and financial systems, and the family (Edwards & Rees, 2006). The two approaches, however, can be viewed as complementary (Sorge, 2004). Sparrow and Hiltrop (1997) distinguished the following four sets of factors to account for differences in the national patterns of HRM in Europe: (1) HR role and competence, (2) business structure, (3) institutional and (4) cultural factors.

In this section of the chapter, following Sparrow and Hiltrop's (1997) national HRM model, we will first provide a brief overview of HRM practices, role and competence in the socialist period, which represents a common past and a unifying starting point in the post-socialist developments of HRM in CEE countries. Next, we will briefly look into the national context differences of CEE countries to reveal their institutional and cultural heterogeneity, which will serve as a premise for our argument on HRM differences across the region. Specifically, we will study eight CEE countries, namely Bulgaria, the Czech Republic, Estonia, Hungary, Lithuania, Slovakia, Slovenia (EU member states) and Serbia (an EU candidate state).

HRM role and competence

Brewster, Morley and Bučiūnienė (2010) noted that charting the HRM landscape in contemporary CEE countries is a difficult task, as in contrast to other European countries, here HRM emerged in management thinking and became established as a management function only after the fall of the socialist regime. Therefore, to understand the current HRM role in CEE countries, it is essential to briefly review personnel management under socialist rule.

Personnel management was relatively uniform in the CEE countries under socialist rule, with a heavy emphasis on centralization and rule-making (Garavan, Morley & Heraty, 1998). The personnel management function, or the so-called cadre department, was typically managed by members of the Communist Party without relevant experience or competence, and first and foremost played a political role (Lucas et al., 2004; Pundzienė & Bučiūnienė, 2009). Management was not considered as a profession (Cakrt, 1993) and decisions regarding promotion were not based on performance assessment (Pearce, 1991). In several cases the selection of specialists and personnel-related decisions were greatly influenced by party and government politics and objectives.

In addition, personnel departments were responsible for some more traditional Western personnel management tasks such as maintaining employee records and overseeing training programmes. Besides, they held a very important responsibility for social and welfare activities (Soulsby & Clark, 1998). Personnel planning and compensation were carried out at the state level; labour markets did not exist in socialist countries, so selection was not relevant and labour turnover hardly existed (Pieper, 1992).

The socialist system was clearly not conducive to the growth of more sophisticated, value-adding activities (Brewster et al., 2010). There was a vacuum of knowledge and lack of organizational-level good practices in the field of managing people. It was only later in the transition period that either the HRM term or the concept, sometimes both with more or less modification, became dominant (Alas & Svetlik, 2004; Karoliny, 2008). After the fall of socialism the personnel management function had to develop the competencies it was lacking and build up the reputation of a strategic partner.

Despite common historical developments, there is, however, evidence of significant variation in current personnel/HRM practices within CEE countries, which are largely explained by different levels of economic and social development, cultural and political factors and the willingness of people to change (Erutku & Valtee, 1997). The latter will be given a closer look in the subsequent sections of this chapter. Here we limit our comparison to prior empirical evidence on HRM differences in the region. Probably one of the most comprehensive studies in the field was carried out by Ignjatović and Svetlik (2003), who studied 24 European countries (4 CEE countries among them) and determined four distinctive clusters, each having different HRM models. The four CEE countries under their study fell into different clusters, that is, the Czech Republic and Slovenia fell under the Central Southern cluster, and Bulgaria and Estonia under the Peripheral cluster, which indicates some HRM differences between CEE countries.

Business structure and environment

The CEE countries followed a uniform management model during the socialist period (Koubek, 2009). In the period of transition, however, the countries have taken different developmental paths, which have met varying levels of success. To demonstrate differences in the institutional context of CEE countries, we draw on two time periods – the years 2004 and 2008 (where data is available). The two points of time were selected to compare CEE country post-socialist developments prior to their joining the EU in 2004 and their achievements four years later. In this chapter we limit the study of the national context of CEE countries to the above-mentioned seven EU-member states. Serbia is excluded from the contextual analysis, for as a candidate country it was not included in the official EU statistics in either 2004 or in 2008 and thus comparable data is unavailable.

Business structure

An important factor of the national economy and one of the antecedents of national HRM developments refers to organizational distribution with respect to size. As seen from data in Table 5.1, there is a clear dominance of micro-sized enterprises in all countries, with about three-quarters of the population employed in SMEs. Slovakia stands out in the region as having the largest proportion of large-sized enterprises, with about half of the country's population working in them. Data for 2008 is not provided by Eurostat; therefore country-specific developments in the course of time cannot be discussed.

The predominance of SMEs has important constraints on the HR function, for as a rule HRM in small firms is costly in terms of time and money, and the HRM resources and expertise they possess are limited. HRM usually

Table 5.1 Firm distribution by size (%) and impact of foreign-controlled enterprises, 2004 (% share of total)

Country	Distribution by size				Foreign-controlled enterprises		
	Large-sized	Medium-sized	Small-sized	Micro-sized	% of enterprises	% of staff	Share of value added
Bulgaria	0.3	1.6	8.0	90.2	2.3	13.5	31.1
Czech Republic	0.2	0.8	3.8	95.3	1.7	20.8	35.1
Estonia	0.4	3.0	15.1	81.5	19.6	31.6	15.3
Hungary	0.1	n/a	n/a	n/a	0.3	16.5	40.3
Lithuania	0.6	4.3	19.7	75.5	3.4	11.0	25.1
Slovakia	1.4	5.5	n/a	n/a	5.7	26.6	44.8
Slovenia	0.3	1.3	5.5	92.9	n/a	n/a	n/a

Source: http://epp.eurostat.ec.europa.eu; n/a not available.

focuses on operational rather than strategic needs, and practices are more informal than in larger organizations and mainly refer to record keeping, staffing and to a lesser degree employee motivation and retention, while responsibility for HRM often lies in the hands of the general manager (Barret & Mayson, 2007).

Another important business structure indicator is the ownership pattern. After the fall of the socialist rule, the majority of enterprises have been privatized and today private enterprises dominate CEE economies. This change in ownership pattern had important implications for the development of the HR function, as to survive and gain competitive advantage firms had to invest more heavily in their human resources and their management. Another factor that was particularly important for economic development, employment and economic growth of CEE countries is foreign direct investment (FDI), which also made a significant contribution to the development of HRM competence and enhancement of its reputation (Lewis, 2005). As seen from Table 5.1, Estonia stands out in the region with the highest proportion of foreign-controlled enterprises. Along with Slovakia it leads in the number of people employed by foreign-controlled enterprises, while the biggest share of the value added is created by foreign-controlled enterprises in Slovakia and Hungary. Data for 2008 is not provided by Eurostat; therefore country-specific developments cannot be discussed.

As seen from the above data, the business structures of CEE countries share some similarities (organizational size and ownership pattern) and demonstrate some differences (FDI levels). Taking into consideration the SME predominance, the HR function in the CEE countries may be expected to perform an administrative rather than a strategic role. However, differences in the numbers of foreign-controlled enterprises lead to a presumption of certain HRM differences between the countries. It is likely that HRM competence and role are more developed in Slovakia and Estonia in comparison to other CEE countries, as MNCs usually introduce managerial practices and missing competences to their subsidiaries and contribute to the promotion of the HR function image and relevance in the host country.

Economy

In between joining the EU and the recent global economic crisis, CEE countries recorded unprecedented economic growth, outscoring many of the older EU members. Overall, however, CEE countries diverge in their economic achievements. As seen from Table 5.2, the selected CEE countries vary in their GDP to a great extent. Slovenia and the Czech Republic are clear leaders in the group, while Bulgaria, a latecomer to the EU, is lagging behind.

It is noteworthy however that, although Slovenia and the Czech Republic demonstrated the highest GDP in both 2004 and 2008, their growth during this period was more modest in comparison to Slovakia, which outperformed other CEE countries and stood in third place according to 2008 indicators. Bulgaria, Estonia and Lithuania also demonstrated faster growth than the leading countries in the group.

Economic growth is one of the key contributors to national HRM developments, as at such times firms have more financial resources and may invest more heavily in their HR function. Firms start investing more in employee training, motivation and retention, which in turn necessitates a more active HR function role and size. Drawing on the GDP data, significant HRM differences may be anticipated among CEE countries, with HRM in Slovenia, the Czech Republic and Slovakia standing out in the region.

Table 5.2   Selected economic and demographic indicators

Country	GDP per capita (EUR; PPS)		Unemployment		% total population having completed at least upper secondary education (25–64)		% tertiary educational attainment (30–34)	
	2004	2008	2004	2008	2004	2008	2004	2008
Bulgaria	7500	10900	12.1	5.6	71.7	77.5	25.2	27.1
Czech Republic	16900	20200	8.3	4.4	89.1	90.9	12.7	15.4
Estonia	12400	17300	9.7	5.5	88.9	88.5	27.4	34.1
Hungary	13600	16000	6.1	7.8	75.3	79.7	18.5	22.4
Lithuania	11000	15400	11.4	5.8	86.6	90.6	31.1	39.9
Slovakia	12300	18100	18.2	9.5	87.0	89.9	12.9	15.8
Slovenia	18800	22700	6.3	4.4	79.7	82.0	25.1	30.9

Source: http://epp.eurostat.ec.europa.eu

Labour market

Upon the end of the socialist period, which was characterized by nearly full employment, CEE countries faced a challenge in fighting against unemployment. As in other spheres of business activity, CEE countries reported varied results. In 2008, however, unemployment in most CEE countries was rather low (EU average of 7.1), which in turn necessitated heavier investment in HRM, as employee retention became a critical issue. Slovenia was a clear leader in the group with the lowest unemployment levels in both periods, which also leads to assumptions of its likely better performance in HRM.

Demographics

Another significant indicator in respect to HRM development is the level of education. All CEE countries score higher (Table 5.2) than the EU average (respectively 68.4 and 71.4 per cent) in the proportion of population with at least upper secondary education. The Czech Republic and Lithuania lead the group. Lithuania also outperforms other CEE countries in tertiary education attainment. This has several implications for HRM. On the one hand, availability of skilled low-cost labour makes a country an attractive destination for outsourcing some functions/operations. On the other hand, the abundance of skilled labour leads to higher employer expectations and excessive demands in recruitment, especially for lower-level positions.

Institutional factors

In this chapter we limit our analysis of institutional context to two factors of the Sparrow and Hiltrop (1997) model – trade union density and power, and corporate social responsibility. Under the socialist model, trade unions were government organizations with nearly 100 per cent membership. They mainly represented the goals of the Communist Party and did little to protect the rights of employees. Unions' main responsibilities included distribution of welfare benefits, social event organizing, overlooking of housing construction and provision of catering services (Kazlauskaitė & Bučiūnienė, 2010). After the fall of the socialist system, the unions lacked the competence to deal with employee relations. Besides, employees wanted to escape from the constraints of union membership and the payment of union membership fees (Zupan & Kase, 2005). Consequently, the level of unionization eroded drastically in CEE countries. During the 2000s, unions in CEE countries lost two million members (European Commission, 2010), with the biggest losses in Lithuania (–47.7 per cent), Estonia (–43.6 per cent), Slovakia (–43.4 per cent) and the Czech Republic (–27.9 per cent). Slovenia is perhaps the only exception in the region, where trade unions retained high density (around 40 per cent) and much of their power (Svetlik, 2009). Serbia demonstrates rather high union density too (about 30 per cent); however being rather fragmented, unions do not have much power (Stajić, 2006).

Trade union power has important implications for the HR function, specifically for the management of employee relations. Respectively such issues as communication, employee involvement, grievance and collective bargaining may be more critical in Slovenian firms in comparison to other CEE countries.

CSR is a relatively new concept in the CEE region; nevertheless, it is gaining more relevance recently, which has to a great extent been encouraged by respective MNCs' policies and practices in the region. The most tangible progress can be seen in Hungary and the Czech Republic, where the highest proportions of companies report on various CSR issues (Noorkoiv & Gröön, 2004). CSR has important implications for HRM, as employees become a relevant stakeholder; thus responsible firms are expected to invest more heavily into HRM.

Cultural environment

Table 5.3 gives some insights into national culture divergence in CEE countries. Looking at this data, we can see that the CEE region is not culturally homogeneous. Slovakia and Serbia demonstrate the highest levels of power distance, while Lithuania, Estonia and Hungary score the lowest. In respect to individualism, Hungary scores highest, while Slovenia, Serbia and Bulgaria can be viewed as the most collectivistic countries. Slovakia and Hungary stand out as most masculine, while Slovenia is most feminine. In respect to uncertainty avoidance Serbia and Slovenia score highest, while Lithuania is least uncomfortable under uncertainty. Thus overall the region can be observed as heterogeneous, where in some cases cultural co-movements, as well as divergent tendencies can be observed (Jarjabka, 2011).

Among the areas where the most obvious links between national culture and HRM can be observed, Sparrow and Hiltrop (1997) refer to (1) attitudes and definitions of effective managers; (2) levels of power distance and uncertainty avoidance with possible implications on recruitment,

Table 5.3 National culture indices

	Power distance	Individualism	Masculinity	Uncertainty avoidance
Bulgaria	70	30	40	85
Czech Republic	57	58	57	74
Estonia	40	60	30	60
Hungary	46	80	88	82
Lithuania*	42	65	60	19
Serbia	86	25	43	92
Slovakia	104	52	110	51
Slovenia	71	27	19	88

Source: www.geert-hofstede.com; * Hüttinger (2008).

communication and participation; (3) expectations of manager–subordinate relationships and their implications for performance management and motivation; and (4) pay systems, socially healthy pay and the individualization of reward. Given the data in Table 5.3, there should be some similarities in the patterns of recruitment, communication and participation within the following country groups – Slovakia, Serbia, Slovenia and Bulgaria (higher power distance countries); Estonia, Lithuania and Hungary (lower power distance countries); and Serbia, Slovenia, Bulgaria and Hungary (higher uncertainty avoidance countries).

To conclude, the contextual analysis of the selected CEE countries suggests that although they share a common past, there are a number of differences between the countries with respect to their business structure, economic development, level of education and national culture, which in turn suggests that significant differences also exist in national HRM patterns in the CEE region.

Research methodology

The present study of HRM patterns in CEE countries is based on 2008–10 Cranet survey data from eight CEE countries (Table 5.4). Our data consist of 1147 organizations. The respondents of the survey were HR directors/managers or employees with HRM responsibility.

The survey employed the standard Cranet questionnaire, which is aimed at a wide range of HRM policies and practices across numerous national contexts, such as staffing, development, compensation and benefits, employee relations and communication etc. This chapter will analyse the survey data following the conceptual model of Sparrow and Hiltrop (1997). Specifically we look at the HRM role, union situation and CSR, and at the HRM practices that are most likely to be affected by national

Table 5.4 Descriptive statistics of survey participants

	Country (N)	Private (%)	Public (%)	Not for profit (%)	Mixed (public/ private) (%)	Other (%)	SME (%)	Large (%)
Bulgaria	267	70.20	17.40	3.30	3.70	5.40	71.90	28.10
Czech Republic	54	n/a	n/a	n/a	n/a	n/a	20.40	79.60
Estonia	74	69.00	25.40	1.40	0.00	4.20	62.20	37.80
Hungary	139	68.30	22.30	1.40	7.20	0.70	60.40	39.60
Lithuania	119	77.60	7.80	0.90	3.40	10.30	52.10	47.90
Serbia	50	69.60	23.90	0.00	2.20	4.30	60.00	40.00
Slovakia	225	88.70	9.50	0.50	1.40	0.00	54.20	45.80
Slovenia	219	63.40	27.30	2.30	3.70	3.20	57.50	42.50

culture and institutional specifics. To determine statistically significant differences between CEE countries, the means of individual countries were compared to the overall mean (sample under the present study), for no overall measures or indices of HRM practices in the CEE region have been determined in prior research that could be used as a point of reference for such a comparison.

Research findings

HR role and competence

The HR role in the selected CEE countries was studied with respect to the following aspects: HR department presence, strategic integration, and devolvement to line management (see Table 5.5).

First we looked into HR department presence. More than half of the respondent organizations have an HR department (Table 5.5). Czech and Lithuanian organizations reported a significantly higher level of HR department presence, while Bulgaria scored lower than the overall mean on this indicator.

Next we looked into HR strategic integration, which was measured by HR strategy availability, HR representation on the board, HR involvement in business strategy development, and evaluation of HR function performance.

Table 5.5   HR strategic integration, mean (standard deviation)

Country	HR department presence	Personnel/ HR strategy availability	HR seat on the board/ equivalent	HR involvement in business strategy development	Extent of HR function performance evaluation
Overall	.65 (.48)	1.18 (.77)	.62 (.48)	2.01 (1.08)	1.78 (1.26)
Bulgaria	.50*** (.50)	1.03*** (.83)	.28*** (.45)	1.72*** (.1.17)	1.50*** (1.33)
Czech Republic	.91*** (.29)	.80*** (.41)	.80*** (.41)	1.73 (1.19)	2.46 (1.00)
Estonia	.68 (.47)	1.31 (.77)	.53 (.50)	2.22 (.80)	2.03 (1.21)
Hungary	.60 (.49)	1.17 (.82)	.88*** (.33)	2.28** (1.02)	1.65 (1.23)
Lithuania	.79*** (.41)	1.23 (.79)	.58 (.50)	1.66*** (1.01)	1.75 (1.12)
Serbia	.53 (.50)	1.27 (.75)	.65 (.48)	1.98 (1.16)	2.02 (1.12)
Slovakia	.69 (.46)	1.35*** (.79)	.80*** (.40)	1.96 (1.10)	1.93 (1.33)
Slovenia	.70 (.46)	1.20 (.63)	.78*** (.42)	2.32 (.92)	1.69 (1.21)

Notes: One sample t-test for equality means comparing with total mean; * $p < .05$, ** $p < .01$, *** $p < .005$.
Measures: HR department presence: 1 = yes; 0 = no; HR strategy availability: 2 = written, 1 = unwritten, 0 = none; HR seat on the board: 1 = yes; 0 = no; HR involvement in business strategy development: 3 = from onset, 2 = subsequent consultation, 1 = on implementation, 0 = not at all; extent of HR function performance evaluation: 0 = not at all, 4 = to a very great extent).

Findings show statistically significant differences between the countries on all four indicators (Table 5.5).

HR strategy availability. Findings show that Slovakia reported higher than average on HR strategy possession, while the Czech Republic and Bulgaria scored lower than the overall mean.

HR seat on the board. Our findings show that HR representation on the board is more common in Hungary, the Czech Republic, Slovakia and Slovenia, while in Bulgaria it is lower than the overall mean.

HR involvement in business strategy development. Similar to HR representation on the board, Hungary scored higher than the overall mean on this indicator, while in Lithuania and Bulgaria the figures were below the mean.

Finally we looked at the *HR function performance evaluation.* Respondents were asked to what extent the HR function was measured in their organization (0 = not at all; 4 = to a very great extent). No statistically significant differences were determined in respect to this indicator, with the exception of Bulgaria, where HR performance evaluation was below the overall mean.

Findings on whose views are taken into consideration in the HR function evaluation process (Table 5.6) revealed some statistically significant differences between the countries. In Lithuania all four groups were involved in HR function performance evaluation to a lesser degree than the overall mean. In Bulgaria employee and personnel function were involved the least, while in Estonia and Slovenia, on the contrary, the views of those two groups were given the highest relevance. In Hungary and Slovakia the HR function was mainly evaluated by top management and line management.

HR decentralization and devolvement to line management. HR decentralization was measured by calculating the percentage of firms where responsibility for

Table 5.6 HR function evaluation, mean (standard deviation)

	Top management	Line management	Employees	Personnel/HR function itself
Overall	.90 (.30)	.80 (.40)	.52 (.50)	.53 (.50)
Bulgaria	.84 (.37)	.80 (.40)	.13*** (.34)	.17*** (.38)
Czech Republic	1.00 (.00)	.93*** (.25)	.66 (.48)	.61 (.50)
Estonia	.91 (.29)	.95*** (.22)	.85*** (.36)	.79*** (.41)
Hungary	.97*** (.18)	.89** (.31)	.59 (.49)	.49 (.50)
Lithuania	.67*** (.47)	.56** (.50)	.26*** (.44)	.24*** (.43)
Serbia	.96 (.19)	.76 (.44)	.42 (.51)	.50 (.51)
Slovakia	.95*** (.21)	.78 (.42)	.52 (.50)	.61* (.49)
Slovenia	.94 (.23)	.85* (.36)	.70*** (.46)	.75*** (.43)

Notes: One sample t-test for equality means comparing with total mean; * $p < .05$, ** $p < .01$, *** $p < .005$.
Measures: 0 = not at all, 4 = to a very great extent.

Table 5.7   Line manager responsibility for major policy decisions (% of firms)

Country	Pay & benefits	Recruitment & selection	Training & development	Industrial relations	Workforce expansion/ reduction
Overall	76.5	61.3	56.7	57.4	70.9
Bulgaria	92.5	81.9	81.7	91.4	91.3
Czech Republic	58.5	52.8	38.5	45.3	67.9
Estonia	81.7	55.6	50.0	50.7	78.9
Hungary	81.5	71.6	61.2	52.2	77.6
Lithuania	73.9	31.9	33.9	32.6	73.5
Serbia	93.8	85.4	79.2	77.1	87.2
Slovakia	60.1	51.6	43.1	43.1	45.2
Slovenia	70.7	54.2	52.1	45.0	60.5

such HR policy decisions as pay and benefits, recruitment and selection, training and development, industrial relations, and workforce reduction/ expansion was given predominantly to line managers – exclusively or in consultation with HR. In the remaining firms policy decisions were mainly made by HR – either exclusively or in consultation with line management. Our findings (Table 5.7) show that Bulgaria and Serbia scored higher than the overall mean on line manager decision-making in respect to all policies. Hungary came close to them, with the exception of line manager responsibility in industrial relations, where HR played a more important role. Slovenia, Slovakia and the Czech Republic stood out in the region, as here decision-making responsibility on all policies rested mainly in the hands of the HR function.

Institutional factors

This section refers to trade unions and CSR issues, which, according to Sparrow and Hiltrop (1997), have significant implications for national HRM patterns. The findings with regard to unionization (Table 5.8) show that trade union influence was strongest in Slovenia, Serbia and the Czech Republic, while in Lithuania, Hungary and Bulgaria trade union impact was significantly lower. In respect to change in trade union impact over the three years of the surveys, the overall figures show that there was no change.

Trade union recognition in collective bargaining was also low in CEE countries (Table 5.8). It was higher in Serbia, the Czech Republic and Hungary. Similar trends are observed with respect to the presence of joint consultative committees/work councils and employer associations, which are not popular in the region. The only country in the region that stood out was Slovenia, with higher scores on both factors.

Table 5.8 Unionism and CSR (mean)

Country	Trade union influence	Change in trade union influence in past three years	Trade union recognition in collective bargaining	Joint consultative committee or works council	Member of employer association	Satisfaction with employer association	CSR statement availability
Overall	.98	1.95	.54	.40	.38	2.15	.73
Bulgaria	.63***	1.88	.33***	.21***	.32*	1.95	.56***
Czech Republic	1.60***	2.00	.83***	.46	.48	1.96	n/a
Estonia	.54	1.92	.29***	.33	.41	2.37	.83
Hungary	.76*	1.95	.71***	.43	.22	2.15	.62
Lithuania	.65***	1.97	.58	.42	.38	1.89	.55
Serbia	1.40*	2.11	.81***	.17***	.36	1.93	.64
Slovakia	.98	1.89	.59	.49*	.27***	2.27	.78
Slovenia	1.56***	2.00	.54	.55***	.60***	2.31*	1.00***

Notes: One sample t-test for equality means comparing with total mean; * p < .05, ** p < .01, *** p < .005.

Measures: trade union influence in organisations: 0 = not at all, 4 = to a very great extent; changes in influence: 3 = increased, 2 = same, 1 = decreased; recognition in collective bargaining: 1 = yes, 0 = no; membership of employer association: 1 = yes, 0 = no; satisfaction with employer association: 0 = not at all, 4 = entirely; CSR statement availability: 2 = written, 1 = unwritten, 0 = none.

Table 5.9   Cultural factors, means (standard deviation)

Country	Reward individualization	Downward communication	Upward communication	Communication on strategy & performance
Overall	.50 (.41)	2.55 (1.07)	1.54 (.76)	.68 (.26)
Bulgaria	.62** (.44)	1.42*** (.80)	.95*** (.57)	.65 (.26)
Czech Republic	.28*** (.37)	2.89** (.77)	1.80* (.60)	.73 (.24)
Estonia	.70*** (.36)	3.14*** (.80)	1.84*** (.63)	.74 (.25)
Hungary	.66*** (.39)	2.45 (.97)	1.32*** (.66)	.66 (.27)
Lithuania	.38** (.40)	2.88** (1.01)	1.57 (.67)	.56*** (.29)
Serbia	.49 (.47)	2.54 (.79)	1.41 (.69)	.70 (.19)
Slovakia	.44 (.41)	2.84*** (.99)	1.63 (.72)	.68 (.21)
Slovenia	.40** (.32)	2.98*** (.80)	2.02*** (.73)	.75*** (.24)

Notes: t-test for equality means comparing with total mean; * $p < .05$, ** $p < .01$, *** $p < .005$. Reward individualization (basic pay determined at the individual pay): 1 = yes, 0 = no; downward communication and upward employee communication: 4 = to a very great extent, 0 = not at all; communication of strategy and performance outcome: 1 = yes, 0 = no.

CSR statement formalization was not given high relevance in CEE countries – not all respondent organizations had a CSR statement, and if they did, these were mostly in an unwritten form. Here Slovenia stood out again with a significantly higher score.

Cultural factors

According to Sparrow and Hiltrop (1997), national culture differences may reveal cross-national differences in such HRM practices as reward individualization and communication. The findings (Table 5.9) show that reward individualization was highest in Estonia, while the Czech Republic, Lithuania, Slovenia, Slovakia and Serbia scored lower than average on the use of this practice. In respect to internal communication, Slovenia stood out as a country that practises both upward and downward communication most in the region, while in Bulgaria both upward and downward communication was at the lowest level in the region. Slovenia also reported a high score with respect to communication on strategy and financial performance.

Conclusions and discussion

The overall aim of this chapter was to provide a comprehensive picture of HRM developments in CEE countries and to break the myth of the region's uniformity in the use of HRM practices. Specifically we compared eight CEE countries in respect to their institutional and cultural contexts and the application of a variety of HRM practices.

First, we looked at some contextual factors in the selected eight CEE countries; the analysis of which provided some support in respect to variances between the countries. As seen from GDP figures, Slovenia, the Czech Republic and Slovakia report the highest economic development, while Bulgaria, the latest EU entrant in the group, is lagging behind the region. Slovenia also stands out with the lowest unemployment rates. The CEE countries share some similarities in business structure, specifically with respect to organizational size and ownership pattern; however, some differences can be seen regarding FDI levels. Overall people in CEE countries are well educated, with Lithuania and Estonia scoring highest in numbers of tertiary education graduates. Most CEE countries reported low and declining trade union density and popularity, with the exception of Slovenia where they are both high in density and power, and Serbia where membership is high but unions lack power. Some national culture differences also differentiate the region; however, no clear culture-specific regional patterns can be observed.

Next we looked into the usage of a variety of HRM practices in the eight CEE countries. Our study revealed some interesting findings with respect to the strategic role of the HR function. For instance, more Czech and Lithuanian firms than those in other CEE countries reported having an HR department; however, the two countries do not reveal similarly high levels with respect to other indicators of HR strategic integration. This suggests that the presence of an HR function in a firm does not suffice. In the Czech Republic, the high HR department incidence rate can be to some extent explained by its sample composition – 80 per cent of the respondents represented large organizations, which are more likely to have an HR department. This most probably also accounts for a higher HR representation on the board in the Czech Republic. In Lithuania it can only be speculatively proposed that HR department presence is associated with a higher level of tertiary education graduates (degrees in management and economics being among the most popular in the country), with higher expectations from the employer and subsequently rising awareness of the HR function relevance. However, it is also noteworthy that in Lithuania HR is predominantly a female-dominated profession, which to some extent accounts for the rather low strategic integration of the function.

If we look at the HR representation on the board, we see that it is highest in the more economically developed countries of the region – Slovenia, the Czech Republic, Slovakia and Hungary. However, Slovakia is the only country in the region that has high HR strategy availability and formalization, while Hungary has high HR involvement in strategy development. The case of Slovakia might be associated with its high FDI and the power distance levels in the region. In Hungary this can also be explained by foreign ownership, which is very high (90 per cent) among large companies and in which HR involvement in strategy development is very common (Poór, Engle & Gross, 2010).

The level of economic development stands out as a significant factor in the development of HR for, in contrast to more economically advanced countries in the region, Bulgaria scored lowest on the HR strategic role. This may to some extent have been influenced by the Bulgarian sample, which comprises considerably more SMEs than in the case of other CEE countries.

In respect to another HR centralization aspect – devolvement to line managers – some rather controversial findings have been revealed. Traditionally a higher devolvement to the line is associated with a more strategic HR role in a firm, as it is line managers who are in more frequent and constant contact with employees and staffing decisions are increasingly made in real time (Larsen & Brewster, 2003). In the CEE, however, we see that devolvement to the line is not related to the overall HR strategic integration, for Slovenia, the Czech Republic and Slovakia score lower than average on this indicator, while Bulgaria, which scored lower or on average on other factors of HR strategic integration, reported the highest levels of devolvement to the line. The above findings lead to an assumption that devolvement to line managers may be associated with a lack of HR competence and resources rather than HR strategic integration, for as mentioned the Bulgarian sample predominantly represents SMEs.

Our findings also reveal differences in trade union influence in the region. Trade union power was reported to be strongest in Slovenia, the Czech Republic and Serbia, which is in parallel to prior research (Svetlik, 2009) and to secondary data in case of Slovenia. The Czech Republic findings may again have been influenced by the predominance of large organizations in the sample, while the Serbian situation may be accounted for by a high union density. Slovenia also reported the highest levels of employer association membership and satisfaction with it.

Some HR differences between the CEE countries have also been revealed in respect to internal communication and reward individualization. Slovenia, along with Estonia and the Czech Republic, stand out in respect to communication (upward and downward), while Estonia also scores the highest in reward individualization. These practices are usually viewed as culture-specific (Sparrow & Hiltrop, 1997). It is noteworthy that CEE countries were relatively heterogeneous with respect to national culture and that no culturally similar groups of countries can be identified. The above scores on reward individualization and communication were more likely to be affected by other factors rather than culture. In the case of Slovenia, where organizations reported using more methods of both upward and downward communication than the CEE average, this was more likely accounted for by strong trade unions and high employer association membership.

Overall, this chapter does show that the CEE countries are heterogeneous in their HRM patterns and that the region should not be taken as a uniform management model based only on their socialist heritage and transitional processes. This is an important finding that both foreign-controlled and domestic companies should take into consideration. The findings provide information that may be useful for MNCs when making business expansion and staffing decisions. With regard to domestic organizations, our findings may serve as a benchmarking tool.

The chapter does, however, have limitations that should be noted here. First, samples of some of the countries under study are small and do not represent the total population. Respondents represent firms with 100 and more employees, which do not represent the typical HRM tendencies in countries with a predominance of SMEs. Our study is limited only to half of the CEE region owing to the fact that other countries did not participate in the Cranet survey. Thus further research needs to be undertaken to achieve an overall picture of the region. Finally, our chapter is purely descriptive and we have not controlled for organizational size, industry and sector. Therefore more sophisticated analyses need to be performed on HRM in the region to make causal inferences.

References

Alas, R. & Svetlik, I. 2004. 'Estonia and Slovenia: Building modern HRM using a dualist approach'. In C. Brewster, W. Mayrhofer & M. Morley (eds), *Human Resource Management in Europe: Evidence of Convergence?* London: Elsevier, 353–83.

Aposporia, E., Nikandrou, I., Brewster, C. & Papalexandris, N. 2008. 'HRM and organizational performance in Northern and Southern Europe'. *The International Journal of Human Resource Management*, 19: 1187–207.

Barrett, R. & Mayson, S. 2007. 'Human resource management in growing small firms'. *Journal of Small Business and Enterprise Development*, 14: 307–20.

Brewster, C. 2007. 'Comparative HRM: European views and perspectives'. *International Journal of Human Resource Management*, 18: 769–87.

Brewster, C., Morley, M. & Bučiūnienė, I. 2010. 'The reality of human resource management in Central and Eastern Europe'. *Baltic Journal of Management*, 5: 145–55.

Cakrt, M. 1993. 'Management education in Eastern Europe: Toward mutual understanding'. *Academy of Management Executive*, 4: 63–8.

Edwards, T. & Rees, C. 2006. *International Human Resource Management: Globalization, National Systems and Multinational Companies.* Harlow: Pearson Education Limited.

Erutku C. & Valtee, L. 1997. 'Business start-ups in today's Poland: Who and how?' *Entrepreneurship and Regional Development*, 9: 113–26.

European Commission. 2010. *Industrial Relations in Europe 2010.* Luxembourg: Publications Office of the European Union.

Garavan, T., Morley, M. & Heraty, N. 1998. 'Managing human resources in a post-command economy: Personnel administration or strategic HRM'. *Personnel Review*, 27: 200–12.

Gooderham P. & Nordhaug, O. 2011. 'One European model of HRM? Cranet empirical contributions'. *Human Resource Management Review*, 21: 27–36.

Hüttinger, M. 2008. 'Cultural dimensions in business life: Hofstede's indices for Latvia and Lithuania'. *Baltic Journal of Management*, 3: 359–76.

Ignjatovic, M. & Svetlik, I. 2003. 'European HRM clusters'. *EBS Review*, Autumn: 25–39.

Jarjabka, A. 2011. 'Similarities and differences in company cultures of Eastern-Europeans'. In J. Poór, P. Boday & V. Kispalne (eds), *Trends and Tendencies in Human Resources Management in Eastern Europe* (in Hungarian). Budapest: Gondolat Publishing House, 76–100.

Karoliny, Z. 2008. 'Reframing the contextual approach based on the experiences gained on analysing empirical findings of HR practices of the new capitalism in Central Eastern Europe'. International Conference on New Trends and Tendencies in the Human Resource Management – East meets West (Pécs: University of Pécs, Faculty of Business and Economics, 13–14 June 2008).

Kazlauskaitė, R. & Bučiūnienė, I. 2010. 'HR function developments in Lithuania'. *Baltic Journal of Management*, 5: 218–41.

Koubek, J. 2009. 'Managing human resourcing in the Czech Republic'. In. M. Morley, N. Heraty & S. Michailova (eds), *Managing Human Resources in Central and Eastern Europe*. London: Routledge, 132–57.

Larsen, H.H. & Brewster, C. 2003. 'Line management responsibility for HRM: What's happening in Europe?' *Employee Relations*, 25: 228–44.

Lewis, P.C. 2005. *How the East Was Won*. New York: Palgrave Macmillan.

Lucas, R., Marinova, M., Kucerova, J. & Vetrokova, M. 2004. 'HRM practice in emerging economies: A long way to go in the Slovak hotel industry?' *International Journal of Human Resource Management*, 15: 1262–79.

Mayrhofer, W. & Brewster, C. 2005. 'European human resource management: Researching developments over time'. *Management Revue*, 16: 36–62.

Michailova, S., Heraty, N. & Morley, M.J. 2009. 'Studying human resource management in the international context: The case of Central and Eastern Europe'. In M.J. Morley, N. Hearty & S. Michailova (eds), *Managing Human Resource in Central and Eastern Europe*. London: Routledge, 1–24.

Nikandrou, I., Apospori, E. & Papalexandris, N. 2005. 'Changes in HRM in Europe – A longitudinal comparative study among 18 European countries'. *Journal of European Industrial Training*, 29: 541–60.

Noorkoiv, T. & Gröön, T. 2004. 'Corporate social responsibility: The concept and its status regionally and nationally in Central and Eastern Europe and Estonia'. *EBS Review*, Winter/Spring: 59–72.

Pearce, J.L. 1991. 'From socialism to capitalism: The effects of Hungarian human resources practices'. *Academy of Management Executive*, November, 4: 75–89.

Pieper, R. 1992. 'Socialist HRM: An analysis of HRM theory and practice in the former socialist countries in Eastern Europe'. *The International Executive*, 34: 499–516.

Poór, J., Engle, A. & Gross, A. 2010. 'Human resource management practices of large multinational firms in Hungary 1988–2005'. *Acta Oeconomica*, 60(4): 427–60.

Poór, J., Karoliny, Z., Alas, R. & Vatchkova, E.K. 2011. 'Comparative international human resource management (CIHRM) in the light of the Cranet Regional Research Survey in Transitional Economies'. *Employee Relations*, 33: 428–43.

Pundziene, A. & Bučiūnienė, I. 2009. 'Managing human resources in Lithuania'. In M.J. Morley, N. Heraty & S. Michailova (eds), *Managing Human Resource in Central and Eastern Europe*. London: Routledge, 55–89.

Sorge, A. 2004. 'Cross-national differences in human resources and organisation'. In A.W. Harzing & J.V. Ruysseveldt (eds), *International Human Resource Management*. London: Sage Publications, 117–40.

Soulsby, A. & Clark, E. 1998. 'Controlling personnel: Management and motive in the transformation of the Czech enterprise'. *The International Journal of Human Resource Management*, 9: 79–98.

Sparrow, P.R. & Hiltrop, J.M. 1997. 'Redefining the field of European human resource management: A battle between national mindsets and forces of business transition?' *Human Resource Management*, 36: 201–19.

Sparrow, P.R., Schuler, R.S. & Jackson, S.E. 1994. 'Convergence or divergence: Human resource practices and policies for competitive advantage'. *The International Journal of Human Resource Management*, 5: 267–99.

Stajić, D. 2006. *Modernizacija sindikata* (The modernization of trade unions). Beograd: Institut za političke studije (Institute for Political Studies).

Svetlik, I. 2009. 'Managing human resources in Slovenia'. In M.J. Morley, N. Heraty & S. Michailova (eds), *Managing Human Resource in Central and Eastern Europe*. London: Routledge, 219–42.

Szerb, L., Richbell, S. & Vitai, Z. 2010. 'HRM in the Hungarian SME sector'. *Employee Relations*, 3: 262–80.

Zupan, N. & Kase, R. 2005. 'Strategic human resource management in European transition economies: Building a conceptual model on the case of Slovenia'. *International Journal of Human Resource Management*, 16: 882–906.

6
Converging and Diverging Trends in HRM between the Nordic Countries and Estonia

Ruth Alas and Sinikka Vanhala

Introduction

Along with the increased focus on comparative HRM research, the role of context and the debate between convergence and divergence of HRM practices have received increasing attention (Martin-Alcazar, Romero-Fernandez & Sanches-Gardey, 2005; Pudelko, 2005; Brewster, 2007; Dewettinck & Remue, 2011). The US-derived vision of HRM as a universalistic paradigm (Delery & Doty, 1996) with highly individualized relationships with employees has faced strong criticism, especially from European HRM scholars (Guest, 1990; Brewster, 1995, 2007). The European view of HRM is seen to be more contingent, a kind of contextual paradigm. Based on the analyses of Cranet empirical contributions, Gooderham and Nordhaug (2010: 34) conclude that 'the practice of HRM cannot be divorced from its institutional context'. This means that history, culture, legislation, trade union representation and the role of the state should be taken into account in understanding the use of HRM practices in particular countries.

Two major changes that have shaped the European political and economic landscape are the collapse of the Soviet Union in 1991, and the EU membership of Central and Eastern European (CEE) post-communist countries starting in 2004, when three former Soviet states, Estonia, Latvia and Lithuania, with four former Soviet-bloc countries, Hungary, Poland, Slovakia and the Czech Republic, as well as Slovenia as part of former Yugoslavia, and Cyprus and Malta, joined the EU. Bulgaria and Romania joined the EU three years later, in 2007. On the one hand, with this historical unification of East and Western Europe, diversity has increased in the EU, partly because of the number of official languages, and partly because the majority of these 12 countries are former communist or Soviet-bloc countries representing different cultural and ideological backgrounds and a lower standard of living than the EU-15 countries, which constituted the European Union between 1995 and 2003. On the other hand, EU-level regulation and legislation are leading to convergence of corporate governance and the rules of working life across member states. These European-level changes offer an exceptionally good opportunity to study how human resource management policies and practices are disseminated, and whether there is a converging trend towards 'one European model' of HRM (Brewster, 1995; Gooderham & Nordhaug, 2010) in general, and more specifically, between older European democracies, like the Nordic countries, and transition countries like Estonia, which are the focus of this chapter. Convergence refers to the increasing similarity between organizational forms and managerial practices, meaning that common management practice overrides cultural differences, while the divergence view focuses on differences in national, cultural and company contexts (Kerr et al., 1960; Brewster, Mayrhofer & Morley, 2004).

The purpose of this chapter is to contribute to European comparative HRM research by identifying converging/diverging trends in HRM practices between Nordic countries, which form a relatively homogeneous and established welfare-state area in the Northern Europe, and Estonia, which represents the Baltic transition economies in the neighbourhood of Nordic countries with close cultural, linguistic and economic connections with Nordic countries, especially with Finland. Estonia makes an interesting case. Part of the Soviet Union until 1991, after regaining its independence it started rapidly to modernize its governance, economy and management of organizations including HRM (Nurmi & Üksvärav, 1994; Vanhala, Kaarelson & Alas, 2006; Kaarelson & Alas, 2009). The Nordic influence on the Estonian economy and management has been especially strong due to investments from Nordic countries in Estonian companies. The proportion of FDI (foreign direct investment) by Finland and Sweden was almost two-thirds of all foreign investments in the early 2000; altogether the Nordic FDI in Estonia has been approximately 70 per cent of all FDI in Estonia (Ehrlich, Kaasik & Randveer, 2002; Sippola, 2009; Bank of Estonia, 2012). The converging and diverging trends are studied by applying data collected in the international Cranet surveys in 2000,[1] 2004 and 2009. The analysis is focused on organizations employing 100 employees or more.

Converging versus diverging European HRM

The rapidly enlarging European Union with three basic freedoms, free movement of capital, goods and services, and labour, is reshaping the European economies and working life. The transformation process going on in Europe together with increasing globalization of companies has raised the question of competitiveness to the primary position both at national and company levels. In this process, the role and position of human capital and human resource management have changed. The HRM function is increasingly expected to contribute to the competitive advantage of companies. This is especially visible in the extant literature focusing on the HRM–performance (HRM-P) link (Huselid, 1995; Guest, 1997; Paauwe, 2004;

Stavrou, Charalambous & Spiliotis, 2007). In this HRM-P literature, HRM scholars have tried to identify 'best' HRM practices (Pfeffer, 1998), 'bundles' of HRM practices (Stavrou & Brewster, 2005; Gooderham, Parry & Ringdal, 2008), or so-called high performance, high commitment and high involvement work/HRM practices (Becker & Huselid, 1998; Boxall & Macky, 2009), all aiming at identifying such HRM practices or systems of work that might lead to superior organizational performance. According to the US Department of Labor (1993), such high-performance HRM practices include careful and extensive systems for recruitment, selection and training, clear job design, local-level participation procedures and monitoring of attitudes. From the point of view of European HRM, the universalistic paradigm has been supported by efforts to identify a European HRM model (Brewster & Hegewisch, 1994; Brewster, 1995); on the other hand, there are a number of studies indicating the existence of several HRM clusters in Europe (Ignjatovic & Svetlik, 2003; Stavrou, Brewster & Charalambous, 2010).

The question of the direction of change – convergence versus divergence – in the adoption of HRM practices and HRM systems in Europe has been widely discussed (Brewster et al., 2004; Paauwe, 2004; Pudelko, 2005; Mayrhofer et al., 2011). The advocates of the 'convergence thesis' base their argumentation on several societal, business and organizational-level mechanisms and trends in Europe, ranging from globalization of companies and the development of European Union-level legislation and regulation, to the selling capabilities of international consultants, and the role of international business schools, textbooks and training programmes of global companies. All these mechanisms are seen to increase similarity in company management and HRM between different countries and cultures. Instead, the advocates of divergence thinking base their argumentation on differences in national, cultural and organizational contexts, and the role of core competencies and the alignment of HRM with corporate strategy in looking for competitive advantage (Clark & Pugh, 1999/2000; see Paauwe & Boselie, 2005).

Partly related to globalization, the neo-institutional theory (DiMaggio & Powell, 1983, 1991) offers an explanation to the convergence–divergence debate: convergence occurs because companies are seeking legitimacy and acceptance in hostile environments by isomorphic developments through mimetic, normative and coercive mechanisms. According to Paauwe and Boselie (2003, 2005), these institutional mechanisms shape HRM in organizations. The mimetic mechanisms related to HRM refer to the imitation of strategies and practices of competitors; the normative mechanisms refer to the relationship between management policies and employee backgrounds (educational level, job experience and professional networks); and the coercive mechanisms include the influence of labour legislation, trade unions and the government. According to Haunchild and Miner (1997), the efforts of organizations to model themselves after successful competitors in the field may lead to different modes of interorganizational imitation: frequency-based imitation (copying of practices adopted by a large number of organizations), trait-based imitation (imitating higher-status organizations), or outcome-based imitation (practices or structures producing positive outcomes for others are imitated). The imitation of practices may lead towards greater similarity, that is, companies adopt similar modes of practices and behaviour, but also to increasing diversity owing to trait or outcome-based imitation. In the selection, adoption and retention of best HRM practices, Paauwe and Boselie (2005: 1002) conclude that 'very often firms adopt HR practices only either out of uncertainty or to avoid being considered old fashioned or for the sake on maintaining or restoring legitimacy...' Best HRM practices are benchmarked and copied.

In European HRM studies, the direction of change (convergence versus divergence or stasis/no change) is widely studied (Mayrhofer, Morley & Brewster, 2004; Papalexandris & Panayotopoulou, 2004; Mayrhofer & Brewster, 2005; Tregaskis & Brewster, 2006; Karoliny, Farkas & Poor, 2009; Mayrhofer et al., 2011). In these studies, two kinds of convergence are identified (Mayrhofer et al., 2004, 2011): final convergence and directional similarity. By final convergence, Mayrhofer et al. (2011: 52) refer to convergence in the literal sense of the word, that is, the situation in which the values of a variable over time develop, for instance in two countries, in a way that would lead to a common endpoint. Directional similarity occurs when the values develop in the same direction, but not to a common endpoint.

The results of prior European convergence–divergence studies in HRM have been mixed: in some cases at least directional similarity could be observed, while in some others studies significant national differences, and thus divergence or stasis, are emphasized. Examples of studies indicating at least directional similarity are those by Mayrhofer et al. (2004) using Cranet data from 22 countries, and Mayrhofer and Brewster (2005) using data from 18 European countries involved in the Cranet studies between 1991 and 2000. Even a minor converging trend was found in a study by Gooderham and Brewster (2003), based on four European countries in 1992, 1995 and 1999; but much remained unchanged. Based on Cranet 1995 and 1999 data from 18 European countries, Nikandrou, Apospori & Papalexandris (2005) identified two major country clusters, North-West and South-East, regarding HRM practices. According to the authors, there was no indication of convergence between these two major country clusters: most differences remained unchanged, some disappeared and some new ones emerged between the two survey data collection rounds. Mayrhofer et al. (2011) analysed the converging trend in HRM policies and practices in large private sector firms in 13 European countries between 1992 and 2004 and found strong directional similarity in employee rewards (use of performance-related and flexible pay) and employee communication. However, no evidence of final convergence could be found.

The whole picture of converging/diverging trends in European HRM looks rather confusing. The strong mimetic and normative mechanism – pressures to imitate 'best' HR practices and the EU-level labour legislation and other steering mechanisms – lends itself to converging management and HRM, while the empirical studies only in part support this thinking. On the other hand, national legislation, culture and business systems may limit the convergence (Whitley & Kristensen, 1996; Witt & Redding, 2009).

The focus of this chapter is the directions of change in HRM between Nordic countries and Estonia. The Nordic countries form an exceptionally homogeneous country cluster according to prior cultural and HR studies, as will be discussed in a subsequent section, while Estonia is a Baltic transition country with close connections with and strong influence of the Nordic countries. Our preliminary hypothesis is that there is evidence for a convergence trend between Nordic and Estonian HRM.

HRM in the Nordic countries and Estonia

Before discussing HRM in the Nordic countries and Estonia, the historical, economic and cultural context of the study is described. The purpose of this contextual positioning is to show the roots of the homogeneity of the Nordic countries and the different road of Estonia to the present Western-type society. We also try to illustrate the influence of the Nordic countries on Estonian economics and HRM.

The Nordic countries and the Nordic model

In addition to geographic and cultural proximity, the Nordic countries (Denmark, Finland, Norway and Sweden) share strong historical, ethnic, linguistic and religious binds fulfilling thus the definition of a country cluster by Clark and Mallory (1996). Moreover, the Nordic countries have a long tradition of cooperation across many areas of social and societal activities. For instance, passport union and free mobility across borders were realized between the Nordic countries almost half a century earlier than the Schengen Treaty was accepted in European Union. Nordic cooperation in the present form started in the early 1950s. The Nordic Council was founded, the Agreement on a Common Labour Market was accepted, and the Nordic Passport Union was established allowing free mobility across the borders of the Nordic countries. The liberation of the labour market had a significant impact on employee mobility inside the Nordic area.

The Nordic model (also known as the Scandinavian model) was originally used to describe the combination of welfare state ideology, social democratic dominance and the Nordic type of corporatism in labour market relations. The Nordic model was offered as a 'third way' between capitalism and communism to industrial and welfare democracy (Byrkjeflot, 2001). The basic features of the model are: a comprehensive, all-embracing, system of social welfare, a historical compromise between labour and capital to ensure industrial peace, and a cooperative approach to day-to-day policy based on negotiation. In the 1980s, the meaning of the Nordic model was broadened to cover a shared cultural heritage, common values and a consensus-seeking approach in a mixed economy. Equality in many meanings is interwoven in the model (Lindeberg, Mansson & Vanhala, 2004).

Estonia in between the cultural blocs

Estonia, in comparison, is a small Baltic country in Northern Europe, bordered to the north by the Gulf of Finland and to the west by the Baltic Sea, with a population of less than 1.5 million people. Estonia lost its independence during the Second World War. The World War and the Soviet era slowed down Estonia's economic growth. Nevertheless, Estonia enjoyed a more developed economy and a higher standard of living than most other parts of the Soviet Union (Hoag & Kasoff, 1999; Nurmi & Üksvärav, 1994). However, a wide wealth gap emerged between Estonia and the Nordic neighbouring countries, Finland and Sweden. The movement towards an independent economy started in Estonia in the late 1980s. With the weakening Soviet Union, Estonia began to liberate its economy and politics with a course towards self-determination. After 50 years of occupation, Estonia regained its independence in 1991.

The role of foreign investors and foreign-owned subsidiaries has been central in shaping the Estonian economy to its internationally competitive scale (Kiriazov, Sullivan & Tu, 2000; Heliste, Kosonen & Mattila, 2007). The foreign direct investments in Estonia have gradually grown since the mid-1990s with a major increase in 2004–7. A significant part of foreign investments in Estonia are made by Finnish and Swedish companies (63 per cent in 2009), with the other Nordic countries, Norway and Denmark, also among the biggest investors (Ehrlich et al., 2002; Sippola, 2009; Bank of Estonia, 2012). The foreign investors are seen as important change agents in turning Estonia into a Western market economy (Heliste et al., 2007). Recently, the influence and legislation of European Union have increased in Estonia. EU membership in 2004 and the membership in the EU Monetary Union (EMU) since the beginning of 2011 have strengthened the impact of the European Union on the Estonian economy.

Nordic and Estonian HRM

Most international comparative cultural (Hofstede, 1980; House et al., 2004), political (Esping-Andersen, 1990; Byrkjeflot 2001) and HRM studies (Brewster & Larsen, 2000; Ignjatovic & Svetlik, 2003; Vanhala, 2008) have resulted in identifying a separate Nordic cluster. The characterizing features of the Nordic HRM cluster are high involvement of employees in HRM and other organizational issues, high formalization of policies and strategies, and decentralized decision-making, importance of employee training and development and the increase of flexible work arrangements along with relatively modest labour turnover (Ignjatovic & Svetlik, 2003; Vanhala, 2008; see also Lindeberg et al., 2004; Rogaczewska et al., 2004). Line management and the head of the HRM department take significant responsibility for HRM.

Compared with the Nordic HRM, Estonian HRM has a shorter history (Vanhala et al., 2006; Kaarelson, 2010). Until 1991, when Estonia was part of the Soviet Union, staff (cadre) departments existed in every Estonian organization, taking care of administrative tasks and working in close cooperation with organizations of the Communist party (Vanhala et al., 2006; Tepp, 2007). After regaining independence, Western-type personnel management appeared in Estonian organizations, and the professional body PARE (the Estonian Association for Personnel Development) was established in 1992. The change from 'personnel' to 'human resources' management thinking and terminology took place in Estonia in the late 1990s – more than a decade later than, for example, in Finland (Vanhala et al., 2006).

In Ignjatovic and Svetlik's analysis (2003) based on Cranet data collected in 2000, Estonia was located in the 'Peripheral' HRM cluster with Bulgaria, Greece, Ireland and Turkey, among others. The underlying characteristic of this 'Peripheral' cluster was managerial-focused HRM. The HRM departments were well staffed, and strategies were less formalized than on average in Europe. In addition, significant shares of money were spent on training of selected groups of employees. Instead, mission statements and strategies tended to be less formalized than the European average.

Even if the differences between Estonian and Nordic HRM were significant according to 2000 Cranet data (Ignjatovic & Svetlik, 2003), the changes in the Estonian economy have been strong in the first decade of 2000. Given the rapid change from a command economy to a capitalist market economy (Hoag & Kasoff, 1999), a significant Nordic impact on Estonian companies through FDIs, and increasing EU legislation along with Estonia's EU membership as well as the results of prior HRM studies, our preliminary hypothesis is that Estonian HRM has converged with the Nordic HRM during the first decade of 2000.

Compared to high formalization of HRM strategies and policies and high line manager involvement in Nordic countries, Estonian HRM has been less strategic, though the more recent studies on Estonian HRM (Kaarelson & Alas, 2009; Poor et al., 2011) emphasize the strengthening role of strategic HRM. In addition, the well-staffed HRM departments refer to lower line manager involvement in Estonian organizations. However, considering the quick changes in the Estonian economy and strong Nordic influence on the Estonian economy and HRM, as well, we suggest the following propositions:

Proposition 1:   *There is a converging trend (directional similarity) in strategic HRM between Nordic and Estonian organizations.*

Proposition 2: *There is a converging trend (directional similarity) in line manager responsibility between Nordic and Estonian organizations.*

As stated, Estonian HRM has been strongly influenced by foreign investors. HRM practices, such as recruiting and selection models, compensation systems and performance management, were first applied in foreign-owned subsidiaries in Estonia (Kiriazov et al., 2000). During the transition period, HRM was also strengthened by incorporating policies and strategies into operational-level HRM decisions (Garavan et al., 1998).

According to prior studies (Ignjatovic & Svetlik, 2003; Vanhala, 2008), the HRM practices adopted in the Nordic countries indicate softer rather than hard practices. Compared with the rest of European organizations, the HRM bundles that scored higher values in the Nordic organizations were, for instance, 'action programmes' (to improve the participation of the following groups in the workforce: ethnic minorities, older employees, the disabled and women), informal managerial and non-managerial career development and briefing for employees, except management, also briefings about strategy, financial performance and organization of work. In Estonian organizations, HRM practices, such as recruiting and selection of employees, compensation and performance management, were first applied in foreign-owned (mainly Nordic) subsidiaries (Kiriazov et al., 2000), from which the practices were transferred to domestic organizations (Kaarelson, 2010). Consequently, we propose as follows:

Proposition 3: *There is a converging trend (directional similarity) in HRM practices between Nordic and Estonian organizations.*

Typical to the Nordic countries are high unionization rates of employees as well as high employers' membership in employer federations, corporatist negotiation structures and a relatively strong influence of trade unions on company-level HRM decisions related to wages and salaries, working conditions, co-determination and communication (Lindeberg et al., 2004; Dølvik, 2007). Finland and Sweden are at the top of the EU statistics with the proportion of over 70 per cent of employees in unions, and Denmark and Norway are also among the top five in Europe (Trade unions, 2012). Instead, the influence of trade unions in Estonia has been weak (Alas, 2012) – the unionization rate is only 10 per cent, which is mainly explained by a reaction to Soviet era compulsory participation (Sippola, 2009, 2011; Trade unions, 2012). In most European countries, including the Nordic countries and Estonia, the unionization rate has been declining (Kallaste & Woolfson, 2009). When considering the Estonian historical roots in the employee unionization we propose as follows:

Proposition 4: *Estonian organizations are diverging from the Nordic ones in labour union membership.*

Methodology

In order to examine the current state and converging versus diverging trends of HRM in Nordic countries (Denmark, Finland, Norway and Sweden) and Estonia, survey data on strategic human resource management policies and practices collected by the Cranet network in 2000, 2004 and 2008 are applied (see, for example, Mayrhofer, 1998; Tregaskis, Mahoney & Atterbury, 2004; Mayrhofer et al., 2011). Based on prior HRM research (Stavrou et al., 2010; Mayrhofer et al., 2011), we focus on the two main factors related to HRM: HRM configuration and HRM practices. The HRM configuration refers to organizing and configuring HRM within the firm (Mayrhofer et al., 2011) – how strategic HRM is, and line manager responsibility, which is seen, in contrast to prior personnel management, as a key characteristic of HRM (Legge, 2005) – and the main HRM practice areas of appraisal, career development, action programmes (to improve the participation of the following groups in the workforce: ethnic minorities, older employees, disabled people and women), flexibility and communication as well as unionization of employees. Employee recruitment and selection as well as remuneration could not be included in the analyses, because questions were not asked identically in the three data collection rounds.

The Cranet data are not panel data but a trend study (Mayrhofer et al., 2011). They allow us to measure changes in the countries involved in the study as well as according to size, sector and industry. Broadly speaking, the Cranet data are representative over time and in each economy despite relatively low response rates (Mayrhofer et al., 2011: 56). The Cranet data applied in this study were based on the questionnaire generated by the Cranet Network.

The organizational sample included private companies and public sector organizations with more than 100 employees. The period under study covers economic fluctuations. Compared with the situation in 2000, 2004 data collection took place at a time of economic growth and an optimistic atmosphere, while the situation in 2008–10 was dramatically different: the annual growth of gross domestic product was –4 per cent in EU-15; in the Nordic countries and Estonia, the decline was even deeper (Nordic Statistical Yearbook, 2010; Statistics Estonia, 2010) (see Table 6.1).

The number of Estonian organizations that employed more than 200 people was only 230 in 2001 (Kaarelson, 2010). The share of large organizations was much smaller in Estonia than in the Nordic countries. This was also visible in the Cranet survey; the Estonian organizations responding in the survey were smaller than the Nordic ones. More than half of Estonian organizations employed fewer than 200 employees. In the Nordic countries, this was the case in about every one-fifth of responding organizations.

Variables

The Cranet questionnaires involve over 100 variables covering the main areas of HRM and HRM practices. In this chapter, we have selected HRM

Table 6.1 Responding organizations according to the size distribution, 2000, 2004 and 2008

	2000		2004		2008	
	Nordic %	Estonia %	Nordic %	Estonia %	Nordic %	Estonia %
100–199 employees	23.7	67.0	19.0	52.5	16.4	51.4
200–499 employees	33.0	19.3	36.2	27.7	35.9	32.4
500+ employees	43.3	13.8	44.8	19.8	47.7	16.2
Total	100.0	100.0	100.0	100.0	100.0	100.0
N	1553	218	1189	118	878	74

variables and bundles of variables that represent the main HRM areas of prior studies (Ignjatovic & Svetlik, 2003; Brewster et al., 2004; Vanhala, 2008; Stavrou et al., 2010). A practical precondition for selecting HRM variables for the analyses was the identical formulation of questions in all three survey rounds. Factor analyses and Cronbach alpha coefficients were applied to reduce the multitude of HRM variables to three combined measures (two strategic HRM bundles and a bundle of HRM practices) and a single question related to trade union membership, as illustrated in Table 6.2. The combined variables (sub-bundles) were constructed by the MEAN modification (SPSS), and the final three HRM bundles by summing the items/sub-bundles.

1. **How strategic HRM is.** SHRM was measured by three items: '*Does your organization have a written personnel/HRM strategy?*' 1 = Yes, 0 = No; '*Does the person responsible for HR have a place on the board or equivalent top executive team?*' 1 = Yes, 0 = No; '*If your organization has a business/service strategy, at what stage is the person responsible for personnel/HR involved in this development?*' 1 = From the outset, 0 = Other. The value of the SHRM bundle ranged between 0 and 3.
2. **Line responsibility.** The question was asked: '*Does line management in consultation with the HR function have primary responsibility for major policy decisions on the following issues: (1) Pay and benefits, (2) Recruitment and selection, (3) Training and development, (4) Industrial relations, and (5) Workforce expansion/reduction?*' All items were coded as: 1 = Yes, 0 = No. The items were summed, and the value of the combined line responsibility bundle ranged between 0 and 5.
3. **HRM practices were measured** by five sub-bundles, which were selected because the questions were the same in all three data collection rounds. They also represented HR practices that are more common in the Nordic countries than the rest of Europe (Ignjatovic & Svetlik, 2003; Vanhala, 2008).

Table 6.2   The variables/combined variables, numbers of items, scales and Cronbach alphas of combined scales

	No. of items/sub-bundles	Scale	Cronbach α Min & Max values in 2000, 2004 & 2009
Strategic HRM	3	0–3	.51–.60
Line responsibility	5	0–5	.71–.74
HRM practices	5	0–5	.56–.77
Trade union membership (76–100%)	1	0–1	–

3a. **Appraisal** was measured by asking: '*Is the appraisal data used to inform decisions in the following areas: (a) Pay, (b) Analysis of training and development needs, and (c) Career?*' The items were coded as: 1 = Yes, 0 = No, and combined by the MEAN modification into a sub-bundle 'Appraisal'. The value of this sub-bundle ranged between 0 and 1. The MEAN modification was used to standardize the values of these sub-bundles of HRM practices.

3b. **Career development** was measured with the item: '*To what extent do you use the following methods for career development: (1) Succession plans, (2) Planned job rotation, and 'High flier' schemes?*' The responses were coded as follows: 1 = Yes (uses the method), 0 = No (does not use the method). The items were combined by the MEAN modification into a sub-bundle 'Career development'. The value of this sub-bundle ranged between 0 and 1.

3c. **Action programmes** were measured by asking: '*Does your organization have action programmes (related to (a) Recruitment, (b) Training, and (c) Career progress) covering any of the following groups to improve their participation in the workforce: (1) Minority ethnics, (2) People with disabilities, and (3) Women?*' The items were coded as: 1 = Yes, 0 = No, and combined by the MEAN modification into three combined variables (three groups of employees or potential employees in 2000 and 2009 data; thus corresponding to the 2004 wording of the alternatives), and further, they were combined (by the MEAN) into a sub-bundle 'Action programmes'. The value of this sub-bundle ranged between 0 and 1.

3d. **Employee-initiated flexibility** was measured by asking: '*Indicate the proportion of those employed by your organization who are on the following working arrangements: (1) Flexi-time and (2) Home-based work.*' The responses were coded as follows: 1 = Yes (the working arrangement was used), 0 = No (the working arrangement was not used). The items were combined by the MEAN modification into a sub-bundle 'Employee-initiated flexibility'. The value of this sub-bundle ranged between 0 and 1.

3e. **Communication** was measured by asking: '*Which employee categories are formally briefed about (1) Business strategy, (2) Financial performance,* *and (3) Organization of work: (a) Management, (b) Professional/Technical, (c) Clerical, and (d) Manual employees?'* Each area and each employee category were coded as: 1 = Yes, 0 = No. The value of this sub-bundle ranged between 0 and 1.

The HRM practices bundle was finally constructed by summing (the SUM modification) the values of the above five sub-bundles related to HRM practices. The value of this combined 'HRM practices' bundle ranged between 0 and 5.

4. **Trade union membership:** The share of organizations with high (76–100 per cent) trade union participation rate was coded: 1 = Yes (the trade union membership rate varies between 76 and 100 per cent) and 0 = No (the trade union membership rate is ≤ 75 per cent).

Company-related variables applied were: Sector: 1 = Private sector, 0 = Public sector, and Size of the company: 1 = 100–199 employees, 2 = 200–499 and 3 = 500+ employees.

The analysis of data was based on comparing the means of Nordic and Estonian organizations by One-way ANOVA. The statistical significance was tested by F-values. The trends are illustrated in the following figures. The impact of sector and size of organizations was analysed by correlate analysis and One-way ANOVA.

Trends in HRM policies and practices between Nordic countries and Estonia

Strategic HRM

The role of HRM generally has changed from the early administrative role during the 1980s towards a more strategic position in the 1990s (Lundy, 1994; Legge, 2005). This was the case in the Nordic countries, as well (Vanhala 1995, 2008; Brewster & Larsen, 2000). By contrast, in Estonia, the change from personnel administration to human resource management thinking and strategic orientation took place a decade later (Vanhala et al., 2006; Tepp, 2007). The strategic role of HRM is measured in this chapter by three typical measures of SHRM as described above.

There was a statistically significant difference in the mean SHRM levels between the Nordic countries and Estonia in all three years of data collection (Table 6.3). According to the ANOVA, the difference between the Nordic countries and Estonia was especially strong in 2000 (F = 160,745; p < 0.001) Figure 6.1 illustrates the trends in the level of SHRM.

The change between 2000 and 2004 indicates a converging trend; however, the change from 2004 to 2008 refers to directional similarity. Both in the Nordic countries and Estonia, the strategic and formalized role of HRM is getting stronger. Sector (private vs public) does not correlate with strategic

Table 6.3   Means, standard deviations and statistical significance of SHRM measure between the Nordic countries and Estonia in 2000, 2004 and 2008

Year	Country cluster/ country	Mean	SD	F-value
2000	Nordic Estonia	1,766 0,848	1,014 0,890	160,745***
2004	Nordic Estonia	1,790 1,079	0,991 1,026	47,717***
2008	Nordic Estonia	2,041 1,361	0,970 1,025	32,369***

Note: $p < 0.05^{*}$, $p < 0.01^{**}$, $p < 0.001^{***}$.

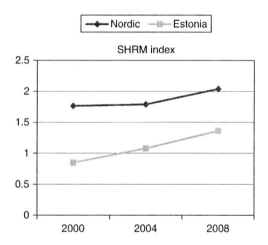

Figure 6.1   Trends in SHRM between the Nordic countries and Estonia

HRM; instead, size of the company has a positive correlation with SHRM, indicating that HRM is more strategic in larger companies (Table 6.4).

The ANOVA confirmed that the sector of the organization was related to SHRM neither in Estonian organizations (except in 2004) nor in the Nordic ones. The impact of the size of the organization on SHRM remained the same in Estonian and Nordic organizations in 2000, 2004 and 2008.

Line manager responsibility

Line manager responsibility was used as an indication of the strategic role of HRM and integration of HRM with other functions of organizations. Devolving HRM decisions and practices to line managers is seen to reserve

Table 6.4 Correlations between HRM bundles
and sector and size, 2000, 2004 and 2008

Year	Sector	Size
SHRM		
2000	.013	,167***
2004	,037	,218***
2008	−.005	,129***
Line responsibility		
2000	,025	−,108***
2004	−,148***	−,081***
2008	−,031*	−,251***
HRM practices		
2000	,100***	,156***
2004	,080***	,150***
2008	,021	,202***
Trade union membership (high)		
2000	−.287***	.149***
2004	−.371***	.194***
2008	−.125***	.110***

Note: $p < 0.05$*, $p < 0.01$**, $p < 0.001$***.

time for HRM professionals to focus on more strategic issues and to lead to full integration of HR into the company's real work (Ulrich, 1998: 125–6). The role of line responsibility in HRM has been increasingly important (Larsen & Brewster, 2003; Papalexandris & Panayotopoulou, 2005; McConville, 2006). Devolvement of HRM to line managers is typically more common in the Nordic countries than in other parts of Europe (Ignjatovic & Svetlik, 2003).

The next table (Table 6.5) indicates the means of major policy decisions for which line management in consultation with the HR function have primary responsibility. In all three points of time, the means of line responsibility were higher in Estonian organizations; however, this difference was statistically significant only in 2000 (Figure 6.2).

The trend in line manager responsibility between Nordic countries and Estonia can be interpreted as indicating convergence. The converging trend is obvious from 2000 to 2004. With a lack of statistical significance in line responsibility between Nordic and Estonian organizations in 2008, the results support final convergence. Both sector (except for 2000) and size correlate negatively with line manager responsibility, indicating that line manager responsibility is higher in the public sector and smaller companies (Table 6.4).

Table 6.5   Means, standard deviations and statistical significance of line responsibilities between the Nordic countries and Estonia in 2000, 2004 and 2008

Year	Country cluster/ country	Mean	SD	F-value
2000	Nordic	3,243	1,576	
	Estonia	3,744	1,518	18,881***
2004	Nordic	3,157	1,571	
	Estonia	3,222	1,529	0,155 (NS)
2008	Nordic	2,764	1,645	
	Estonia	3,138	1,746	3,403 (NS)

Note: $p < 0.05$*, $p < 0.01$**, $p < 0.001$***, NS = not significant.

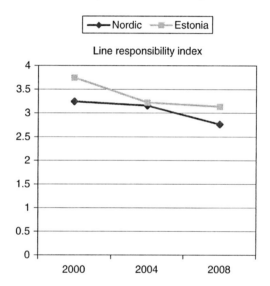

Figure 6.2   Trends in formal line responsibilities between the Nordic countries and Estonia

HRM practices

In prior research, the lists of 'best' or 'advanced' HRM practices and bundles of practices vary considerably. For example, Steven Wood (1999) in his review article identifies 222 such 'best' HRM practices. However, in most studies, the HRM practices or practice bundles are related to employee staffing, training and development, compensation, and communication and participation (Pfeffer, 1994; 1998; Delery & Doty, 1996).

The bundle of HRM practices applied in this study covers appraisal, career development, action programmes, flexibility and communication. The trends in the use of these HRM practice bundles indicate a movement towards final convergence between Nordic countries and Estonia. The Nordic means were higher in 2000 and 2004 becoming lower in 2008, and Estonian means were rising linearly from 2000 to 2008 (Table 6.6 and Figure 6.3).

The trends in HRM practices indicate a trend towards final convergence between Estonian and Nordic organizations. It is however true that there is no evidence that this will continue the same in the future. That is why this 'final convergence' can be interpreted only as a trend, not as a final state of affairs. Organizations in the private sector (except 2008) and larger organizations were more likely to use the HRM practices studied (Table 6.4). In Estonian organizations, sector was not related to use of HRM practices; in Nordic organizations, this was the case in 2008. The size of the organization was strongly related to use of HRM practices ($p < 0.001$) in the Nordic organizations but not in the Estonian ones.

Table 6.6 Means, standard deviations and statistical significance of HRM practices between the Nordic countries and Estonia in 2000, 2004 and 2008

Year	Country cluster/ country	Mean	SD	F-value
2000	Nordic	2,302	0,875	
	Estonia	1,941	0,854	32,732***
2004	Nordic	2,546	0,928	
	Estonia	2,246	0,817	9,890**
2008	Nordic	2,376	0,870	
	Estonia	2,436	0,953	0,310 (NS)

Note: $p < 0.05*$, $p < 0.01**$, $p < 0.001***$, NS = not significant.

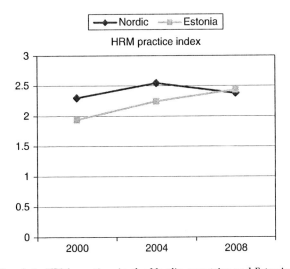

Figure 6.3 Trends in HRM practices in the Nordic countries and Estonia

Employee relations

Trade union membership level has traditionally been high in the Nordic countries, while in Estonia the unionization level has remained low through its 20 years of independence. According to Kallaste and Woolfson (2009), trade union density is falling in most of the world, especially in the Baltic countries, where it is the lowest in the European Union. Instead, the Nordic countries have traditionally held the top positions in the unionization rates of employees (Worker participation, 2012). The main reasons for the low union density in Estonia can be traced back to the history of trade unions during the Soviet era as a part of ideological propaganda apparatus, the development of 'a Soviet person' (Alas, 2012). It is interpreted that the legacy of the Soviet Union has played an especially big role in the decline of trade unions in the Baltic countries (Kallaste & Woolfson, 2009).

According to Cranet studies, the proportion of firms with zero trade union membership has grown in Estonia from 32.9 per cent in 2000 to 52.2 per cent in 2004 and, further, to 58.8 per cent in 2009. It means that we are now in a situation in which over half of large Estonian organizations report that none of their employees is a member of a trade union. In the Nordic countries such is the case in less than one per cent of organizations. The next figure illustrates the opposite side of the coin, organizations with high unionization rates (see Figure 6.4).

In Figure 6.4, we can see a lowering trend in the proportion of organizations with high (76–100 per cent) unionization rates in the Nordic

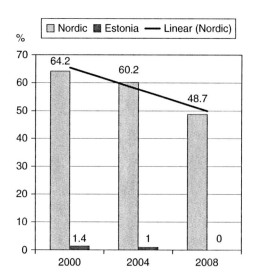

Figure 6.4   Shares of organizations with high union membership (76–100%) rates in the Nordic countries and Estonia, 2000, 2004 and 2008

organizations. The rate of change is much lower in Estonian organizations, where the share of organizations with high unionization is almost non-existent. The trend is converging, that is, towards lower unionization rates both in the Nordic countries as well as in Estonia. As Table 6.4 indicates, high trade union membership rates are more common in public organizations than in the private sector and in larger organizations than in smaller ones. The correlations between high unionization rate and sector and size of organizations were highest in 2004 and lowest in 2008.

Summary and discussion

The purpose of this chapter was to analyse and identify converging versus diverging trends of certain HRM policies and practices between Estonia and the Nordic countries. Estonia is an especially interesting case as it was part of the Soviet Union until 1991 and with close connections to and geographical proximity with the Nordic countries. In addition, the Nordic influence on Estonian organizations has been significant owing to a high influx of FDI from Nordic organizations to Estonia involving also their business and HR models and practices (Kiriazov et al., 2000; Sippola, 2011). Our preliminary hypothesis was that there would be a converging trend (or at least directional similarity) between Estonian and Nordic organizations in strategic HRM, line manager responsibility and HRM practices bundles, while there would be a diverging trend in the high unionization level of employees.

The propositions related to the converging trend in SHRM, line manager responsibility and HRM practices were supported. In the HRM practices bundle and the line manager responsibility bundle, a trend towards final convergence could be identified from 2000 to 2008, while in SHRM directional similarity could be observed. Instead, the industrial relations system differs between Nordic countries and Estonia. Contrary to our proposition related to a diverging trend in unionization, the percentages of high unionization rates of employees (76–100 per cent) indicate a lowering (and thus) converging trend in the Nordic countries in a situation in which the percentages vary between 0 and 1 per cent in Estonia.

The era of strategic human resource management started in Estonia later than in the Nordic neighbouring countries. The motivation of companies to adopt advanced HRM policies and practices has thus been strong (Vanhala et al., 2006; Tepp, 2007; Kaarelson, 2010). Also, the recession of 2008–9 directed the HRM functions in Estonia to adopt a more strategic orientation (Vösa, 2010). The upward trend in Estonian SHRM during 2000–9 was sharper than in the Nordic highly formalized SHRM (Ignjatovic & Svetlik, 2003). A similar upward trend was observable in the Estonian HRM practices bundle. Instead, the trends in line manager responsibility were downward in both Nordic and Estonian organizations, indicating the strengthening role of the HRM function in major policy decisions, especially in large private companies. Although there is a downward trend, it is starting from high levels. High line manager responsibility is a typical Nordic feature of HRM (Ignjatovic & Svetlik, 2003; Vanhala, 2008), which is related to the strategic role of HRM (Storey, 1992). The result of this study refers to the centralization trend in HRM decision-making.

This study as well as many other studies (Sippola, 2009) shows that HRM practices and policies are relatively easily distributed to other countries and cultures, while the industrial relations model is much more difficult to transfer (DiMaggio & Powell, 1983, 1991; Sippola, 2011). According to Sippola (2011: 370), 'a lack of model transfer (employee relations system from Nordic to Baltic countries) seems to be a rule rather than exception'. In Estonia, the low and still lowering unionization rate is a direct result of the collapse of Soviet-era unions at the end of the 1980s, when union membership was compulsory, and the Soviet regime used the unions as its ideological weapon. The Nordic investors in Estonia have not brought any change. Sippola (2009) refers to 'regime shopping' when companies from highly unionized Nordic countries invest in sparsely unionized countries (e.g. Baltic states), and take advantage of the situation. It is true however that the unionization rate is decreasing in Nordic countries, as well (Kallaste & Woolfson, 2009). In spite of the lowering trend, the difference between Nordic countries and Estonia is so big that perhaps convergence terminology should not be used in this connection at all.

Compared with prior convergence/divergence studies with relatively modest indications towards convergence in European HRM (Mayrhofer et al., 2004; Papalexandris & Panayotopoulou, 2004; Mayrhofer & Brewster, 2005; Tregaskis & Brewster, 2006; Karoliny et al., 2009; Mayrhofer et al., 2011), the results of this study reveal both directional similarity and a trend towards final convergence. This was an expected result owing to an exceptionally strong influence of Nordic, especially Finnish and Swedish, companies on the Estonian economy and business through FDI (Ehrlich et al., 2002; Heliste et al., 2007; Statistics Estonia, 2010; Sippola, 2011). The special position of Estonia as an advanced part of the Soviet Union, and a rapid adoption of Western values and practices after the collapse of the Soviet Union, also help explain the results. It is true that the main change in personnel issues happened when the Soviet cadre system was replaced by Western-type personnel administration (Vanhala et al., 2006; Tepp, 2007; Kaarelson, 2010); however, the change has continued.

Conclusions and limitations

The results of this study confirm the converging trend of HRM between Nordic countries and Estonia, a Baltic transition state. The present state of Estonian HRM, as well as the converging nature of Estonian and Nordic HRM, can be understood when considering the post-war history of Estonia with a special position as a Soviet state, a rapid transfer towards a market economy after the collapse of the Soviet Union, and the adoption of Western values and practices. Estonia started rapidly to integrate with the Western institutions and obtained membership in the European Union (2004), NATO (2004) and the European Monetary Union (2011). At the same time the Nordic companies invested strongly in Estonian industry. An interesting detail is that Estonian foreign policy-makers have tried to change the public image of the country by redefining it as part of the Nordic countries rather than the Baltic region (Largerspetz, 2003). Applying neo-institutional theory (DiMaggio & Powell, 1983, 1991), the strong orientation towards Western values and Northern neighbours may thus be used to explain the adoption of management and HRM policies and practices in Estonia, and further the converging trend revealed in the study.

This study involves several limitations. Based on Cranet data, it is important to note that Cranet is a trend study, not a panel study (Mayrhofer et al., 2011). In a panel design, the same organizations are studied in different points of time, while in a trend study a representative sample of organizations is taken in different countries at different points of time. Owing to the rapid rate of change of companies and businesses, a trend study gives a more reliable view of management and HRM over time compared with a panel. Relatively low response rates are an obvious limitation. The average response rate in the Nordic countries was 22 per cent in 2000 and 20 per cent in 2004. In 2008, the response rates dropped dramatically, to 10.5 per cent in the Nordic countries. The trend was similar in Estonia, while not fully comparable, because of multiple data collection methods. However, while the response rates of this study are somewhat low, they are very comparable to other international company-level surveys (Baruch & Holton, 2008). Another limitation mainly emerging from a vast international network with over 20 years' history is related to changes in the questionnaire (Dewettinck & Remue, 2011). All questions are not available in trend studies; only part of them is exactly in the same format, which limits the range of HRM practices that could be chosen for the comparison. In addition, a questionnaire that is applicable in all contexts, for all kinds of organizations in different countries and cultures, cannot go deeply into topics that might be relevant in a certain research design such as in comparing trends in Nordic and Estonian HR practices.

In spite of these limitations, the results of this study increase our understanding of the adoption of HR practices in a transition country with a relatively short history in Western-style HRM and the converging trends between neighbour countries with close historical, economic and cultural links.

Note

1. All Cranet data collection rounds have taken two to three years. In this chapter, the first data collection round (2000) covers the years 1999–2000, the second one (2004) covers the years 2004–5 and the third one (2009) covers the years 2008–10.

References

Alas, R. 2012. 'The reasons for low popularity of trade unions in Estonia'. In V.-M. Autio (ed.), *Contemporary Corporate Culture under Globalization*. Helsinki: JTO Publications.

Bank of Estonia, Key Economic Indicators 1995–2010. http://statistika.eestipank. ee/?lng=en#listMenu/1017/treeMenu/MAJANDUSKOOND [accessed 16 March 2012].

Baruch, Y. & Holton, B.C. 2008. 'Survey response rate level and trends in organizational research'. *Human Relations*, 61: 1139–60.

Becker, B.E. & Huselid, M.A. 1998. 'High performance work systems and firm performance: A synthesis of research and managerial implications'. In K.M. Rowland & G.R. Ferris (eds), *Research in Personnel and Human Resource Management*, Vol. 16. Greenwich, CT: JAI Press, 53–101.

Boxall, P. & Macky, K. 2009. 'Research and theory on high-performance work systems: Progressing the high-involvement stream'. *Human Resource Management Journal*, 19: 3–23.

Brewster, C. 1995. 'Towards a European model of human resource management'. *Journal of International Business Studies*, 26: 1–22.

Brewster, C. 2007. 'Comparative HRM: European views and perspectives'. *International Journal of Human Resource Management*, 18: 769–87.

Brewster, C. & Hegewisch, A. (eds), 1994. *Policy and Practice in European HRM*. London: Routledge.

Brewster, C. & Larsen, H.H. 2000. 'The Northern European dimension: A distinctive environment for HRM'. In C. Brewster and H.H. Larsen (eds), *Human Resource Management in Northern Europe: Trends, Dilemmas and Strategy*. Oxford: Blackwell.

Brewster, C., Mayrhofer. W. & Morley, M. (eds), 2004. *Human Resource Management in Europe: Evidence of Convergence?* Oxford: Elsevier Butterworth-Heinemann.

Byrkjeflot, H. 2001. 'The Nordic model of democracy and management'. In H. Byrkjeflot, S. Myklebust, C. Myrvang & F. Schersted (eds), *The Democratic Challenge to Capitalism*. Bergen: Fagbokforlaget.

Clark, T. & Mallory, G. 1996. 'The cultural relativity of human resource management: Is there a universal model?' In T. Clark (ed.), *European Human Resource Management*. Oxford: Blackwell Publishers.

Clark, T. & Pugh, D. 1999/2000. 'Similarities and differences in European conception of human resource management'. *International Studies of Management & Organization*, 29: 84–100.

Delery, J.E. & Doty, D.H. 1996. 'Modes of theorizing in strategic human resource management: Tests of universalistic, contingency and configurational performance predictions'. *Academy of Management Journal*, 39: 803–35.

Dewettinck, K. & Remue, J. 2011. 'Contextualizing HRM in comparative research: The role of the Cranet network'. *Human Resource Management Review*, 21: 37–49.

DiMaggio, P.J. & Powell, W.W. 1983. 'The iron cage revisited: Institutional isomorphism and collective rationality in organizational fields'. *American Sociological Review*, 35: 147–60.

DiMaggio, P.J. & Powell, W.W. 1991. 'Introduction'. In W.W. Powell & P.J. DiMaggio (eds), *The New Institutionalism in Organizational Analysis*. Chicago: University of Chicago Press.

Dølvik, J.E. 2007. 'The Nordic regimes of labour market governance: From crisis to success-story?' Fafos Rådsprogram 2006–2008 (Fafo-paper 2007:07).

Ehrlich, L., Kaasik Ü. & Randveer, A. 2002. *The Impact of Scandinavian Economies on Estonia via Foreign Trade and Direct Investments.* Working Papers 2002–4. Tallinn: Bank of Estonia.

Esping-Andersen, G. 1990. *The Three Worlds of Welfare Capitalism.* Princeton: Princeton University Press.

Garavan, T., Morley, M., Heraty, N., Lucewicz J. & Suchodolski, A.1998. 'Managing human resources in a post-command economy: Personnel administration or strategic HRM'. *Personnel Review,* 27: 200–12.

Gooderham, P.N. & Brewster, C. 2003. 'Convergence, stasis or divergence? Personnel management in Europe'. *Beta – Scandinavian Journal of Business Research,* 17: 6–18.

Gooderham, P. & Nordhaug, O. 2010. 'One European model of HRM? Cranet empirical contributions'. *Human Resource Management Review,* 21: 27–36.

Gooderham, P., Parry, E. & Ringdal, K. 2008. 'The impact of bundles of strategic human resource management practices on the performance of European firms'. *The International Journal of Human Resource Management,* 19: 2041–56.

Guest, D. 1990. 'Human resource management and the American dream'. *Journal of Management Studies,* 27: 377–97.

Guest, D. 1997. 'Human resource management and performance: A review and research agenda'. *The International Journal of Human Resource Management,* 8: 263–76.

Haunschild, P.R. & Miner, A.S. 1997. 'Modes of interorganizational imitation: The effects of outcome salience and uncertainty'. *Administrative Science Quarterly,* 42: 472–500.

Heliste, P., Kosonen, R. & Mattila, M. 2007. *Suomalaisyritykset Baltiassa tänään ja huomenna: Liiketoimintanormien ja – käytäntöjen kehityksestä.* Helsinki: Helsingin kauppakorkeakoulu.

Hoag J. & Kasoff, M. 1999. 'Estonia in transition'. *Journal of Economic Issues,* 33: 919–31.

Hofstede, G. 1980. *Culture's Consequences: International Differences in Work-Related Values.* Beverly Hills, CA: Sage Publications.

House, R.J., Hanges, P.J., Javidan, M., Dorfman, P.W. & Gupta, V. (eds), 2004. *Culture, Leadership, and Organizations: The GLOBE Study of 62 Societies.* Thousand Oaks, CA: Sage Publications.

Huselid, M.A. 1995. 'The impact of human resource practices on turnover, productivity and corporate financial performance'. *Academy of Management Journal,* 38: 635–70.

Ignjatovic M. & Svetlik, I. 2003. 'European HRM clusters'. *EBS Review,* Autumn: 25–39.

Kaarelson, T. 2010. 'Human resource management in Estonian organizations: Formation of the characteristics in the institutional and cultural context'. Unpublished PhD Thesis, Tallinn: The Institute of Management, Estonian Business School.

Kaarelson T. & Alas, R. 2009. 'Human resource management in Estonia'. In M. Morley, N. Heraty & S. Michailova (eds), *Managing Human Resources in Central and Eastern Europe.* London: Routledge.

Kallaste E. & Woolfson, C. 2009. 'The paradox of post-communist trade unionism: You can't want what you can't imagine'. *The Economic and Labour Relations Review,* 20: 93–110.

Karoliny, Z., Farkas F. & Poor, J. 2009. 'In focus: Hungarian and Central Eastern European characteristics of human resource management – an international comparative survey'. *Journal for East European Management Studies,* 1: 9–47.

Kerr, C., Dunlop, J.T., Harbison, F. & Myers, C.A. 1960. *Industrialism and Industrial Man*. Cambridge, MA: Harvard University Press.

Kiriazov, D., Sullivan, S.E. & Tu, H.S. 2000. 'Business success in Eastern Europe: Understanding and customizing HRM'. *Business Horizons*, 43: 39–44.

Largerspetz, M. 2003. 'How many Nordic countries? Possibilities and limits of geopolitical identity construction'. *Cooperation & Conflict*, 38: 49–61.

Larsen H.H. & Brewster, C. 2003. 'Line management responsibility of HRM: What is happening in Europe?' *Employee Relations*, 25: 228–33.

Legge, K. 2005. *Human Resource Management: Rhetorics and Realities*. Basingstoke: Palgrave Macmillan.

Lindeberg, T., Mansson, B. & Vanhala, S. 2004. 'Sweden and Finland: Small countries with large companies'. In C. Brewster, W. Mayrhofer & M. Morley (eds), *Human Resource Management in Europe: Evidence of Convergence?* Oxford: Elsevier Butterworth-Heinemann.

Lundy, O. 1994. 'From personnel management to strategic human resource management'. *The International Journal of Human Resource Management*, 5: 687–720.

Martin-Alcazar, F., Romero-Fernandez, P.M. & Sanches-Gardey, G. 2005. 'Strategic human resource management: Integrating the universalistic, contingent, configurational and contextual perspectives'. *International Journal of Human Resource Management*, 16: 633–59.

Mayrhofer, W. 1998. 'Between market, bureaucracy, and clan – coordination and control mechanisms in the Cranfield Network on European Human Resource Management (Cranet-E)'. *Journal of Managerial Psychology*, 13: 241–58.

Mayrhofer, W. & Brewster, C. 2005. 'European human resource management: Researching developments over time'. *Management Revue*, 16: 36–62.

Mayrhofer, W., Morley, M. & Brewster, C. '2004. 'Convergence, stasis, or divergence?' In C. Brewster, W. Mayrhofer & M. Morley (eds), *Human Resource Management in Europe: Evidence of Convergence?* London: Elsevier Butterworth-Heinemann, 417–36.

Mayrhofer, W., Brewster, C., Morley, M. & Ledolter, J. 2011. 'Hearing a different drummer? Convergence of human resource management in Europe – A longitudinal analysis'. *Human Resource Management Review*, 21: 50–67.

McConville, T. 2006. 'Devolved HRM responsibilities, middle-managers and role dissonance'. *Personnel Review*, 35: 637–53.

Nikandrou, I., Apospori, E. & Papalexandris, N. 2005. 'Changes in HRM in Europe: A longitudinal comparative study among 18 European countries'. *Journal of European Industrial Training*, 29: 541–60.

Nordic Statistical Yearbook 2010, Nord 2010:001 http://www.norden.org/en/publications/publications/2010-001 [accessed 6 October 2011].

Nurmi, R. & Üksvärav, R. 1994. *Estonia and Finland: Culture and Management. A Conjectural Presentation*. Publications of the Turku School of Economics and Business Administration, Series A-9: 19.

Paauwe, J. 2004. *HRM and Performance: Achieving Long Term Viability*. Oxford: Oxford University Press.

Paauwe, J. & Boselie, P. 2003. 'Challenging strategic human resource management and the relevance of institutional setting'. *Human Resource Management Journal*, 13: 56–70.

Paauwe, J. & Boselie, P. 2005. 'Best practices ... in spite of performance: Just a matter of imitation'. *The International Journal of Human Resource Management*, 16: 987–1003.

Papalexandris, N. & Panayotopoulou, L. 2004. 'Exploring the mutual interaction of societal culture and human resource management practices: Evidence from 19 countries'. *Employee Relations*, 26: 495–509.

Papalexandris, N. & Panayotopoulou, L. 2005. 'Exploring the partnership between line managers and HRM in Greece'. *Journal of European Industrial Training*, 29: 281–91.

Pfeffer, J. 1994. *Competitive Advantage through People: Unleashing the Power of the Workforce*. Boston, MA: Harvard Business School Press.

Pfeffer, J. 1998. 'Seven practices of successful organizations'. *California Management Review*, 40: 96–124.

Poor, J., Karoliny, Z., Alas, R. & Vatchkova, E.K. 2011. 'Comparative international human resource management (CIHRM) in the light of the Cranet regional research survey in transitional economies'. *Employee Relations*, 33: 428–43.

Pudelko, M. 2005. 'Cross-national learning from best practice and the convergence–divergence debate in HRM'. *International Journal of Human Resource Management*, 16: 2045–74.

Rogaczewska, A.P., Larsen, H.H., Nordhaug, O., Dølviknd E. & Gjelsvik, M. 2004. 'Denmark and Norway: Siblings or cousins?' In C. Brewster, W. Mayrhofer & M. Morley (eds), *Human Resource Management in Europe: Evidence of Convergence*. Oxford: Elsevier Butterworth-Heinemann.

Sippola, M. 2009. 'The two faces of Nordic management? Nordic firms and their employee relations in the Baltic States'. *The International Journal of Human Resource Management*, 20: 1929–44.

Sippola, M. 2011. 'Nordic subsidiaries in the Baltic States: Is model transfer possible?' *Employee Relations*, 33: 356–74.

Statistics Estonia, Main indicators 2010–2011. www.stat.ee [accessed 11 March 2011].

Stavrou, E. & Brewster, C. 2005. 'The configurational approach to linking strategic human resource management bundles with business performance: Myth or reality?' *Management Revue*, 16: 186–201.

Stavrou, E.T., Brewster, C. & Charalambous, C. 2010. 'Human resource management and firm performance in Europe through the lens of business systems: Best fit, best practice or both?' *The International Journal of Human Resource Management*, 21: 933–62.

Stavrou, E.T., Charalambous, C. & Spiliotis, S. 2007. 'Human resource management and performance: A neural network analysis'. *European Journal of Operational Research*, 181: 453–67.

Storey, J. 1992. *Developments in the Management of Human Resources*. Oxford: Blackwell.

Tepp, M. 2007. *HR Profession in Estonia: Content and Contradictions*. Working Papers in Economics, School of Economics and Business Administration, Tallinn University of Technology (TUTWPE), No. 170. http://deepthought.ttu.ee/majandus/tekstid/TUTWPE_07_160.pdf [accessed 25 May 2011].

Trade Unions in Europe. http://www.fedee.com/labour-relations/trade-unions-in-europe/ [accessed 24 May 2011].

Tregaskis, O. & Brewster, C. 2006 'Converging or diverging? A comparative analysis of trends in contingent employment practice in Europe over a decade'. *Journal of International Business Studies*, 37: 111–26.

Tregaskis, O., Mahoney, C. & Atterbury, S. 2004. 'International survey methodology: Experiences from the Cranet network'. In C. Brewster, W. Mayrhofer & M. Morley (eds), *Human Resource Management in Europe: Evidence of Convergence?* Oxford: Elsevier Butterworth-Heinemann.

Ulrich, D. 1998. 'A new mandate for human resources'. *Harvard Business Review*, January–February: 124–34.

US Department of Labor. 1993. *High Performance Work Practices and Firm Performance*. Washington, DC.

Vanhala, S. 1995. 'Human resource management in Finland'. *Employee Relations*, 17: 31–56.

Vanhala, S. 2008. 'Nordic model of HRM? HR practices in the Nordic and other European countries'. In *HRM Global 2008: Sustainable HRM in the Global Economy*. Turku: Publications of Turku School of Economics.

Vanhala, S., Kaarelson, T. & Alas, R. 2006. 'Converging human resource management: A comparison between Estonian and Finnish HRM'. *Baltic Journal of Management*, 1: 82–101.

Vösa, H. 2010. *The Impact of Economic Crisis on HRM in Estonia*. Helsinki: Aalto University School of Economics.

Whitley, R. & Kristensen, P.H. (eds), 1996. *The Changing European Firm: Limits to Convergence*. London/New York: Routledge.

Witt, M.A. & Redding, G. 2009. 'Culture, meaning, and institutions: Executive rationale in Germany and Japan'. *Journal of International Business Studies*, 40: 859–85.

Wood, S. 1999. 'Human resource management and performance'. *International Journal of Management Review*, 1: 367–413.

Worker participation.eu. The gateway to information on worker participation issues in Europe. http://www.worker-participation.eu/National-Industrial-Relations/Across-Europe/Trade-Unions2 [accessed 16 March 2012].

7
HRM in Scandinavia – Embedded in the Scandinavian Model?

Tina Lindeberg, Bo Månson and Henrik Holt Larsen

The Scandinavian arena

The purpose of this chapter is threefold: first, to identify similarities and differences between HR practice in the Scandinavian countries (Denmark, Norway and Sweden); second, to analyse how the HR practice is embedded in the historical, cultural, social and political characteristics of the Scandinavian countries, including Scandinavian management; and third, to compare the Scandinavian HR practice with HR practice in a number of (deliberately chosen) similar or different European countries. In order to understand – and be able to interpret – the Scandinavian management and HR practices, a brief analysis of the societal situation in these areas will be provided.

We will also use Cranet data to illustrate some HR practices in nine European countries. In our comparison for this chapter we have chosen countries based on the following criteria: they are physically close to the Scandinavian countries, they are similar in terms of socio-economic features, and/or they are countries with which the Scandinavian countries have close ties, such as by trade. We have chosen Finland (SF), being a very close neighbour, France (F), Germany (D), the United Kingdom (UK), Belgium (B) and the Netherlands (NL). We use Cranet (2008–10) data when available for illustration, and we also use other sources of information and research to describe the typical traits of Scandinavian countries regarding work–life and characteristics of management practice.

Four European social models

The Belgian economist André Sapir (2005) has developed a typology for different models of employment and social welfare in Europe. His typology is based on earlier work by Esping-Andersen (1990), who partitioned welfare systems into three regimes: a liberal regime (encompassing Anglo-Saxon countries); a conservative regime (encompassing Continental and

Mediterranean countries); and a social democratic regime (encompassing the Nordic countries).

Sapir extended the Esping-Andersen model into four regimes by dividing the Continental regime into a Continental and a Mediterranean regime, a typology that will be used in this chapter. The Nordic model will be discussed below together with brief descriptions of Sapir's three other models for comparison.

The Nordic model refers to the economic and social models of the Nordic countries (sometimes with the inclusion of the Netherlands). The basis for the model has been described as a combination of collective risk sharing and openness to globalization (Andersen et al., 2007). Collective risk sharing helps make globalization acceptable to citizens by facilitating adjustments that allow the economy to benefit from changing markets and to raise productivity and wealth. This particular adaptation of the mixed market economy is characterized by universal welfare provision, aiming specifically at enhancing individual autonomy, ensuring the universal provision of basic human rights and stabilizing the economy. It is distinguished from other welfare states with similar goals by its emphasis on maximizing labour force participation, promoting gender equality, egalitarian and extensive benefit levels, a large magnitude of redistribution, and liberal use of expansionary fiscal policy (Esping-Andersen, 1990).

The model is characterized by a set of labour market institutions that include strong labour unions and employer associations, significant elements of wage coordination, relatively generous unemployment benefits and, although labour markets are relatively unregulated, a prominent role for active labour market policies.

The Anglo-Saxon model (Ireland and the UK) is of countries that provide relatively large social assistance as a last resort, with cash transfers going mainly to people of working age. Active measures to help the unemployed get jobs and schemes that link access to benefits to regular employment are important ('workfare'). Unions are weak and the labour market relatively unregulated, resulting in comparatively wide wage dispersion and a relatively high incidence of low-pay employment.

The Continental model (Austria, Belgium, France, Germany and Luxembourg) relies on social insurance for those out of work, as well as provision of pensions. Employment protection is stronger than in the Nordic countries. The latest available OECD figures indicate, however, that while this is true for Sweden, Denmark and Finland, Norway has actually got stronger employment protection than Germany, Austria and Belgium (Venn, 2009). Unions are also powerful or enjoy legal support for extension of the results of collective bargaining.

The Mediterranean model (Portugal, Spain, Italy and Greece) concentrates public spending on old-age pensions. Heavy regulation protects (and lowers) employment while generous support for early retirement seeks to reduce the number of job-seekers. The social welfare system typically draws on employment protection and early retirement provisions to exempt segments of the working age population from participation in the labour market. The wage structure, at least in the formal sector, is covered by collective bargaining and strongly compressed.

Boeri (2002) and Sapir (2005) compare the four models in terms of three criteria: first, reduction of income inequality and poverty; second, protection against uninsurable labour market risk; and third, rewards to labour market participation.

Figure 7.1 summarizes their findings along two dimensions: equity and efficiency. *Equity* (criterion 1) is whether the model achieves a relatively low poverty risk. *Efficiency* (criteria 2 and 3) is whether the model provides the incentives so as to achieve the largest possible number of employed persons, that is, the highest employment rate.

Figure 7.1 can be read in terms of a trade-off between efficiency and equity. The best performance is achieved by the Nordic model, which delivers both efficiency and equity, whereas the Mediterranean model delivers neither efficiency nor equity. The Anglo-Saxon and Continental models both seem to face a trade-off between efficiency and equity where the former should improve its equity and the latter its efficiency.

Protection against uninsurable labour market risk (criterion 2) can either be provided by employment protection legislation, which protects workers against firing, or by unemployment benefits. Legislation protects those who already are employed and does not impose any tax burden, whereas benefits provide insurance to the population at large and are typically financed by tax on those who work. Having a generous unemployment insurance system reduces the need for restrictions against getting fired, and vice versa.

The four models differ when it comes to employment protection legislation and unemployment benefits. The Mediterranean model has generally strict employment legislation (at least for permanent workers) and a rather low coverage of unemployment benefits. In contrast, the Nordic model

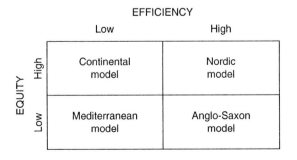

Figure 7.1   Social models, efficiency and equity (Sapir, 2005)

provides unemployment benefits that are generous and comprehensive, but with less strict employment protection legislation. The Continental model also provides generous unemployment benefits, but with stricter employment protection legislation. Finally, the Anglo-Saxon model has comparatively less employment legislation but as much unemployment insurance as the Continental and Nordic Models.

Rewards for labour market participation (criterion 3) also vary across the models. Employment rates are far higher in Nordic and Anglo-Saxon countries than in Continental and Mediterranean countries, with much of the difference attributable to the two ends of the age spectrum. The Nordic and Anglo-Saxon countries are more successful in keeping the employment rate for older workers high and the unemployment rate for young workers low.

The institutional framework in the Scandinavian countries

After having compared the Nordic region with other European regions, we now look specifically at the Scandinavian countries. When using the term 'Scandinavian countries' we refer to Sweden, Norway and Denmark. The term 'Nordic countries' also includes Finland and Iceland in this group. There are two reasons for focusing in particular on Scandinavia. First, the Scandinavian countries are typical examples of the Nordic social model. Second, we draw on Cranet data generated in the Scandinavian countries – and not the entire Nordic region.

The Scandinavian countries have many historical, cultural, social and political features in common. Hence, the Scandinavian languages, a branch of the Germanic family, are very close, and Scandinavians can fairly easily understand each other. The dominant religion in all countries is Lutheranism/Protestantism, although a majority of the populations would label themselves as atheists or agnostics. In fact, the Scandinavian countries count as some of the most non-religious societies in the world.

The three states are constitutional monarchies and parliamentary democracies with highly developed economies. The kings in Norway and Sweden and the Danish queen are heads of the respective states, but their functions are reduced to primarily ceremonial ones. The countries are Unitarian states with administrative subdivisions on two levels known as regions/counties and municipalities.

The countries share similar traits in the policies implemented under the post-war period, especially in the socio-economic area. All Scandinavian countries have large tax-funded public welfare sectors and extensive social legislation. In most cases, this is due to the political ideology of the many social democratic governments that came to power during the interwar period in each of the countries. The three countries rank among the top five in world comparisons of the highest level of income equality (UNDP, 2011).

Sweden, Denmark and Norway form a relatively homogeneous group in spite of different positions in respect of EU membership, participation in the European Monetary Union and membership of NATO. The three countries are all knowledge-based economies and have large knowledge- and service-based sectors, which employ more than 75 per cent of the workforce. They have the largest proportion of employment in knowledge-intensive service sectors in the EU, ranging from 43.5 per cent (Denmark) and 45.9 per cent (Norway) to 47.8 per cent (Sweden), with an EU (27) average of 32.9 per cent (Eurostat, 2002).

This partly explains why the labour cost constitutes a significant part of total operating cost in Scandinavian organizations. This is illustrated in Figure 7.2, which is based on Cranet data for 2008. The three Scandinavian countries (and also Finland) are at the very top, as 50–60 per cent of total operating cost is labour. There are two possible explanations for this: either that a large proportion of the labour force is highly educated and well paid, or that considerable social costs are imposed on the employer (Papalexandris & Poor, 2011). However, relative to other European countries, the latter is not the case in Scandinavian or the Nordic region, as a large proportion of social, safety, health and pension costs are financed through the welfare state as such – and not by the individual employer.

Does the fact that the labour force is generally highly educated and well paid also imply that investments in training and development are also

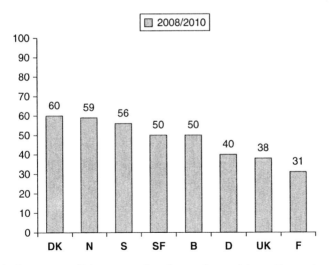

Figure 7.2 Percentage of labour cost of total operating cost (operating cost accounted for by labour costs)
Acronyms: DK (Denmark), N (Norway), S (Sweden), SF (Finland), B (Belgium), D (Germany), UK (United Kingdom), F (France).
Note: Data from the Netherlands are missing in this figure.

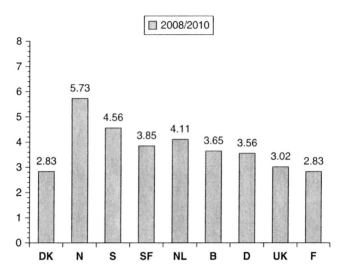

Figure 7.3   Percentage of annual payroll cost spent on training and development
Acronyms: DK (Denmark), N (Norway), S (Sweden), SF (Finland), NL (The Netherlands), B (Belgium), D (Germany), UK (United Kingdom), F (France).

high? Figure 7.3 shows the percentage of annual payroll cost spent on training and development, using Cranet data. Norway, Sweden, Finland and the Netherlands spend considerable resources on training and development, whereas this is not the case to the same extent in Denmark (possibly owing to a heavy emphasis on less expensive learning-on-the-job methods). However, on the whole, the mentioned countries are characterized by, not only employing highly educated people, but also for providing continuing in-service training. Not only is the emphasis on employee training seen by the employer as a rational investment in a resource of crucial importance to the organization, but also is a typical expectation of knowledge workers – and hence influencing the psychological contract between employer and employee – that the employer should provide ample opportunities for maintaining and developing the employees' professional competence.

Scandinavian management and HRM practices

After having examined the institutional framework in the Scandinavian countries, we now turn to the characteristics of Scandinavian management, hypothesizing that this has some very distinct features.

General characteristics of Scandinavian management

Scandinavian management indeed has roots into – and reflects – the Scandinavian welfare state. Embedded in the management style are the old ideals of freedom equality, liberty and fraternity. The democratic mentality has created a unique set of values in the Scandinavian countries, and this influences the actual management style.

According to Larsen, Schramm-Nielsen and Stensaker (2011) and Larsen and Bruun de Neergaard (2007a, 2007b), in Scandinavian organization the *organizational structure is typically flat*, and managers and co-workers work closely together. Communication is informal and is marked by natural respect, not just level-based formal authority. There is less symbolism and ceremonies concerning level-based authority, and managers spend a significant part of their time with subordinates.

It is a characteristic of the Scandinavian countries that workplaces are very *knowledge-intensive*. This means that a great proportion of the employees have an identity strongly connected to their occupation and professional training rather than the specific organization they work for (Hein, 2009). Although this feature is also found in other European regions, it has great impact on the culture of Scandinavian organizations. It matches something that is very specifically Scandinavian (namely cooperation and involvement of employees in management-related issues) – Schramm-Nielsen, Lawrence and Sivesind (2004).

Profession-based management typically implies promotion from within and that someone with similar educational background as the subordinates is put in a management position and hence manages people who used to be his or her colleagues. It is not necessarily regarded as attractive to become a manager as it means that you have to 'leave behind' a job where you could fully apply and enjoy your professional field since the reputation of people stems from their capacity of being a professional expert and role model for the peers.

Cooperation, involvement and influence

Participation and cooperation, involvement and influence are also significant features of Scandinavian management and are related to the low power distance culture (Schramm-Nielsen et al., 2004). The co-determination of the employees falls into two categories: the formal one (often through agreements or negotiations) and the informal one, which expresses actual management practice in daily working life. Concerning the first category, the general principles and agreements are basically the same for all Scandinavian countries. The informal co-determination reaches – despite variations from organization to organization – much further because of the consequences of the low power distance in the Scandinavian countries. Managers expect their subordinates to be competent, reliable and able to act independently. When the trust that this reflects is confirmed, it becomes natural to involve the employees to a greater extent.

Turning now to whether the HR director is a *member of the top executive team*, differences between the Scandinavian countries can be seen (see

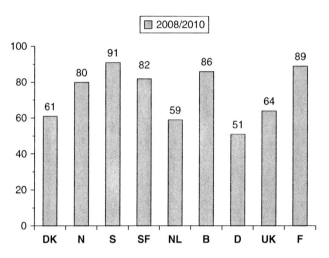

Figure 7.4 Proportion of persons responsible for HR who have a place on board or equivalent top executive team

Acronyms: DK (Denmark), N (Norway), S (Sweden), SF (Finland), NL (The Netherlands), B (Belgium), D (Germany), UK (United Kingdom), F (France).

Figure 7.4). Sweden and Norway have a very high rate of HR managers on the top executive team, while Denmark shows the lowest percentage of the three Scandinavian countries. This makes Denmark diverge from the Scandinavian characteristic of involvement and influence when it comes to HRM issues. One explanation for this is the somewhat smaller company size in Denmark. Another possible reason is a less intensive knowledge sharing in the Danish community of HR practitioners regarding the importance of being a member of the board than in Norway and Sweden.

Cooperation with the unions is often carried out through the HR manager. Since this plays an important role in the Scandinavian management arena, the representation of the HR manager on the top executive team should logically be of great necessity and importance.

Collaboration also affects *decision-making*. It is important in Scandinavian management that employees are generally heard and involved when it comes to decision-making. This often makes the process of decision-making much more complicated and time-consuming:

> Any understanding of Scandinavian management necessarily implies the realization of the strong impetus for consensus and cooperation. This attitude implies an emphasis on discussion and bargaining as participants work towards an acceptable compromise. The key word here is the very notion of cooperation which means working together towards a common goal. Larsen et al. (2011: 335)

Involvement in policies and strategies

Another area where employees in Scandinavia are informally involved in managerial processes is the implementation of *values and strategies*. Involving the individual employee in this turns the employee into a co-creator of the process, hence it is influenced by will, desire and motivation instead of just performing a task merely because someone told the employee to do so. In this way the drivers of *engagement* are embedded in the Scandinavian management style: openness, flat structures, dialogue, democracy, communication and collaboration as well as decentralization of responsibility and decision-making power.

HR policy or HR strategy

When it comes to policy documents of different sorts, the Scandinavian countries tend to have a high proportion of organizations with written or unwritten policies. Regarding HR practices – like an HR policy or HR strategy – Cranet data suggest that the Scandinavian countries and Finland seem to have these in the majority of the organizations. The Scandinavian countries seem to be more inclined to write down their policies than their European neighbours in this sample. In some countries, having an *unwritten* strategy or policy is as common to having a written one, as in Germany, France and the Netherlands (see Figure 7.5).

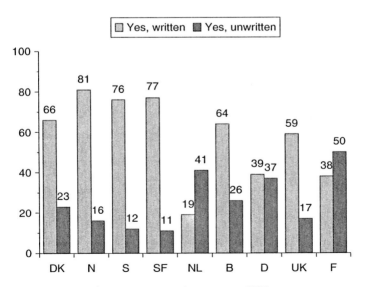

Figure 7.5 Proportion of organizations with a personnel/HR strategy
Acronyms: DK (Denmark), N (Norway), S (Sweden), SF (Finland), NL (The Netherlands), B (Belgium), D (Germany), UK (United Kingdom), F (France).

Something that has attracted much attention recently in Scandinavia is working on organizational ethics and values and as a consequence of that formulating some kind of value statement. This has become an important issue both in private and public organizations. The work of finding and formulating the common values of the organization is often done involving all employees.

Looking at Cranet data on whether the organizations have a value statement, we see the same tendency as in having an HR policy. This means that it is quite common for the Scandinavian countries to have a value statement, especially a written one. It is even more common than having an HR policy/strategy. In Norway practically all organizations respond that they have a value statement, and in 90 per cent of the cases this is a written one (see Figure 7.6).

Scandinavian management puts heavy emphasis on – and requires – *communication* with employees. It is very difficult for a person to obtain and maintain a management position if the person does not have good communication skills – and gives priority to dialogue. The manager is close to his or her subordinates, and this is why it is necessary that he or she understands what they are thinking, and helps them come up with ideas, values and projects.

Cranet data show that in Norway, Sweden and Finland the proportion of HR managers involved from the outset in developing business strategies is comparatively high. Denmark, on the other hand, shows a low percentage of initial involvement of the HR manager in strategy-making (see Figure 7.7).

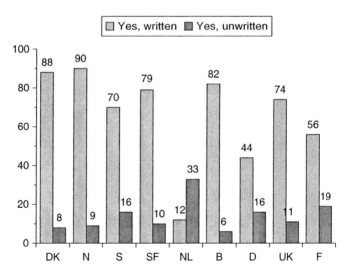

Figure 7.6 Proportion of organizations that have a value statement, written or unwritten

Acronyms: DK (Denmark), N (Norway), S (Sweden), SF (Finland), NL (The Netherlands), B (Belgium), D (Germany), UK (United Kingdom), F (France).

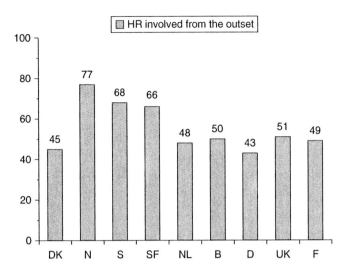

Figure 7.7 At what stage is the person responsible for HR in your organization involved in development of the business/service strategy?
Acronyms: DK (Denmark), N (Norway), S (Sweden), SF (Finland), NL (The Netherlands), B (Belgium), D (Germany), UK (United Kingdom), F (France).

Decentralization of HR

Another important aspect to be mentioned is the *decentralized responsibility for human resources to line managers*. It has for approximately 20 years been documented through the Cranet survey that the Scandinavian countries are characterized by a high degree of decentralization of HR responsibility to the individual line manager (Brewster & Larsen, 2000; Cranet, 2011). This is a consequence of the very expensive and demanding workforce in Scandinavia. The 'product' of knowledge-intensive organizations is non-material, and the human resources are of strategic importance and contribute to the vertical integration of business strategy and HRM strategy. This vertical integration requires – and is strengthened by – emphasis on the human resource role of the line manager. The reason for this is that the immediate superior (typically middle managers) has the best insight and possibilities for optimizing the competence, commitment and performance of the individual employee.

In the accompanying figures we can see that the Scandinavian countries have a large part of the responsibility in different HRM areas allocated to line managers. As shown in Figure 7.8, the responsibility distribution between line managers and HR in the area *Recruitment and selection* is weighted more towards the line managers in the Scandinavian countries as compared to the other countries in this comparison. The Cranet survey 2008/10 shows that the Scandinavian countries differ less from other countries within areas like *Training and development* and *Workforce expansion/reduction*. However,

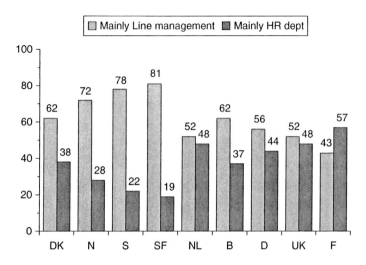

Figure 7.8   Who has the primary responsibility for major policy decisions on recruitment and selection?

Acronyms: DK (Denmark), N (Norway), S (Sweden), SF (Finland), NL (The Netherlands), B (Belgium), D (Germany), UK (United Kingdom), F (France).

they are always among the countries that emphasize line management responsibility the most.

Regarding *Industrial relations* most countries, including the Scandinavian countries, have their HR department primarily responsible. Industrial relations have traditionally been an area of expertise of HR professionals, and since it is of major importance to the organization that it is being handled correctly, it remains within the HR function (see Figure 7.9).

Compared with the results from the Cranet survey 2004, the results show that the differences between countries have diminished. We can see from the data set that the Scandinavian countries since 2004 have retransferred some of the responsibilities from line managers back to the HR function, while some of the other European countries in this sample have increased line management responsibility regarding HRM issues – more towards the Scandinavian model.

If line managers are carrying such a heavy load of HR work, how does it come about that they are so seldom mentioned in the theoretical models of HRM organization and structure of the HR function? One researcher who claims that line managers are one of the main actors in HR work is Dave Ulrich. He states that many of the HR tasks in large organizations are carried out by the line managers. They are the ones responsible in the end for decisions regarding their workers (Ulrich & Brockbank, 2005). The advice he gives to HR specialists is to involve line managers in HR tasks and strategies and not take on the role of serving them. The responsibility should not rest

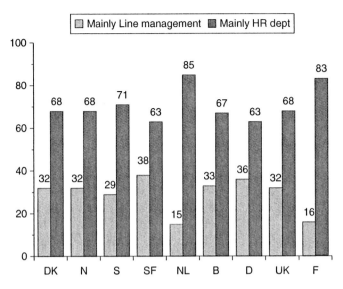

Figure 7.9 Who has the primary responsibility for major policy decisions on industrial relations?
Acronyms: DK (Denmark), N (Norway), S (Sweden), SF (Finland), NL (The Netherlands), B (Belgium), D (Germany), UK (United Kingdom), F (France).

on the shoulders of the HR department alone. HR specialists should act as coaches and consultants for line managers when they make the decisions in most HR issues, according to Ulrich. It seems that in Scandinavia this has been adopted as a regular procedure in most organizations.

Pay and benefits

The bonus salary can be based either on individual goals/performances or on team goals/performances. In most countries it is more frequent to base the bonus on the individual goal/performance. However, in the Scandinavian countries it is nearly equally common to base the bonus on the goals/performance of the team. In the UK no large differences exist in what the bonus is based on. The frequency of bonuses or performance-related pay in Scandinavia compared to the other countries is also lower (see Figure 7.10).

Conclusion

The Scandinavian countries share a number of historical, cultural, societal and political features. These fit with the so-called Nordic social model (Esping-Andersen), which is a mixed market economy, characterized by a combination of universal welfare provision, individual autonomy,

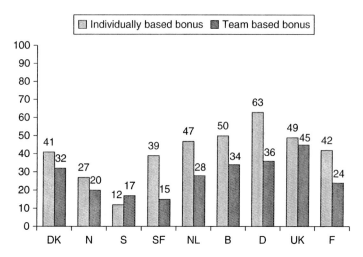

Figure 7.10   Do you offer bonus based on individual or team goals/performance?
Acronyms: DK (Denmark), N (Norway), S (Sweden), SF (Finland), NL (The Netherlands), B (Belgium), D (Germany), UK (United Kingdom), F (France).

emphasis on maximizing labour force participation, promoting gender equality, egalitarian and extensive benefit levels, a large magnitude of redistribution etc.

Scandinavian management is characterized by the following characteristics (Larsen et al., 2011): participation, involvement and collaboration; responsibilities being shared and taken; co-creativity/influence; leadership arises in relations – and is nothing on its own; equality; dialogue; flat hierarchies; short power distances; openness; honesty; justification; and leadership that is less 'macho' than in other cultures. Despite the fact that management in Scandinavian countries shares a vast range of common characteristics, actual HRM practice varies considerably among these countries. We *do* see some universal practices across the Scandinavian borders, mainly where the implications of knowledge-intensive organizations and highly educated employees are predominant. Given the strong tradition of consensus, the democratic decision-making process and the relatively strong unions that defend the rights of employees, Scandinavian organizations have a long history of emphasizing commitment to human resources. This has perhaps contributed to a faster development of HRM in the Scandinavian countries than in many other countries. Examples are the high rate of HR professionals being represented in the top management team, as well as having written HR policies and other documents related to the human resources of the organization.

However, we also see significant *differences* among the Scandinavian countries. In particular, Denmark stands out as being more similar to Europe as a whole than to Sweden and Norway. An example of these intra-Scandinavian differences is the study by Gooderham et al. (2011) showing how the 'working life regimes' in Denmark and Norway are drifting from each other, which is partly related to the principle of 'flexicurity', which is somewhat unique for Denmark. Flexicurity implies that the employer has a large opportunity to use numerical flexibility (i.e. hire and fire), but that this flexibility goes hand in hand with the security of the welfare state, consisting of a financial unemployment package and a proactive labour market policy aiming at bringing the unemployed back into the labour market. These three aspects are sometimes called 'the golden triangle'.

It does not only apply to Scandinavia, but to Europe in general that HRM practices are very divergent. This is partly related to cultural differences and differences in the organizational climate, which often reflect the political and social climate of society. The tradition in which HRM routines and tasks have been conducted in the past certainly affects today's way of handling these issues.

This interpretation is supported by the research by Gooderham & Nordhaug (2011), who investigated:

> whether there is so much variety of HRM at the national level that it is problematic to refer to a European model of HRM. Our conclusion is that Europe consists of a set of distinctive HRM regimes both in terms of culture and institutions. …Thus, treating various European countries together may disguise interesting differences that have an impact on HRM as well as performance. Gooderham & Nordhaug (2011: 34)

The same researchers also state that European HRM shows little sign of becoming more uniform or convergent. They conclude:

> Clearly the findings we have reviewed indicate that little or no convergence is taking place within Europe. On the contrary, the studies equally emphasize persistent national differences. In other words the findings from the convergence studies point to different 'European models of HRM' rather than to 'a European model of HRM'. Gooderham & Nordhaug (2011: 34)

Hence, based on this finding as well as the analysis of the Cranet data in the previous section, we can conclude that despite the *common* cultural, political, social and economic features in the various Scandinavian countries, it is far too simplistic and optimistic to talk about an overall, universal HRM and/or management model in Scandinavia. There certainly *are* significant similarities between the three countries, but also significant differences – and these differences do *not* tend to get smaller as a result of a process of convergence. In contrast, status quo or even a slight move in the direction of increasing divergence is currently taking place.

References

Andersen, T.M., Holmstrom, B., Honkapohja, S., Korkman, S., Soderstrom, H.T. & Vartiainen, J. 2007. *The Nordic Model: Embracing Globalization and Sharing Risks.* The Research Institute of the Finnish Economy (ETLA), ETLA Report B232.

Boeri, T. 2002. 'Let Social Policy Models Compete and Europe Will Win'. Paper presented at a conference hosted by the Kennedy School of Government, Harvard University, 11–12 April.

Brewster, C. & Larsen H.H. 2000. *Human Resource Management in Northern Europe.* Oxford: Blackwell.

Cranet, 2011. *International Executive Report: Cranet Survey on Comparative HRM.* Cranfield: Cranfield University.

Esping-Andersen, G. 1990. *The Three Worlds of Welfare Capitalism.* London: Polity Press.

Eurostat, 2002. www.ec.europa.eu/eurostat (retrieved 11th December 2012).

Gooderham, P., Navrbjerg, S.E., Olsen, K.M. & Steen, C.R. 2011. 'Arbeidslivsregimer i Danmark og Norge – går de hver sin vei?' *Tidsskrift for Arbejdsliv,* 13(3): 30–44.

Gooderham, P.N. & Nordhaug, O. 2011. 'One European model of HRM? Cranet empirical contributions'. *Human Resource Management Review,* 21: 27–36.

Hein, H.H. 2009. *Motivation – motivationsteori og praktisk anvendelse.* København: Hans Reitzels forlag.

Larsen, H.H. & Bruun de Neergaard, U. 2007a. *Nordic Lights: A Research Project on Nordic Leadership and Leadership in the Nordic Countries.* Copenhagen: Kommunernes Landsforening.

Larsen, H.H. & Bruun de Neergaard, U. 2007b. *Nordic Lights: Executive Summary. A Research Project on Nordic Leadership and Leadership in the Nordic Countries.* Copenhagen: Kommunernes Landsforening.

Larsen, H.H., Schramm-Nielsen, J. & Stensaker, I. 2011. 'Talent development as an alternative to orthodox career thinking: The Scandinavian case'. In M. London (ed.), *The Oxford Handbook of Lifelong Learning.* Oxford: Oxford University Press.

Papalexandris, N. & Poor, J. 2011. 'HRM roles'. In Cranet, *International Executive Report: Cranet Survey on Comparative HRM.* Cranfield: Cranfield University.

Sapir, A. 2005. 'Globalisation and the reform of European social models'. *Bruegel Policy Brief,* Issue 2005/01.

Schramm-Nielson, J., Lawrence, P. & Sivesind, K.H. 2004. *Management in Scandinavia: Culture, Context and Change.* Cheltenham: Edward Elgar.

Ulrich, D. & Brockbank, W. 2005. *The HR Value Proposition.* Boston, MA: Harvard Business School Press.

UNDP (United Nations Development Programme). Presented in Wikipedia under 'List of countries by income equality' [accessed 20 October 2011].

Venn, D. 2009. *Legislation, Collective Bargaining and Enforcement: Updating the OECD Employment Protection Indicators.* www.oecd.org/els/workingpapers.

8
Divergent Norwegian and North American HRM Regimes: Implications for Norwegian MNEs

Paul Gooderham, Birgitte Grøgaard and Odd Nordhaug

Purpose

As Norwegian companies internationalize by establishing major business units in a variety of locations such as North America they have to confront different local human resource management (HRM) policies and practices. These differences are not arbitrary but products of different industrial relations regimes. Using a comparative data set the initial purpose of this chapter is to assess the 'distance' between the Norwegian and the North American HRM regimes in terms of 'calculative' and 'collaborative' HRM practices (Gooderham, Nordhaug & Ringdal, 1999). In line with measures of institutional and cultural distance our findings indicate substantial differences. Thereafter we employ interview data to investigate how these differences have an impact on the selection of HRM practices in the North American operations of a Norwegian multinational enterprise (MNE). In particular we investigate the degree to which the Norwegian MNE 'exports' Norwegian HRM practices and the degree to which it succumbs to local pressures to adapt to the North American context. We conclude by discussing the implications of our findings for the HRM strategies of Norwegian companies in the North American setting.

Calculative and collaborative HRM

The origins of HRM lie in the insight that as the US economy in the 1980s moved from mass-production to fast-moving batch production and professional services, competitive advantage is increasingly derived from firms' human resources. Managers subsequently faced the challenge of how to succeed in creating inclusivity and commitment and how to create a linkage between the ambitions of increasingly highly educated employees and the strategic aims of the firm. When comparing HRM practices across different national settings in Europe, Gooderham et al. (1999) identified that institutional factors influenced two key, although not mutually exclusive, dimensions of HRM: calculative and collaborative HRM. These HRM dimensions have since been applied in a number of cross-national studies of HRM practices and policies. The findings have confirmed the influence of institutional factors on the deployment of calculative and collaborative HRM practices (e.g. Lunnan et al., 2005; Gooderham, Nordhaug & Ringdal, 2006; Gooderham, Parry & Ringdal, 2008; Poutsma, Lightart & Veersma, 2006; Rizov & Croucher, 2009).

Calculative HRM

Fombrun, Tichy and Devanna (1984) launched the 'Michigan' model of HRM, which emphasized that organizational effectiveness is dependent on achieving a tight fit between human resource strategy and the overall business strategy of the firm. It is a largely prescriptive perspective and may be conceived of as being based on a rational model of efficiency-seeking through the creation of an 'optimal degree of fit' between the input of human resources and the productive activities of the firm that stem from its business strategy. As Sparrow and Hiltrop (1994: 7) phrase it, within this HRM paradigm human resources are 'to be obtained cheaply, used sparingly, and developed and exploited as fully as possible in accordance with the demands determined by the overall business strategy'. The core recommendation in this perspective is that, once performance requirements have been strategically specified, the firm must develop a clearly defined system for individual performance appraisal and a system of rewards that differentiates between varying levels of performance.

Collaborative HRM

An additional core imperative of rational HRM models is to simultaneously fulfil the needs of the firm and the needs of the employees in a harmonious way. This stems from a consensus-oriented perspective in which mutual expectations and goals are to be coordinated and met. The 'Harvard' model developed by Beer et al. (1985) argues that employee commitment is of crucial importance for firm success regardless of the type of strategy being pursued. As a consequence, Beer et al. recommend tapping into employees' intrinsic motivation. Typically, to achieve this, considerable effort is expended on creating mission statements that communicate the business strategy to employees. Coupled to mission statements are employee communication policies and systems for conducting employee briefings at all levels. It is important to note, though, that none of these North American collaborative techniques are rooted in governance systems that involved any role for the employees' trade unions. On the contrary, as HRM established itself in North America unions became even more marginalized in an institutional environment characterized by increasing management autonomy and shareholder power.

The Norwegian and North American HRM regimes

Previous research on the effect of national institutional environments indicates that firms in Scandinavia, and particularly Norway, have developed HRM practices that are highly distinctive in relation to those of other European contexts (Gooderham et al., 1999; Gooderham et al., 2006). One factor is the high level of unionization combined with the fact that unions exert a considerable influence on the management of firms. Another factor is that Norwegian HRM practices are markedly less 'calculative' than, for example, UK firms, but they are also highly 'collaborative'. In Gooderham et al. (1999) four distinct HRM regimes were identified. UK firms have a particularly high score in terms of the calculative dimension and a somewhat high score in terms of the collaborative dimension. French and Spanish firms are weaker than UK firms in terms of both dimensions, and German firms even more so. Danish and Norwegian firms form their own unique cluster. First, they are much weaker in terms of the calculative dimension than of the other countries and not least the UK. Second, they exhibit strong scores in terms of the collaborative dimension. Norwegian firms, in particular, have an extremely high score in relation to the collaborative dimension. As such Norwegian firms in the European context have a very distinctive set of HRM practices.

Positioning US firms in relation to the calculative and collaborative dimensions has been hindered by the lack of comparative data for North American firms: indeed our chapter is one of the first studies to include such data from North America. However, measures of institutional distance (Botero et al., 2004; Hall & Gingerich, 2004) as well as measures of cultural distance (Hofstede, 1980; House et al., 2004) all suggest that both Canada and the USA have a culture similar to that of the UK and dissimilar to Norway in regard to HRM. In other words, we should suppose that, like UK firms, North American firms make more use of calculative HRM and less use of collaborative HRM than Norwegian firms. A study of the HRM practices of the subsidiaries of US MNEs in Europe supports this (Gooderham et al., 2006). In terms of their use of calculative HRM, US subsidiaries are similar to indigenous UK firms and dissimilar to Norwegian/Danish firms. It would therefore seem reasonable to 'hypothesize' that the North American and Norwegian HRM regimes are considerably different. To the extent that this is the case, Norwegian MNEs with North American operations are confronted by a significant managerial challenge: do they implement their own set of HRM practices or do they adapt their HRM practices to the local North American setting?

Research strategy

In order to test our general hypothesis we draw on the 2010 Cranet data set. The overall strategy of the Cranet survey is to mail identical, appropriately translated questionnaires to HRM managers in representative national samples of firms with more than 100 employees. Problems in ensuring that the selection and interpretation of topic areas are not biased by one country's approach, as well as problems related to the translation of concepts and questions, were largely overcome by close collaboration between business schools located in each country. The Cranet survey includes data for Norwegian (n = 92) and US (n = 413) organizations. Data were not available for Canadian organizations but, given the discussion above, we would expect findings similar to that of the USA. We use a series of cross-tabulations to compare and contrast calculative HRM and collaborative HRM in connection with industrial relations.

Thereafter, we present key findings from 32 interviews we conducted in a natural resource-seeking Norwegian MNE operating in North America. The MNE in focus has operations in over thirty countries spanning five continents, but the North American operations have grown into becoming the organization's largest foreign interest. The North American operations currently comprise a greenfield site in the US and an acquisition in Canada with the Canadian operation reporting to the US operation. The size and the strategic importance of the North American units is such that one would expect that local employees could bring pressure to bear on the Norwegian MNE to adapt to local needs. Furthermore, this pressure may increase particularly as the US operations become increasingly embedded in the local business community. The face-to-face[1] interviews were conducted at the multinational's local North American offices, tape-recorded and transcribed in verbatim. Each interview lasted between 1 and 2 hours. The respondents include a mix of managers and employees located either in the US or Canadian subsidiaries or with experience from both countries (totalling 21 interviews) as well as Norwegian expats working in Canada and the US (totalling 11 interviews). The interviews were coded using computer-assisted qualitative data analysis software (CAQDAS), Atlas t_i to increase reliability (Weber, 1990). The coding was based on theoretically derived characteristics of collaborative and calculative HRM practices (Gooderham et al., 1999).

Findings

The Cranet survey

In the following we briefly present findings derived from the Cranet survey that address the overall issue of a substantial difference in the North American and Norwegian HRM regimes.

Although institutional distance as conceived by Botero et al. (2004) and Hall and Gingerich (2004) is multi-dimensional, one key indicator is that of industrial relations. Table 8.1 serves as an indicator of the profound differences in the Norwegian and US industrial relations regimes not just in terms

Table 8.1 Industrial relations (all cross-national comparisons statistically different at the 95% level)

	USA	N
Proportion of employees that are **not** members of a trade union	66%	4%
Extent to which trade unions do **not** influence organization at all/small extent	76%	7%
Firms that do **not** recognize trade unions for collective bargaining	67%	4%

Table 8.2 Calculative HRM (all cross-national comparisons statistically different at the 95% level)

	USA	N
Formal appraisal system for:		
Management	92%	54%
Professional	96%	44%
Clerical	94%	44%
Manual	72%	42%
Performance-related pay for:		
Management	77%	32%
Professional	74%	20%
Clerical	67%	15%
Manual	52%	10%

of trade union membership, but more significantly also in terms of union influence on management.

Unlike their Norwegian counterparts, US managers generally do not operate under the constraint of union influence and therefore have latitude to choose their HRM practices. Indeed, Table 8.1 indicates that the majority of US organizations are 'union-free', while this is the exception for Norwegian organizations. This is in line with previous research (e.g. Dølvik & Stokke, 1998) indicating that the Norwegian and US organizations in our sample constitute a representative sample.

As the upper section of Table 8.2 indicates, formal appraisal at all levels is commonplace in US organizations. This is far less the case for Norwegian organizations.

However, secondary analysis indicates that those Norwegian organizations that do have appraisal systems use them in the same way as their US counterparts, that is, to inform pay decisions, training and development decisions and to inform career moves.

The lower section of Table 8.2 reinforces the contrast between Norway and the US in terms of calculative HRM. Among US organizations the use of performance-related pay is much more widespread than in Norwegian organizations.

Table 8.3   Collaborative HRM (all cross-national comparisons statistically different at the 95% level apart from those marked 'n.s.')

	USA	N	
The organization has a:			
Written mission statement	90%	91%	n.s.
Written code of ethics	89%	85%	n.s.
Employee communication:			
Verbally to employees to a great extent	78%	53%	
Written to employees to a great extent	84%	57%	
Team briefings to a great extent	70%	56%	
Via representative staff bodies to at least some extent	31%	87%	
Employees communicate their views to a great extent direct to:			
Senior managers	57%	21%	
Through immediate supervisor	87%	82%	n.s.
Through team briefings	51%	43%	n.s.
Through trade union representative to a great extent	15%	60%	
Formal briefings about business strategy for:			
Management	97%	100%	n.s.
Professional	83%	92%	n.s.
Clerical	59%	85%	
Manual	49%	82%	

In terms of formally communicating the organization's mission statement and code of ethics, Table 8.3 indicates no differences between Norwegian and US organizations.

However, in terms of the channels of employee communication there are noteworthy differences. In particular while US managers are more likely to communicate directly with individual employees, verbally or in writing, Norwegian organizations have a considerably greater tendency to communicate indirectly with employees through representative staff bodies.

In regard to employees communicating their views there is a much greater tendency for employees in US organizations to do this directly to senior managers than employees in Norwegian organizations. However, communicating via the immediate supervisor is very common for organizations in both countries. A common added communication channel for employees in Norwegian organizations, as opposed to their US counterparts, is through the trade union representative.

Finally, Table 8.3 indicates a significant difference in regard to involving employees at lower levels within the organization. Norwegian organizations are significantly more likely to brief employees at lower levels about strategy than is the case for US organizations. In other words, collaborative HRM is practised by Norwegian organizations in a more collective manner than is the case for US organizations. In short, collaborative HRM is more comprehensively applied by Norwegian organizations than their US counterparts.

To summarize: the Cranet survey data confirm our general hypothesis that profound differences exist between the Norwegian and the North American HRM regimes. First, industrial relations are very different. Second, calculative HRM is much more widespread in US organizations than Norwegian organizations. Third, collaborative HRM is more comprehensively applied in Norwegian organizations than US organizations, and is associated with the Norwegian system of industrial relations, unlike in the US, where it is a managerial choice. The issue we turn to now is how these differences manifest themselves in the HRM practices of Norwegian MNEs in North America.

Interviews in the North American operations of a Norwegian MNE

The interviews we conducted within a Norwegian MNE in North America indicated a complete lack of union involvement either in the Canadian or the US operations. In the case of the US operation this was entirely consistent with the findings for the US in Table 8.1 as well as with the institutional distance measures we have referred to. Unions are thus not viewed by either locals or expatriates as affecting the Norwegian MNE's HRM practices in North America. It was also recognized that this was significantly different from the Norwegian context where union membership is high and organizations consult, inform and interact with union representatives on HRM issues. Table 8.4 illustrates the common sentiments expressed in the interviews.

Given this lack of constraint by unions at its North American operations the issue was therefore what the Norwegian MNE would seek to apply of its Norwegian HRM practices. We observed a pronounced application of collaborative HRM where employees are seen as active partners and their involvement is encouraged (Gooderham et al., 1999). The approach was referred to by several interviewees as 'bringing the "Norwegian model" to North America'. Reactions to this HRM policy were twofold. On the one hand, interviewees commented that they appreciated that the North American operations were valued to such an extent that effort was made

Table 8.4　Interview responses to industrial relations

Local respondents	Expatriates in North America
'Unions have no impact at this level, they only have an impact on people that are working on field projects' (Canada)	'No, it's very different from Norway ... they play no role in what we are doing here' (US) 'They're non-existent' (Canada)

to integrate them in a MNE-wide HRM approach. On the other hand, local employees found some aspect of the collaborative HRM practices difficult to understand and therefore irritating. Collaborative HRM practices were generally seen by local employees as non-value-adding, time-consuming and ineffective. The emphasis on active involvement and collaboration was not only identified in relation to communicating the strategy and corporate culture but also the underlying values that were communicated and reinforced through many aspects of daily business. The quotes in Table 8.5 are representative of both perceived strengths and weaknesses communicated in the interviews.

Table 8.5   Perceived strengths and weaknesses of collaborative HRM in the North American affiliates

Perceived strengths	Perceived weaknesses
'The company has developed a strategy and actually invests tremendously in its people … it's tremendous for me to be able to engage in that and actually have a view' (Local manager, Canada)	'We can spend weeks and months off-sites and talk about organizational development and talk about our strategies and goals, do conflict resolution and do all the right moves. … If we are going to do it that way, we are not focusing on the bottom line. We can't spend our time like this. It's not efficient' (Local employee, Canada)
'In the Norwegian model, everybody gets to have a voice, which is a positive thing. And they encourage that, that's all good' (Local employee, US)	
'The values, and maybe that's part of the culture, but the values of the company, you know, it is a value-based company, that's for me everything. It is a really important part of why I think most people stay' (Local employee, Canada)	'Sometimes you just want somebody just to, you know, make a decision. And you feel like, if you got 10 people in a room and only two of them really have the background, why should everybody else be involved in the decision?' (Local employee, US)
	'People that get into some kind of authority have worked hard for twenty years to get into these positions and then feel they should have some responsibility for decision-making. What then happens is that they say "this is the way it is" and all the peers and groups say "now it's time to talk about it" … by the time the decision gets made, you end up with the lowest common denominator decision' (Local employee, Canada)

As the quotes in Table 8.5 illustrate, some of the aspects of the Norwegian MNE's collaborative HRM practices created both resistance and frustration locally. Although top management's investment in communicating the vision, strategy and culture was recognized as important, the extensive allocation of time to ensure that the geographically dispersed organizations were aligned, integrated and actively involved created frustration among several North Americans. These collaborative HRM practices necessitated significant internal focus, which was perceived by some as taking the focus away from the local 'fast-paced external business environment'. Increasing frustration was particularly identified in collaborative characteristics permeating the daily operations such as decision-making processes and expectations of internal communication and involvement. Several interviewees expressed concern that the North American operations might not be operating as efficiently in the market as their competitors, particularly as the extended emphasis on collaboration differed from the practice of most local competitors.

The interviews further revealed that as the Norwegian MNE registered the frustrations and scepticism it had begun to engage in significant moderations of its HRM policies to succeed locally. The local pressures for adaptation were particularly expressed in terms of expectations of individual accountability and efficiency, as exemplified by representative quotes in Table 8.6.

The differences in external environments and explicit local expectations of calculative HRM practices resulted in a number of local adaptations intended not only to increase perceived efficiency but also to attract and retain local talent. As Table 8.7 indicates, local adaptations include compensation such as performance-related pay and general hiring conditions.

Table 8.6 Quotes illustrating local expectations and pressures in North America

'A North American style would be more "if we have the talent, we don't need to rely so much on having the best processes" but talent wins the day rather than processes and organizational design' (Local employee, Canada)

'It's a much tougher workforce [in North America]' (Local employee, US)

'They [North Americans] are used to quick decisions, a lot of autonomy, quick turnaround, very *not* process oriented. A very different culture' (expatriate in Canada)

'Well, to the company's credit the learning curve was very quick and they were able to more or less adopt to this faster pace here … the pace here is like warp ten compared to what it is in Norway and it's constantly changing' (Local manager, US)

'I think the frustration is sometimes not being sure of which direction they should be speaking because there are so many different interest groups that seem to come in at different levels. … People feel a little bit as if they are spinning wheels' (Local employee, Canada)

Table 8.7 Quotes illustrating local adaptations in North America

---

'We pay well, we're competitive, give good bonuses, give good pay rises. We are competitive in the market here; we've made sure of it. But I don't know how much protection they have. I know it's not the protection that Norwegians have' (Expatriate, US)

'When you get down to the hire, how you fire, how you run your annual compensation system, that's very local and very specific' (Local manager, Canada)

The interviews thus suggest that despite an ingrained commitment to developing a collaborative culture, active steps were being taken towards incorporating calculative HRM practices. In other words, our interviews revealed a process that involved the Norwegian MNE responding to local expectations that resulted in a somewhat hybrid form of HRM. Although primarily Norwegian, there were also elements of North American HRM practices. As one US employee summarized:

> although this office has kind of moved to be a little more Americanized out of need ... there is much more openness. You can push back, you can have your voice, everybody's voice counts. ... The Norwegian consensus and all that which at times is frustrating ... everybody has an opportunity to say their piece.

Conclusions

Both institutional and cultural distance measures had caused us to assume considerable differences between the Norwegian and North American HRM regimes. The findings from the Cranet survey support this. The North American regime is characterized by a much greater use of calculative HRM practices than the Norwegian regime. Using in-depth interviews enabled us to explore the consequences of these differences for HRM policy in the North American operations of a Norwegian MNE. We observed that the introduction of Norwegian HRM in a North American setting received a mixed reception both in the greenfield US operation and the brownfield Canadian operation. The relatively extreme use of collaborative HRM by the Norwegian MNE was regarded as frustrating in both operations, and pressures arose for the introduction of significantly more calculative HRM.

Adopting a purely North American perspective, it could be argued that making greater use of calculative HRM and more direct communication with employees would enhance the subsidiary's external relationships (e.g. speed of decision-making) and the subsidiary's ability to attract and retain local employees. However, this would mean that the North American operations would diverge significantly in terms of HRM from the Norwegian operation. Such a divergence would make it highly problematic to forge a common

MNE-wide corporate culture, thereby undermining communication between US and Norwegian co-workers (Gooderham, 2007). The interviews indicate how vital the Norwegian MNE perceives its common corporate culture to be and how local adaptations so far have been balanced with a continued emphasis on underlying collaborative values. However, our interviews suggest that the process of adapting HRM practices to the North American model may not be over.

Given that Norwegian companies in North America accede to normative pressure and choose to implement a substantial element of calculative HRM, while decreasing their use of collaborative HRM, this poses a managerial challenge in terms of getting these adaptations to work in practice. Case studies of a Norwegian MNE developing and applying US-style performance management show this inherent difficulty (Lervik, 2005; Lunnan et al., 2005). Similarly, the MNE studied in this chapter illustrates the potential for conflict as concessions are made to local pressures for calculative HRM practices such as performance-based pay, while attempting to restrict the effect of these calculative measures by, for instance, maintaining collaborative characteristics that affect business processes such as decision-making.

The Cranet survey data compares aggregate data for Norway and North America. Although our interviews serve to confirm the aggregate data and enable us to view how the differences between the Norwegian and North American regimes have an impact on the HRM of the North American operations of a Norwegian MNE, there is clearly a need to go beyond these findings. In particular we need studies that draw on data collected over an extended period of time so that we can observe the 'final outcome' of the processes that had led to a degree of HRM hybridization. The insights gained from our interviews indicate an enormous complexity in terms of both positive and negative perceptions of entering the North American market with a significantly more 'people-oriented' approach to employee engagement and commitment. Remaining too collaboratively oriented seems to create frustration that can alienate North American employees. On the other hand, giving individuals at all levels a voice through collaborative HRM practices and positioning the organization as strongly value-based can possibly attract certain types of individuals in a context characterized by 'hiring and firing'. We argue that further case studies would enable us to better understand the multiplicity of the contexts Norwegian MNEs are confronted by (cf. Marschan-Piekkari et al., 2004) and the potential pressures to engage in local adaptations of HRM.

Implications for Norwegian companies in North America

On the basis of our analyses of Cranet findings and interviews in a Norwegian MNE, we will now draw out some HRM implications for Norwegian MNEs with operations in North America.

Norwegian companies have developed their HRM policies and practices in a very different institutional setting from that of North America. Whereas managerial latitude is largely unconstrained by trade unions in North America, particularly in the US, Norwegian companies have developed their HRM policies and practices in relation to this constraint. This has given rise to the extensive use of calculative HRM in North American organizations and its limited use in Norwegian organizations. In regard to collaborative HRM the imprint of trade unions is noticeable in respect of communication and in terms of strategy briefings. In US organizations direct communication between employee and management is used more, whereas in Norwegian organizations management is clearly obliged to take into account the union channel. The interviews suggest that this collaborative imprint continues to permeate the daily business processes and practices of the North American operations. In other words, we observe a marked 'country-of-origin' effect.

However, extant studies show that HRM policies and practices tend to differ significantly across MNE operations in response to the local business contexts that the foreign subsidiaries are embedded in (Bjorkman, Fey & Park, 2007; Gooderham et al., 2006). Thus it is reasonable to expect that Norwegian companies setting up operations in North America will sooner or later respond to normative pressures to make much greater use of calculative HRM and also to engage in direct communication with employees. However, this is no more than speculation. Not only do we lack large-scale empirical studies of the practices of Norwegian MNEs in North America but we also lack in-depth case studies that examine which HRM practice and policies Norwegian MNEs 'insist' on applying when operating in North America. The only previous in-depth relevant case study available is one that that features the implementation of performance management in a Norwegian MNE (Lervik, 2005; Lunnan et al., 2005). The study showed that immediate adoption of calculative HRM practices originating from the USA required substantial time and effort to implement. Our interviews in one Norwegian MNE suggest that local adaptations are primarily related to hiring/firing practices and compensation systems (such as performance-related bonuses) while key collaborative characteristics such as internal communication and employee involvement are maintained. The continued emphasis on collaborative HRM practices, however, appears to create resistance and frustration among North American employees.

Although our study has been confined to Norwegian MNEs entering North America the basic dilemma Norwegian MNEs face is hardly unique. When MNEs expand into settings characterized by substantial cultural and institutional distance the issue of adapting HRM practices to the local environment almost inevitably arises. Any substantial local adaptation by an MNE means that it comprises business units with distinct and possibly even conflicting identities. This may constitute a barrier for the development of common understandings and trust without which the exchange of knowledge becomes highly problematic (Gooderham, 2007).

Note

1. With the exception of one phone interview which was taped through a speakerphone.

References

Beer, M., Spector, B., Lawrence, P., Quinn Mills, D. & Walton, R. 1985. *Human Resource Management: A General Manager's Perspective*. New York: Free Press.

Bjorkman, I., Fey, C.F. & Park, H.J. 2007. 'Institutional theory and MNC subsidiary HRM practices: Evidence from a three-country study'. *Journal of International Business Studies*, 38: 430–46.

Botero, J. Djankov, S. La Porta, R. Lopez-de-Silanes, S. & Shleifer, A. 2004. 'The regulation of labor'. *Quarterly Journal of Economics*, 119: 1339–82.

Dølvik, J.E. & Stokke, T.A. 1998. 'Norway: The revival of centralized concentration'. In A. Ferner and R. Hyman (eds), *Changing Industrial Relations in Europe*. Oxford: Blackwell, 118–45.

Fombrun, G.R., Tichy, N.M. & Devanna, M.A. 1984. *Strategic Human Resource Management*. New York: John Wiley & Sons.

Gooderham, P.N. 2007. 'Enhancing knowledge transfer in multinational corporations: A dynamic capabilities driven model'. *Knowledge Management Research and Practice*, 5: 34–43.

Gooderham, P.N., Nordhaug, O. & Ringdal, K. 1999. 'Institutional and rational determinants of organizational practices: Human resource management in European firms'. *Administrative Science Quarterly*, 44: 507–31.

Gooderham, P.N., Nordhaug, O. & Ringdal, K. 2006. 'National embeddedness and HRM in US subsidiaries in Europe'. *Human Relations*, 59: 1491–513.

Gooderham, P.N., Parry, E. & Ringdal, K. 2008. 'The impact of bundles of strategic human resource management practices on the performance of European firms'. *International Journal of Human Resource Management*, 19(11): 2041–56.

Hall, P.A. & Gingerich, D.W. 2004. 'Varieties of capitalism and institutional complementarities in the macroeconomy'. MPIfG Discussion Paper 04/5. Berlin: Max Planck Institut für Gesellschaftsforschung.

Hofstede, G. 1980. *Culture's Consequences: International Differences in Work-related Values*. Thousand Oaks, CA: Sage.

House, R.J., Hanges, P.J., Javidan, M., Dorfman, P.W. & Gupta, V. 2004. *Culture, Leadership and Organizations; The GLOBE Study of 62 Societies*. Thousand Oaks, CA: Sage.

Lervik, J.E. 2005. 'Managing matters – Transfer of organizational practices in MNC subsidiaries'. Unpublished Doctoral Dissertation. Oslo: Norwegian School of Management.

Lunnan, R., Lervik, J., Traavik, L.M., Nilsen, S.M., Amdam, R.P. & Hennestad, B.W. 2005. 'Global transfer of management practices across nations and MNC subcultures'. *Academy of Management Executive*, 19(5): 77–80.

Marschan-Piekkari, R., Welch C., Penttinen, H. & Tahvanainen, M. 2004. 'Interviewing in the multinational corporation: Challenges of the organizational context'. In

R. Marschan-Piekkari & C. Welch (eds), *Handbook of Qualitative Research Methods for International Business*. Cheltenham: Edward Elgar.

Poutsma, E., Lightart, P.E.M. & Veersma, U. 2006. 'The diffusion of calculative and collaborative HRM practices in European firms'. *Industrial Relations*, 45: 513–46.

Rizov, M. & Croucher, R. 2009. 'Human resource management and performance in European firms'. *Cambridge Journal of Economics*, 33: 253–72.

Sparrow, P. & Hiltrop, M. 1994. *European Human Resource Management in Transition*. London: Prentice Hall.

Weber, R.P. 1990. *Basic Content Analysis*. Newbury Park, CA: Sage.

Section Three
HRM Practices and Outcomes

9
The Development of Employee Financial Participation in Europe

Erik Poutsma, Paul Ligthart, Andrew Pendleton and Chris Brewster

Introduction

Financial participation is a key human resource management practice, extending democracy at the workplace and, as the success of the organization becomes directly linked to employee rewards, altering the relationship between employees and the organization. In this chapter we discuss the incidence and characteristics of financial participation in eight European Union countries. We address the following questions in the chapter. One, what is the incidence of financial participation schemes in these eight Member States? Two, to what extent are financial participation schemes selective for specific employee groups, such as managers? Three, what was the extent of development of these schemes in the decade 1995–2005? Four, what are the determinants of the use of these schemes? In the chapter we focus on narrow-based schemes targeted at management and broad-based schemes where all employees are eligible to participate. We focus on two types of schemes through which employees and managers participate financially in the performance of their companies: profit sharing and share ownership.

The data used to address these questions are of two types. The first involves qualitative data on the development of financial participation in the selected countries based on reports by national experts (see Pendleton & Poutsma, 2004). These data facilitate interpretation of the results arising from the second data source. This analysis is based on eight countries covered by the Cranet survey: Belgium, Finland, France, Germany, the Netherlands, Spain, Sweden and the UK. We draw on data from the 1995, 1999/2000, and 2004/2005 surveys to consider the incidence, development and determinants of financial participation.

The results show that country-level factors are a key influence on the character and incidence of broad-based employee financial participation and are more important than organizational factors. Tax concessions appear to be a key element of these country-level factors. By contrast, management-only schemes appear to be driven by factors other than regulatory regimes and taxation.

Financial participation schemes: Instruments and concepts

Profit sharing

Profit sharing can take a number of forms: it can be paid in cash, shares or bonds. Alternatively, profit-sharing bonuses may be invested in company savings schemes (which may invest in the employer's stock). Usually, where shares are paid in some form other than cash, a minimum retention period is given. So far, profit sharing has been most widely developed in France, where it is required by law for firms with over 50 employees (see Poutsma, 2001; Mabile, 1998 for further details).

Government support for profit sharing can take the form of legislation, which gives schemes a specific legal identity, and tax concessions to the employee and employer (Pendleton & Poutsma, 2004). Usually, the tax concessions to the employee take the form of some exemption from income tax and social security contributions, while the employer may benefit from social security exemptions and a company tax deduction for the money paid as a profit share. On the whole, tax concessions are not given to simple cash bonus schemes because they can encourage 'cosmetic' schemes and tax avoidance. An exception was the Profit-Related Pay scheme in the United Kingdom in the 1990s, where substantial tax concessions were available for the portion of wages classified as profit-related. However, the tax concessions were withdrawn from this scheme precisely because in many cases the profit share component of wages was being widely used as a means of tax avoidance.

Employee share ownership

Employee share ownership provides for participation in ownership. As a result of share ownership employees may benefit from the receipt of dividends, the capital gains that accrue to company equity, or a combination of the two. While share ownership schemes are not necessarily financed out of company profits, they are related to company profitability in that growth in market value of the shares will be a function of profits and performance (at least in part). The size of dividend payments will also be based on company profit performance.

Employees may acquire shares in one of three main ways: by direct purchase of shares; by taking out options to buy shares at some point in the future; or by transfers financed by company profits. Shares may take the form of ordinary share capital of the firm, or a special class of employee shares (such as preference shares with a pre-specified level of interest payments).

Government support for share ownership can take the form of legislation to give schemes a distinct legal entity and to provide a clear framework for monitoring a scheme (Pendleton & Poutsma, 2004). Tax concessions are usually mainly directed at employees rather than firms and take the form of exemptions from income tax on share acquisition. However, tax concessions are not usually available on dividend payments. It is common for the employee's taxation liability to take the form of capital gains tax liability on the growth in share value over time (which may be offset by Capital Gains Tax allowances). If the costs of financing share ownership schemes are included on the profit and loss account, corporation tax deductions may be available to the firm.

The coverage of share ownership

A key issue is whether financial participation covers all or most employees, or is highly selective (Pendleton, Poutsma & Brewster, 2003). In other words, what proportion of the workforce is eligible to participate in financial participation schemes? Are all groups of employees offered participation, or is it restricted to certain classes of employee? On the whole, selective schemes are likely to be restricted to executives/managers or senior key professionals.

The distinction between selective (narrow-based) schemes and all-employee (broad-based) schemes is important for several reasons. One, very different motives may lie behind the introduction of selective schemes and broad-based schemes. Whereas broad-based schemes might be introduced to enhance employee identification with the firm, selective schemes might be aimed at improving specific managerial performance or aligning the interests of managers with those of shareholders as a response to the 'agency' problem (Jensen & Meckling 1976; Murphy, 1999). Two, if participation is restricted to management or other sub-groups in the workforce, financial participation may increase rather than reduce existing inequalities of income and wealth.

We predict that the presence of legislation and tax concessions will affect the balance of selective and broad-based schemes at a country level. Where legislation is not present, it is likely that a higher proportion of schemes will take a selective form, based on the agency perspective (Eisenhardt, 1989; Jensen & Meckling, 1976; Murphy, 1999; Tihanyi et al., 2009). The reasoning for this is that the impetus for using schemes will come either from owners concerned to align managerial interests with theirs or from top managers seeking to provide incentives for their subordinate managers.

Financial participation research

Research has a tradition of studying the causes, characteristics and effects of financial participation. Much of this research has taken place in the USA, reflecting the considerable interest in Profit Sharing and Employee Share-Ownership Plans (ESOPs) since the mid-1970s (see Blasi 1988; Blasi, Conte & Kruse 1996; Blinder, 1990; Cheadle 1989; Kruse 1993, 1996; Kruse, Freeman & Blasi, 2010). A number of important research studies have been conducted in Europe also, mainly based on data from individual European countries (e.g. Fitzroy & Kraft 1987; Wilson & Peel 1991; Fakhfakh & Pérotin, 2000; Pérotin & Robinson, 2003; Kraft & Ugarkovic, 2006; Robinson & Wilson, 2006; Bryson & Freeman 2010; Pendleton & Robinson 2010, 2011).

The current wave of interest, especially in broad-based financial participation in Europe, suggests the desirability of recent comparative research studies, especially studies able to compare nations at the firm level. Vaughan-Whitehead (1995), in a study published by the International Labour Office, brought together information on a number of European countries. An updated version of the PEPPER (Promotion of Employee Participation in Profit and Enterprise Results) Report was produced by the European Commission in 1997, in response to one of the stipulations of the 1992 Council Recommendation. The information in this report has been updated further by Poutsma (2001), in a report for the European Foundation for the Improvement of Living and Working Conditions. Also, the data collected across Europe for the Employee Participation in Organisational Change (EPOC) project of the European Foundation for the Improvement of Living and Working Conditions have been used to investigate the characteristics of firms with broad-based employee share ownership (Poutsma & Huijgen, 1999). A second report for the European Foundation summarized the development of financial participation (including profit sharing) for the European Union (Pendleton & Perotin, 2001). A third report reviewed more recent developments and provided in-depth coverage of the nature and extent of financial participation in Eastern European countries (Lowitsch, Hashi & Woodward, 2009). Despite these pioneering studies, comparative research on financial performance has been scarce. We start with the basic question of the extent of financial participation in different countries.

National incidence of financial participation

A key question for this chapter concerns the incidence of financial participation schemes in different countries and the reasons for the differences between countries. It has been widely observed that government legislation on financial participation, and the availability of tax concessions, are key determinants of national differences in the incidence of schemes (Uvalic, 1991; IPSE, 1997, Poutsma, 2001; Poutsma, Hendrickx & Huijgen, 2003). These studies show that differences exist in cultural attitudes, and in regulatory and fiscal regimes that create variation between countries in the use and incidence of financial participation. As a first step, we examine the incidence of selective and broad-based profit sharing and employee share ownership in eight Western European countries. These countries are selected to provide coverage of various types of fiscal regulatory regimes and business systems within Western Europe.

We use two major data sources. The first is data coming from an investigation of the national frameworks and policies of governing bodies and social partners concerning executives and all employee share ownership. These data come from national reports and excerpts of these are published in Pendleton and Poutsma (2004).

The second data source for the project is the Cranet survey. Eight of the current Member States of the European Union have been included in the survey throughout the time period we analyse: Belgium, Finland, France, Germany, the Netherlands, Spain, Sweden and the United Kingdom. This provides broad coverage of the European Union, with the Mediterranean, Benelux, Scandinavian, northern and western regions of Europe included in the survey. In this research we mainly utilize three consecutive Cranet surveys, namely 1995, 1999/2000 and 2004/2005. Use of the three waves not only allows for replication of results, but also provides some indication of whether results are robust to differing economic conditions, since the first time period (1995/2000) reflects the culmination of a decade of economic growth, while the second (2000/2005) encloses a period of economic downturn. It should be emphasized, however, that the three data sets do not form a panel, although it is likely that some establishments participated in multiple waves. Besides limiting the study to the eight Member States, we also limit it to the private sector. A further criterion for inclusion is that the establishment should employ at least 100 employees, providing us with a total of 5840 cases for all three waves.

We employ the following measures: we distinguish between narrow-based and broad-based plans (Poutsma, Ligthart & Schouteten, 2005). Narrow-based means that the plan applies to management only. Broad-based plans are targeted to include all other employees, and those plans usually include management.

Overview of incidence

What is the average incidence of financial participation in Europe in the period 1995–2005? Table 9.1 presents an overview, based on pooling the data from the three points of observation, for the two forms of financial participation included in this study. Table 9.1 indicates that nearly 31 per cent of establishments of companies with more than 100 employees have a share ownership scheme (ESO) for one or more employee groups (management-only 11 per cent; broad-based 20 per cent). The overall incidence of profit sharing (PS) is much higher, that is, 47 per cent establishments adopted this form of financial participation (management only 10 per cent; broad-based 37 per cent). Furthermore, there is some overlap between the two forms of participation. These large variations of incidence rates across the employee groups underline the relevance of taking these differences into account when studying the diffusion of financial participation in Europe.

Table 9.1   Incidence rates of financial participation in establishments (>100 employees) in the selected countries

Pooled data	Proportion[1]
Employee share ownership	
No ESO	69%
Management ESO	11%
Broad-based ESO	20%
Profit sharing	
No profit sharing	53%
Management profit sharing	10%
Broad-based profit sharing	37%

Note: [1] 100% = N = 5840.

An overview of the developments and the main characteristics of financial participation in these countries are summarized in Table 9.2. The proportion of companies with only narrow-based share ownership ranges from 10 to 20 per cent in 2005, with the UK and France having the lowest proportions and Belgium and Spain the highest. In most countries the incidence of these schemes increased between 1995 and 2005, though usually the increase was concentrated in the five years from 1995. The pattern of broad-based employee share ownership schemes is rather different: the UK and France have the highest incidence (38 and 35 per cent respectively in 2005) and Spain the lowest (8 per cent). Belgium, France, Finland, the Netherlands and Sweden display substantial increases in incidence over the period, though mostly the increase is concentrated in the second half of the 1990s, the period of economic growth.

The incidence of profit sharing just for management grades is very low in all countries except Germany throughout the period. Germany has a high incidence of these schemes, with profit-based payments forming part of performance pay schemes for managers. However, the incidence of these schemes declines substantially during the period from 44 to 24 per cent. To some extent this decline is related to the increasing availability of other instruments such as stock options and share ownership, and also to broadening the scheme to all employees.

The pattern of broad-based profit sharing is highly varied between the countries. France has the highest incidence, reflecting the compulsory nature of profit sharing. Profit sharing is also widely used in Finland, the Netherlands and Germany, with substantial increases observed in each from 1995 onwards. The UK is the only country to show a decline between 1995 and 2005, and this is probably owing to the withdrawal of the tax concessions for the Profit-Related Pay scheme in the late 1990s.

Table 9.2 An overview of development and characteristics of financial participation in eight selected countries

Country	Incidence					Characteristics of national system
		ESO	ESO	PS	PS	
EUC8	Year	NB	BB	NB	BB	
Finland	1995	3%	7%	4%	17%	Elaborate system of personnel
	1999	12%	22%	4%	32%	funds; tax concessions; employee
	2005	16%	18%	5%	86%	representatives (unions) involved in plan monitoring
Sweden	1995	3%	6%	2%	19%	No national incentive policies to
	1999	14%	15%	7%	20%	promote financial participation;
	2005	12%	17%	8%	28%	employers against any involvement of employees or unions
The Netherlands	1995	4%	10%	4%	33%	Tax concessions through wage savings
	1999	19%	19%	0%	53%	system; no direct involvement of
	2005	13%	26%	8%	54%	unions, but involvement of works council; outside collective bargaining
Germany	1995	5%	9%	44%	28%	Regulated tax concessions and
	1999	8%	11%	33%	37%	benefits for capital savings for low
	2005	14%	11%	24%	60%	earners, indirectly linked to ESO; outside collective bargaining; unions started discussions but are sceptical
United Kingdom	1995	15%	34%	6%	34%	Legal framework for ESO, tax
	1999	13%	34%	6%	31%	concessions; employees and unions
	2005	10%	38%	8%	24%	not involved
Belgium	1995	8%	7%	8%	11%	Only in last period legislative
	1999	15%	14%	9%	11%	initiatives, especially for NB; BB
	2005	21%	21%	7%	16%	discussed with unions who are critical regarding ESO
France	1995	8%	9%	0%	81%	State-regulated BB PS, gradually
	1999	18%	23%	0%	88%	evolved in ESO funds; tax incentives;
	2005	10%	35%	0%	92%	limited employee representative involvement
Spain	1995	6%	7%	7%	12%	Minor regulations and developments,
	1999	11%	10%	9%	15%	some tax exemptions for NB ESO, but
	2005	20%	8%	8%	30%	tightened after scandals; schemes not discussed in collective agreements negotiations

Note: NB = narrow-based; BB = broad-based; ESO = employee share ownership; PS = Profit sharing.

In the next section we explore these differences by investigating the national frameworks in the eight countries. The frameworks make clear that incidence and developments of financial participation are related to regulations and availability of tax concessions in countries, in some cases with a long history.

National frameworks of share ownership[1]

Belgium

In *Belgium* the development of share schemes is quite recent. Unlike many of the other countries, Belgian establishments showed an increase in use the second half of the time period, that is, 1999/2000–2004/5 (Table 9.2). In this period, Belgium acquired a legal framework for financial participation that consolidated earlier diffuse and fragmentary provisions. Moreover, the law in relation to fiscal scheme of values allocated to employees, whether they should be taxed as remuneration and reckonable for social security charges, was unclear.

In general, employers in Belgium are in favour of these schemes while the trade unions had been opposed. Hence it was only in the late 1990s and the early 2000s that important and wide-ranging legislative initiatives were taken in response to factors including European pressure and demands from employers' associations and enterprises themselves. Financial participation became a priority on the agenda of the 'rainbow' government of Liberals, Socialists and Ecologists, and the government reached a compromise in 2001 on a law 'relating to employee share ownership and profit-sharing schemes'.

In Belgium, labour statutes and labour law mean that only trade unions are entitled to negotiate on terms and conditions of employment. Employment relations and labour terms are highly formalized in central labour agreements and labour law, which creates a cooperative situation in Belgian workplaces but limits managerial room for manoeuvre in changing the employment relations and labour terms (Baisier & Albertijn, 1992). Of course, as in other European countries, management has more individualized contracts with owners of companies, which allow space for the use of management-only stock (options) plans. The Belgian government favours this with specific tax provisions in order to raise the competitiveness of enterprises and the incidence of narrow-based share schemes increased in the period of investigation.

Finland[2]

The Finnish financial participation landscape is dominated by the typical Finnish Personnel Fund (PF). Along with broad-based stock options (Jones, Kalmi & Mäkinen, 2006), PFs represent the major form of financial participation in Finland. The Personnel Funds (PF) law was enacted in the beginning of the 1990s, inspired by US employee stock ownership plans (ESOPs) and Swedish wage-earner funds. A PF typically distributes its shareholdings quite widely and invests also in other securities, whereas employee share ownership plans invest only in their own firm. Personnel funds are deferred profit-sharing plans, with the capital paid into the fund dependent on the company's financial results, allowing investment into the equity of the company and thus involving an element of employee share ownership. In practice many of the companies invest part of the assets in their own company and the rest in other assets. PFs are company-level agreements, established by a collective decision of the employees in the company, but in Finland both share schemes and profit-sharing schemes are largely developed outside the domain of collective bargaining. The PF is owned by the employees and administers the assets it receives from the company, and hence the Finnish PFs are more participative than schemes in other countries.

The funds do not pay any taxes on their earnings and for the employees, 20 per cent of the payouts from the fund are tax-free. Employers do not have to pay pension or social security contributions for the profit shares paid to the fund. These funds developed gradually in the 1990s, and they boomed in the second period of our investigation, 1995–2000, as a result of the expanding market (see Table 9.2). Share schemes (mainly stock options plans) experienced a similar increase, but when stock market performance plunged, the adoption of broad-based share schemes declined in favour of an increase of narrow-based share schemes and broad-based profit sharing.

France

France has a framework that consists of state-regulated (mandatory) broad-based deferred profit sharing with the aim of enhancing employee savings and achieving a wider distribution of wealth and wage flexibility. Started by President De Gaulle with the aim of bridging the gap between labour and capital, the development of deferred profit sharing (mandatory for companies with 50 or more employees) and voluntary Mutual Fund Savings schemes have been supported by French governments with tax incentives ever since. To secure approval, financial participation systems must be agreed by employees or their representatives. The financial participation system has evolved into a system where employee savings are invested in funds, which in turn either invest in a diversified fund or in the shares of the employer. This development of share-related schemes was supported by new legislation in 1997, and the gradual increase of more share-based systems (PEE) related to the widely used profit-sharing system. The 1997 law promotes more specific investments in the company's own capital, resulting in the very high incidence rate of profit-sharing schemes in France (85 per cent) relative to other European countries (see Table 9.2). In this way employee share ownership has been promoted in the French system: evidence from 2001 indicates that nearly half of savings plans are used as a means for employee share acquisition (see Incomes Data Services, 2001).

Germany

Share ownership schemes have not been well developed in Germany, though there is a considerable body of regulations designed to encourage employee asset accumulation, and there have been attempts to promote share ownership schemes recently. In the elaborate German system of industrial relations, collective agreements set the standards and, for instance, works councils have a legal right to negotiate on agreements about broad-based financial participation plans. Trade unions appear to have started discussions on plans, but in general they are sceptical, which may explain the slow diffusion of share schemes.

The regulated asset accumulation programmes encourage redistribution of capital and development of employee savings by investment plans. Employees have been encouraged to participate in their own and other companies' capital primarily within specific savings schemes. In most cases these capital savings plans do not take the form of company-related share ownership plans and certainly not share options plans (although there may be elements of share option savings related to the plan). This helps to explain why the incidence of employee share ownership plans in the Cranet survey is low (between 9 and 11 per cent for broad-based, and 5 and 14 per cent for narrow-based schemes). In contrast to share ownership schemes, profit-sharing schemes are more popular in Germany. Relative to the UK, for example, the incidence of broad-based schemes is higher, and the incidence of the narrow-based schemes is much higher.

The last observation may also relate to stock options developments. The issue of stock options to management and employees was prohibited by company law until 1998. Since then it has grown for management and selected staff, which explains the increase in narrow-based share schemes in the second period of our investigation, and may have substituted for narrow-based profit sharing. A further interpretation is that the stock market is less extensive in Germany than in some other European countries such as the UK, and many firms are privately owned, which leaves little scope for the development of full employee share ownership. This supports the observation that profit sharing is much more developed in Germany and that gradually the incidence of broad-based profit sharing became substantial.

The Netherlands

As in France and Germany, employee savings schemes are at the centre of financial participation in the Netherlands, though the national philosophy behind financial participation is different. While in France and Germany promoters talk about social objectives such as wealth redistribution, in the

Netherlands part of the philosophy was to find ways to influence collective bargaining outcomes to increase workforce flexibility and to moderate wage increases. Therefore, any incentives for financial participation were regulated within a system that also promoted general wage savings.

Two forms of company savings schemes were introduced in 1994. One (premium savings schemes) provides for employees to subscribe to a savings plan from post-tax salary, with a one-for-one match by the employer. The other scheme provides for employees to subscribe pre-tax pay or the proceeds of a profit-sharing scheme, but without the employer match. In both cases, the employee can withdraw sums from the fund after four years, tax-free. The profit share form is by far the most popular, with nearly 3 million participants in 2000. Savings funds may be used to operate broad-based stock options schemes, with the exercise of shares financed by savings in the fund. This type of stock options scheme allows employees to receive double the amount of options tax-free than is normally permitted. These schemes are required to be open to three-quarters of the workforce and to be approved by the Works Council. This offering of tax concessions explains the gradual increase of financial participation as found in our data (Table 9.2).

Spain

Spain has a limited framework for share ownership and share-based profit sharing. Table 9.2 shows an increase in narrow-based share schemes from 6 per cent to 20 per cent between 1995 and 2005, whereas there has been stable development of broad-based schemes. In the second period, from 1999/2000 to 2004/2005, an increase of broad-based profit sharing was experienced. In fact, the policy on broad-based employee share ownership was much more determined by concerns about the development of the co-operative sector and the social economy. The co-operative movement and the use of labour societies are important in Spain, and are gradually diffusing into small employee-share-ownership companies. The development in this SME sector is not covered by our data, since we have only data from larger (>100 employees) companies.

In the case of (public) joint stock companies there has been not much development in policy concerning employee share ownership or any substantial development in the uses of schemes, despite some upswing owing to the privatization of national bodies. Following a scandal (Telefonica), where top management made use of these tax exemptions from stock options to enrich themselves during the privatization, regulation was tightened by setting a maximum amount on the received benefit.

Spain has a long tradition of negotiations and collective agreements on variable pay. However, stocks (options) were seldom included in the debates. Given the weak institutional structures of industrial relations and a limited countervailing power of trade unions, management is granted much autonomy. An increase of individual contracts 'outside' collective agreements, mainly for management and higher staff, may boost schemes but, on the other hand, as in France, the terms and working conditions for the main labour force are regulated in detail, and this has set legislative and administrative constraints that leave little scope for broad-based schemes.

Sweden

Sweden has a strong industrial relations framework where trade unions are legally entitled to be consulted on changes in the terms and conditions of work at the workplace level. Although there is some managerial autonomy in the setting of HRM practices, this restricts the possibilities for widespread adoption of financial participation. There are no national incentive policies to promote employee share ownership or stock options in Sweden. In effect, there is some hostility towards collectively instigated financial participation schemes in general in Sweden. This follows painful attempts to do so in the 1980s. The intention of trade unions was to develop Wage Earners Funds, and it was envisaged that a shift would occur in corporate ownership to trade union-led funds. These plans received a lot of criticism and were eventually abolished. This experience has led to important political divisions that prevented a resolution to any debate on financial participation, with the result that no substantial developments took place, as we found in our data (Table 9.2).

The United Kingdom

The UK has a well-developed framework for employee share ownership. A series of schemes have been introduced by statute since the late 1970s, with two new schemes (Share Incentive Plan and Enterprise Management Incentives) introduced in 2000. Most schemes are option-based, with the Share Incentive Plan the main exception. In the Share Incentive Plan, companies can issue shares to employees free of charge, and employees can purchase shares on highly favourable terms. Two of the UK schemes are broad-based and open to all eligible employees. The other two are discretionary and are primarily aimed at managers. However, in some cases (around one-third of Enterprise Management Incentive companies) they are used as all-employee schemes. This explains a substantial level of broad-based share ownership as found in our data (Table 9.2). Profit sharing as such is not equally supported, but since the forms of financial participation correlate, adoption of broad-based profit sharing is also found in the UK.

The introduction of financial participation schemes in the UK is rarely covered by collective bargaining, and the decision to introduce schemes is usually taken solely by management. Although the UK introduced two new schemes during the period, the overall incidence of companies using most of the schemes has remained broadly stable, though there has been a decline since the late 2000s. The main exception to this picture has been the steep growth in awards of options by small companies under the Enterprise Management Incentives arrangements. This is not captured by the data presented here, which is mainly derived from larger companies.

Developments

What are the developments in financial participation in the 1990s and early twenty-first century?

We find, with some exceptions, common trends for financial participation in the eight countries. The development of selective narrow-based and broad-based Employee Share Ownership (ESO) and Profit Sharing in the eight countries for the three consecutive surveys is presented in Figures 9.1 and 9.2.

For share ownership, broad-based schemes show higher incidence rates in the last two waves compared to the 1995 wave, except for Germany and Spain. Whereas most countries show further increases or stabilization in broad-based ESO in the 2005 wave, the development of narrow-based ESO (i.e. the management-only scheme) shows much more divergence, that is, its incidence rate increases in half of the countries and decreases in the other half. An increase is noticeable in Finland, Germany, Belgium and Spain. A decrease is shown in Sweden, the Netherlands, France and the United Kingdom. It is interesting to see that the developments in narrow-based and broad-based ESO are diametrically opposed in the second period. A change in narrow-based ESO in 2005 is mirrored by a change in the opposite direction of broad-based ESO in 2005 for almost all countries except Belgium. Possibly, the economic downturn around 2000 incited the establishments to adapt more focused ESO schemes whether being a selective narrow-based or a broad-based scheme.

In the case of profit sharing, in most countries there is a stability of incidence rates for the low level of management-only schemes, except for Germany. The higher incidence rate of management-only schemes found in Germany in 1995 decreased in the following periods. Two factors may account for this. Until 1998 stock options to management and employees were prohibited by company law. Since the liberalization of this there is an increase in the use of stock options for management and selected staff, which explains the increase in narrow-based share schemes in the second period of our investigation. Secondly, there is a stronger increase in broad-based profit sharing, suggesting a further broadening of eligibility of these schemes. In fact, most countries show higher incidence rates for broad-based profit sharing in the second period except for the Netherlands and the UK.

After 2005 there was limited further growth in financial participation, and differences between the countries persisted (see, for recent developments, Pendleton & Poutsma, 2012). The UK and France further refined legislation

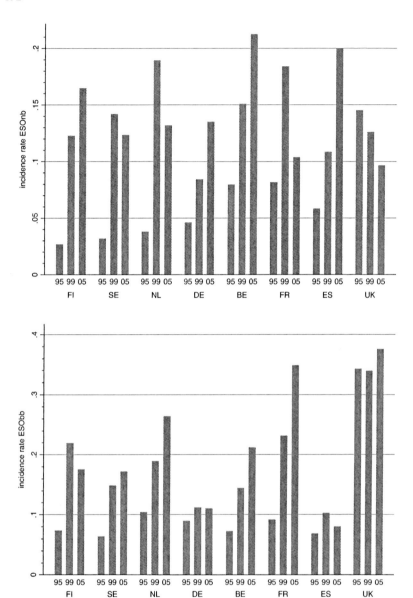

Figure 9.1 Distribution of observed narrow-based (ESOnb) and broad-based (ESObb) employee share ownership for the eight countries and the three consecutive surveys

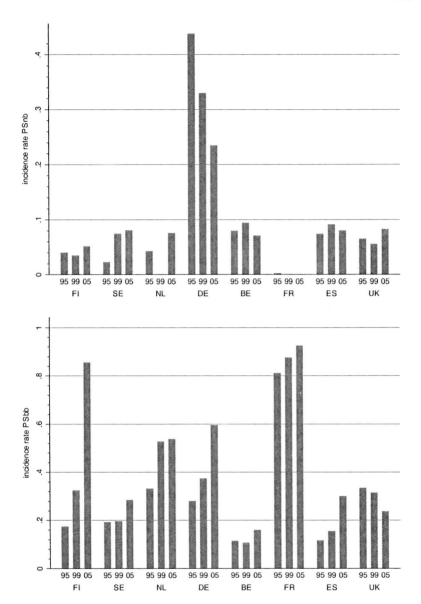

Figure 9.2 Distribution of observed narrow-based (nb) and broad-based (bb) profit sharing schemes for the eight countries and the three consecutive surveys

and continued to promote their specific national systems of financial participation. In Belgium there were recent government initiatives to promote financial participation. In Germany the tax concessions on acquiring employer shares have been increased, as have the size of the bonuses on savings arrangements. Eligibility to receive these benefits has also been widened somewhat. The concessions and benefits remain relatively small compared with those in other countries. Most recently in the Netherlands the tax concession for the savings arrangement, which covers also shares, options and profit shares, was abolished in January 2012 and, as a consequence, a decrease of broad-based financial participation is expected.

Determinants of financial participation

In this section we consider the influences upon the use of financial participation schemes. Why do companies do it? We ran a multi-nomial logistic regression analysis with the data of the eight countries. These regressions included most of the determinants found in the relevant literature, as will be presented and discussed below. Each regression has a dependent variable where the values are either no share ownership (or profit sharing) scheme, or a narrow-based scheme, or a broad-based scheme. For ease of presentation the results are presented separately for narrow-based and broad-based schemes within the table. Below we summarize the literature briefly and compare the results with the outcomes of our multiple wave-analysis in Table 9.3. In this analysis we controlled for the year when the data were collected. Beside year, the following independent variables are used (Appendix Table 9.1): country dummies with UK as the reference category; industry with manufacturing as the reference category; if the firm is listed on the stock exchange; is the firm part of a multinational company and where is the headquarters (HQ) located, in the United States of America or Europe, US-based HQ and EU-based HQ (national firm is the reference category); unionization degree with 0% as the reference category; joint consultative committee at the firm, with no the reference category; and communication practices (see later for scale explanation). Since unionization and joint consultative committee had a substantial amount of missing values we added missing as a separate category. The odds ratios reported in the tables indicate a positive effect if higher than 1 and a negative effect if lower than 1. In the Appendix information is provided on the analysis per year of observation (Appendix Table 9.3a, b for employee share ownership and 4 a, b for profit sharing).

In general, the analysis confirmed the importance of country as a determinant of financial participation. This was especially relevant for broad-based schemes. The analysis per year (see Appendix Tables 9.3 and 9.4) showed that the importance of country for management-only schemes diminished in later periods whereas this remained for broad-based schemes.

Table 9.3 Determinants of the use of narrow-based (i.e. management only) and broad-based financial participation in establishments (y = 1 = employees) (employee share ownership (ESO) and profit sharing (PS)) (multi-nomial logistic regression, refcat = No ESO or No PS, N = 5480)

Financial participation	ESO Narrow-based	Robust SE	ESO Broad-based	Robust SE	PS Narrow-based	Robust SE	PS Broad-based	Robust SE
Country								
Finland	0.526**	[0.120]	0.237**	[0.048]	1.045	[0.321]	1.920**	[0.295]
Sweden	0.611*	[0.132]	0.224**	[0.043]	0.862	[0.229]	0.851	[0.130]
Netherlands	0.420**	[0.092]	0.244**	[0.043]	0.998	[0.287]	2.072**	[0.292]
Germany	0.356**	[0.066]	0.185**	[0.029]	13.545**	[2.207]	5.271**	[0.669]
Belgium	0.802	[0.140]	0.232**	[0.039]	1.196	[0.245]	0.412**	[0.066]
France	0.418**	[0.075]	0.227**	[0.035]	0.109*	[0.110]	18.493**	[2.621]
Spain	0.370**	[0.076]	0.102**	[0.021]	1.314	[0.299]	0.568**	[0.095]
United Kingdom (refcat)								
Industry								
Construction	1.266	[0.285]	1.072	[0.213]	1.775*	[0.406]	1.941**	[0.324]
Transportation	1.385	[0.292]	1.183	[0.219]	0.445**	[0.126]	0.524**	[0.086]
Banking, Finance	1.113	[0.183]	1.511**	[0.193]	0.906	[0.174]	1.478**	[0.170]
Chemicals	1.403*	[0.217]	1.516**	[0.208]	0.662*	[0.115]	0.985	[0.115]
Other industries (e.g. services)	1.032	[0.133]	1.031	[0.107]	0.796	[0.104]	0.740**	[0.066]
Manufacturing (refcat)								
Year								
1995	0.401**	[0.048]	0.412**	[0.042]	0.955	[0.143]	0.894	[0.080]
1999 (refcat)								
2005	1.24	[0.162]	1.498**	[0.165]	1.297	[0.185]	1.498**	[0.142]
Stock listing	2.798**	[0.308]	5.292**	[0.510]	0.802	[0.092]	1.227**	[0.096]
Lnsize	1.343**	[0.050]	1.347**	[0.041]	1.118**	[0.046]	1.128**	[0.033]
Headquarters company								
Nationals (refcat)								
EU-based HQ	1.903**	[0.226]	1.611**	[0.160]	1.298*	[0.158]	1.173	[0.099]
US-based HQ	3.552**	[0.488]	1.826**	[0.231]	1.295	[0.222]	0.814	[0.090]

(continued)

Table 9.3 Continued

Financial participation	ESO Narrow-based	Robust SE	ESO Broad-based	Robust SE	PS Narrow-based	Robust SE	PS Broad-based	Robust SE
Joint Consultative Committee								
No JCC (refcat)								
JCC	0.893	[0.120]	0.881	[0.099]	1.062	[0.169]	1.084	[0.106]
JCC (missing)	0.63	[0.167]	0.902	[0.182]	1.452	[0.325]	0.877	[0.142]
Unionization (proportion)								
0% (refcat)								
13%	1.195	[0.201]	1.006	[0.132]	0.933	[0.194]	0.95	[0.114]
38%	1.046	[0.214]	0.945	[0.153]	1.019	[0.226]	0.680**	[0.099]
63%	0.995	[0.207]	0.829	[0.136]	0.917	[0.219]	0.782	[0.114]
88%	0.67	[0.154]	0.654*	[0.119]	0.786	[0.197]	0.672*	[0.106]
missing unionization	0.873	[0.174]	1.096	[0.170]	0.919	[0.207]	0.813	[0.114]
Financial participation								
Narrow-based PS	2.487**	[0.395]	1.498**	[0.218]				
Broad-based PS	2.418**	[0.262]	1.945**	[0.179]				
Narrow-based ESO					2.536**	[0.411]	2.389**	[0.260]
Broad-based ESO					1.500**	[0.217]	1.873**	[0.174]
Communication practices	1.070**	[0.020]	1.104**	[0.017]	0.992	[0.018]	1.106**	[0.015]
Constant	0.007**	[0.002]	0.014**	[0.003]	0.043**	[0.014]	0.057**	[0.013]
Model statistics	ESOx3c				PS3c			
Cragg-Uhler (Nagelkerke) R2:	0.411				0.402			
log likelihood (model)	–3913				–4342			
log likelihood (intercept)	–4780				–5472			
chi2 (df_m)	1260 (56)				1637 (56)			
p-value	0.000				0.000			
Cragg-Uhler (Nagelkerke) R2	0.319				0.379			

Note: ** p < 0.01, * p < 0.05.

The literature on determinants of financial participation focused mainly on those determinants that may represent indicators for the principal–agency problem. For instance, the argument for adoption of narrow-based schemes is that the performance-based pay contract, which links pay to share prices, provides a powerful way of incentivizing managers to pursue shareholders' objectives (Conyon & Leech, 1994). Share options and equity-based pay provide the direct performance link to shareholder wealth. According to Hall (1998), much of the increase in executive pay can be attributed to the explosion of share options over the period of stock market growth. Most stock markets in Europe experienced considerable growth in the late 1990s, and we expect that this is a strong determinant of narrow-based share schemes in the first half of the period 1995–2004. Our analysis shows that stock listing is a strong determinant of narrow-based share schemes. This holds for all periods of investigation.

National differences in corporate organizations and ownership also appear likely to influence the incidence of schemes. For instance, share ownership schemes seem likely to be facilitated by the extensive use of stock market performance in countries such as the UK, and limited by cross-ownership structures and stakeholder performance in continental European countries such as Sweden and Germany (Gospel & Pendleton, 2004). Our analysis shows that most continental countries have lower adoption of narrow-based financial participation compared with the UK. However, this seems to disappear in the later periods, as is shown in Table 9.3a in the Appendix. In addition, MNCs originating from the USA appear to adopt more share schemes for management of its subsidiaries in Europe than European MNCs and local companies, which suggests a transfer of shareholder-focused practices. This holds for all periods.

However, the sometimes enormous self-enrichment of top management has created public debate and may have had the effect of limiting the narrow-based schemes. This will be the case especially when other stakeholders publicly announce their intention to vote against or try to influence government to take preventive measures. One of these stakeholders is the trade union. Probably, with strong union influence the internal pay settlement may be set within limitations. Our analysis shows no significant influence of unionization on narrow-based schemes and some inhibiting effects on broad-based schemes.

The literature on the determinants of broad-based participation (Poole, 1989; Poole & Whitfield, 1994; Kruse, 1996; Pendleton, 1997; Poutsma & Huijgen, 1999; Festing et al., 1999; Kato & Morishima, 2002) uses also a set of predictions drawn from principal–agent/optimal contracting theory. For instance, it is widely thought that information asymmetries and monitoring become more problematic as firm size increases. Therefore size may be an important predictor of the adoption and use of share ownership, and indeed many studies find this to be the case. However, the problem with interpreting this evidence is that size of firm is likely to be inversely related to the incentive effects of employee share ownership, because of 'free-rider' effects. Thus, the effects of size are likely to be ambiguous. A strong positive relation with size is less commonly found with profit sharing than share ownership, possibly because profit sharing is more targeted at providing direct incentives than share ownership (and hence the free-rider limitations of its use in large firm settings are more relevant). Most of the above literature finds a positive relationship with size. We also find this positive relationship. An additional interpretation is that smaller companies are constrained in adoption owing to the higher set-up and monitoring costs of these schemes.

The analysis for broad-based share schemes showed also the importance of stock market and (US/EU) MNCs for the incidence, suggesting a similar development of stronger emphasis on stock market performance and share value for adopting these schemes. The effects were especially strong in the second period (2000–5), as is shown in the Appendix Table 9.3b and 4b.

An important strand of the HRM literature views financial participation schemes as part of a high-performance work system, composed of several, interacting HRM instruments (see Kaarsemaker & Poutsma, 2006 for an overview). This literature identifies 'bundles' of human resource measures, which, by interacting positively with each other, lead to performance outcomes that are greater than would be achieved by the sum of each measure independently. In a similar vein, the financial participation literature focuses especially on the complementarities thesis, combining several other participative practices with financial participation. If employees are to share in the performance of the firm, it is arguable that they should actively contribute to performance outcomes. We therefore expect to find firms with financial participation also having a range of other human resource management practices directed to increase participation, such as an explicit policy for employee communication, with briefing of the firm's strategy for different employee groups. We calculated from the Cranet survey such a policy with a set of communication practices. The selected practices are listed in the Appendix Table 9.2 and appeared to form a reliable scale (KR-20 coefficient: 0.793). Our analysis (Table 9.3) shows some proof of the complementarities thesis where participative practices such as communication and briefing with employees are positively related to broad-based financial participation.

Evidence on linkages between indirect representative participation, such as consultation committees and works councils, and financial participation is mixed, with some studies finding that financial participation is more prevalent in unionized environments (Gregg & Machin, 1988; Pendleton, 1997) and others finding the opposite (Heywood, Hubler & Jirjahn, 1997; Festing et al., 1999;). Trade unions and other representative bodies generally do not resist collaborative practices, but they may put pressure on management to have strategy talks through channels such as works councils and/or collective bargaining bodies. We find no evidence of any relationship between works councils and financial participation, and some evidence of negative influence on broad-based employee share ownership in the case of moderate to high levels of unionization. However, for profit sharing the significant negative effects of unionization disappeared in 2005 with even positive signs and a significant positive effect of high unionization.

Conclusions

In this chapter we have addressed some key issues concerning the development of financial participation of employees in Europe. We were able to compare the incidence of the two forms of financial participation in 1999 with data from 1995 and 2005. Because the data sets do not form a panel we cannot say, for instance, how many business units use financial participation for the first time, or how many cease to use it during the decade. Caution should be exercised in interpreting these results since this is based on cross-sectional data and not longitudinal data, although we cannot exclude the possibility that an unknown number of establishments participated in multiple waves. On the other hand, by ensuring that the surveys were representative of the economy at each stage of data-collection, rather than being a panel survey, we can have more confidence that our findings show a true picture of the developments in each country over time and a true representation of the comparative position.

The chapter shows clear differences in the character and incidence of financial participation between countries. The differences are related to the presence, nature and extent of legislation and tax concessions, to ownership structures (presence of well-developed stock market), trade union influence and industrial relations arrangements, and broader ideological considerations. In other words, the institutional environment in which firms operate is likely to structure and influence the decision to adopt or not to adopt financial participation. The findings provide support for the critical importance of legislation and tax concessions, especially for broad-based financial participation schemes. Selective narrow-based schemes appear to be less influenced by institutional factors and more by corporate characteristics. Trade unions and industrial relations arrangements have a limited and mainly legitimizing effect on specific financial participation arrangements. Left-wing unions tend to oppose these schemes in most countries, while other unions have a sceptical attitude but find themselves in a position of very low influence since most of these schemes are negotiated outside the bargaining institutions. It is typical that in the two countries with ample profit-sharing arrangements, Finland and France, employee representatives and trade unions are involved in schemes.

The findings show also that US-owned multinational companies and EU-owned multinationals to a lesser degree have a positive influence on employee share ownership, especially narrow-based schemes, in all countries. They may be considered as outsiders who challenge the existing employment practices and norms.

Financial participation is also related to major changes in institutions, especially in systems of collective bargaining. In many of the more regulated and centralized national systems of collective bargaining, such as Germany, the Scandinavian countries and the Netherlands, collective bargaining has been decentralized. Alongside these changes, pay systems have become more individualistic. Financial participation is often seen as being a key component of these trends. These trends relate also to alternative ways to commit employees and align their interest with that of the company in the development of so-called high performance work systems (Kaarsemaker & Poutsma, 2006). This perspective of the use of financial participation is supported with our last finding: communication practices in the firm affected financial participation positively.

This chapter has shown how different financial participation practices are all embedded in their national context and, using a rare longitudinal analysis, has developed the institutional explanation for the differences between countries. Overall, our analysis confirms some of the findings in the extant literature on financial participation and adds others, particularly concerning the changes in extent and type of scheme over time. A practical implication is that although those involved have some scope to introduce and vary schemes, that scope is not unbounded: a detailed knowledge of the opportunities and constraints in the national approach to pay and rewards and the fiscal and other legal rules applying in each country will be necessary if the benefits of such schemes are to be realized.

Clearly, there is much more that we need to understand. Further research bringing this evidence up to date and extending it to a wider range of countries is necessary. The evidence here has examined the extent and antecedents of these practices, but our understanding would be enhanced by more knowledge of specific decisions to introduce, withdraw or amend such schemes and the views of the relevant parties to such changes.

Appendix Table 9.1 The descriptive statistics of the determinants and the two schemes of Financial Participation in establishments (>100 employees)

Financial participation and determinants	Per cent[1]	Mean (stdev)
Financial participation		
Employee share ownership		
no_ESO (refcat)	69.1%	
Management ESO	10.8%	
Broad-based ESO	20.1%	
Profit sharing		
no_Profit Sharing (refcat)	53.2%	
Management Profit Sharing	10.3%	
Broad-based Profit Sharing	36.5%	

(continued)

Appendix Table 9.1   Continued

Financial participation and determinants	Per cent[1]	Mean (stdev)
Determinants		
Country		
United Kingdom (refcat)	31.9%	
France	12.8%	
Germany	16.3%	
Sweden	9.5%	
Spain	7.1%	
Netherlands	6.7%	
Finland	6.2%	
Belgium	9.6%	
Industry		
Construction	4.6%	
Transportation	4.9%	
Banking, Finance	11.3%	
Chemicals	9.2%	
Other industries (e.g., services)	24.8%	
Manufacturing (refcat)	45.1%	
Year		
1995	43.3%	
1999 (refcat)	32.6%	
2005	24.1%	
Stock listing		
Stock Listing	39.4%	
Lnsize		6.47 (1.23)
size (median)		500
Headquarters company		
Nationals (refcat)	55.8%	
EU-based HQ	32.9%	
US-based HQ	11.3%	
Unionization (proportion)		
0% (refcat)	12.3%	
13%	31.9%	
38%	11.5%	
63%	12.6%	
88%	17.6%	
missing unionization	14.1%	
Joint Consultative Committee		
No (refcat)	21.8%	
Yes	67.5%	
missing jcc	10.7%	
Communication practices		8.18 (2.85)

Note: [1] 100%: N = 5840.

Appendix Table 9.2 Share of companies using a communication practice

Communication practice	Label	Mean
Financial briefing: managers	FBmg	0.96
Strategy briefing: managers	SBmg	0.96
Workforce meetings	E2Mwm	0.87
Financial briefing: professionals	FBpr	0.80
Communication policy employees (written)	Wcos	0.72
Mission statement (written)	Wmis	0.71
Financial briefing: clerks	FBcl	0.69
Strategy briefing: professionals	SBpr	0.65
Financial briefing: manuals	FBma	0.57
Attitude Employees assessment	E2Mas	0.56
Strategy briefing: clerks	SBcl	0.46
Strategy briefing: manuals	SBma	0.37

Note: Kuder-Richardson coefficient of reliability: 0.793.

Appendix Table 9.3a Determinants of the use of Management (a) and Broad-based (b) Employee Share Ownership (ESO) per year (multi-nomial logistic regression, refcat = No ESO)

Financial participation	ESO 1995 Narrow-based	Robust SE	ESO 1999 Narrow-based	Robust SE	ESO 2005 Narrow-based	Robust SE
Country						
Finland	0.185**	[0.108]	1	[0.373]	1.086	[0.443]
Sweden	0.130**	[0.087]	1.215	[0.413]	0.858	[0.292]
Netherlands	0.119**	[0.053]	1.218	[0.441]	0.879	[0.369]
Germany	0.108**	[0.064]	0.469*	[0.139]	0.815	[0.266]
Belgium	0.424**	[0.129]	1.063	[0.319]	2.059*	[0.702]
France	0.139**	[0.040]	1.068	[0.310]	0.852	[0.374]
Spain	0.224**	[0.085]	0.431**	[0.136]	0.758	[0.327]
United Kingdom (refcat)						
Industry						
Construction	1.281	[0.504]	1.558	[0.555]	0.837	[0.389]
Transportation	1.36	[0.556]	1.662	[0.568]	1.253	[0.477]
Banking, Finance	1.099	[0.294]	1.195	[0.325]	0.95	[0.341]
Chemicals	1.098	[0.280]	1.491	[0.395]	1.693	[0.544]
Other industries (e.g., services)	1.061	[0.255]	1.256	[0.249]	0.881	[0.222]
Manufacturing (refcat)						
Year						
1995	1	[0.000]				
1999 (refcat)			1	[0.000]		
2005					1	[0.000]
Stock listing	2.363**	[0.470]	3.185**	[0.539]	4.582**	[0.883]
Lnsize	1.480**	[0.090]	1.166*	[0.074]	1.339**	[0.104]
Headquarters company						
Nationals (refcat)						
EU-based HQ	1.816**	[0.359]	2.217**	[0.400]		
US-based HQ	5.206**	[1.327]	3.039**	[0.748]	2.987**	[0.745]

(continued)

Appendix Table 9.3a Continued

Financial participation	ESO 1995 Narrow-based	Robust SE	ESO 1999 Narrow-based	Robust SE	ESO 2005 Narrow-based	Robust SE
Joint Consultative Council						
No JCC (refcat)						
JCC	0.798	[0.167]	1.023	[0.243]	0.93	[0.262]
JCC (missing)	1.108	[0.562]	1.078	[0.721]	0.000**	[0.000]
Unionization (proportion)						
0% (refcat)						
13%	1.711	[0.482]	0.747	[0.202]	1.456	[0.521]
38%	0.945	[0.328]	0.851	[0.286]	1.326	[0.546]
63%	1.185	[0.404]	0.596	[0.212]	1.299	[0.552]
88%	0.893	[0.358]	0.439*	[0.160]	0.768	[0.352]
missing unionization	0.979	[0.390]	0.585	[0.180]	1.056	[0.417]
Financial participation						
Narrow-based PS	3.596**	[0.999]	1.893*	[0.509]	2.044*	[0.639]
Broad-based PS	4.084**	[0.770]	1.677**	[0.306]	1.479	[0.328]
Narrow-based ESO						
Broad-based ESO						
Communication practices	1.012	[0.031]	1.070*	[0.032]	1.128**	[0.045]
Constant	0.003**	[0.002]	0.016**	[0.008]	0.004**	[0.002]
Model statistics						
Observations	2531		1903		1406	
log likelihood (model)	-1419		-1372		-987.8	
chi2	52		52		50	
P	615.9		413.5		2177	
p-value	0.000		0.000		0.000	
Cragg-Uhler (Nagelkerke) R2	0.342		0.300		0.411	

Note: ** $p < 0.01$, * $p < 0.05$.

Appendix Table 9.3b Determinants of the use of broad-based employee share ownership (ESO) per year – see Table 3a for the model statistics

Financial participation	ESO 1995 Broad-based	Robust SE	ESO 1999 Broad-based	Robust SE	ESO 2005 Broad-based	Robust SE
Country						
Finland	0.090**	[0.033]	0.601	[0.209]	0.382*	[0.153]
Sweden	0.109**	[0.059]	0.465*	[0.147]	0.422**	[0.136]
Netherlands	0.128**	[0.037]	0.394**	[0.142]	0.449*	[0.146]
Germany	0.205**	[0.104]	0.270**	[0.060]	0.202**	[0.068]
Belgium	0.096**	[0.027]	0.381**	[0.118]	0.585	[0.197]
France	0.091**	[0.024]	0.416**	[0.104]	0.715	[0.252]
Spain	0.096**	[0.032]	0.127**	[0.038]	0.072**	[0.047]
United Kingdom (refcat)						
Industry						
Construction	1.327	[0.397]	0.912	[0.309]	0.75	[0.307]
Transportation	1.186	[0.391]	1.121	[0.337]	1.3	[0.496]
Banking, Finance	0.918	[0.196]	1.676*	[0.386]	2.239**	[0.556]
Chemicals	1.192	[0.257]	1.314	[0.327]	2.847**	[0.883]
Other industries (e.g., services)	0.915	[0.161]	0.991	[0.175]	1.263	[0.259]
Manufacturing (refcat)						
Year						
1995	1	[0.000]				
1999 (refcat)			1	[0.000]		
2005					1	[0.000]
Stock listing	4.019**	[0.689]	5.476**	[0.805]	8.292**	[1.383]
Lnsize	1.352**	[0.070]	1.220**	[0.064]	1.456**	[0.091]
Headquarters company						
Nationals (refcat)						
EU-based HQ	1.350*	[0.190]	1.594**	[0.239]		
US-based HQ	1.188	[0.276]	1.869**	[0.432]	2.480**	[0.565]

(*continued*)

Appendix Table 9.3b Continued

Financial participation	ESO 1995 Broad-based	Robust SE	ESO 1999 Broad-based	Robust SE	ESO 2005 Broad-based	Robust SE
Joint Consultative Council						
No JCC (refcat)						
JCC	0.86	[0.155]	0.911	[0.183]	0.96	[0.204]
JCC (missing)	0.602	[0.271]	1.39	[0.735]	2.9	[2.176]
Unionization (proportion)						
0% (refcat)						
13%	1.082	[0.237]	1.101	[0.258]	0.781	[0.196]
38%	1.178	[0.294]	0.883	[0.272]	0.517*	[0.165]
63%	0.809	[0.214]	0.951	[0.281]	0.53	[0.174]
88%	0.97	[0.269]	0.612	[0.202]	0.265**	[0.103]
missing unionization	1.878*	[0.538]	0.978	[0.247]	0.619	[0.191]
Financial participation						
Narrow-based PS	1.869**	[0.442]	1.065	[0.268]	1.444	[0.431]
Broad-based PS	2.135**	[0.340]	1.974**	[0.302]	1.533*	[0.301]
Narrow-based ESO						
Broad-based ESO						
Communication practices	1.110**	[0.027]	1.067*	[0.029]	1.149**	[0.038]
Constant	0.010**	[0.004]	0.025**	[0.010]	0.006**	[0.003]

Note: ** p < 0.01, * p < 0.05.

Appendix Table 9.4a Determinants of the use of management (a) and broad-based (b) profit sharing (PS) per year (multi-nomial logistic regression, refcat = No PS)

Financial participation	PS 1995 Narrow-based	Robust SE	PS 1999 Narrow-based	Robust SE	PS 2005 Narrow-based	Robust SE
Country						
Finland	0.859	[0.428]	0.703	[0.426]	7.233**	[4.265]
Sweden	0.25	[0.192]	1.231	[0.512]	1.321	[0.530]
Netherlands	1.002	[0.418]	0.000**	[0.000]	1.997	[0.927]
Germany	12.424**	[7.276]	14.256**	[3.670]	14.655**	[4.445]
Belgium	1.273	[0.423]	1.315	[0.486]	0.86	[0.377]
France	0.202	[0.211]	0.000**	[0.000]	0.000**	[0.000]
Spain	1.1	[0.400]	1.471	[0.527]	1.505	[0.900]
United Kingdom (refcat)						
Industry						
Construction	1.576	[0.590]	1.884	[0.736]	1.835	[0.883]
Transportation	0.459	[0.236]	0.725	[0.302]	0.198*	[0.129]
Banking, Finance	0.92	[0.266]	0.977	[0.356]	0.83	[0.322]
Chemicals	0.65	[0.168]	0.684	[0.203]	0.536	[0.242]
Other industries (e.g., services)	0.569*	[0.127]	1.07	[0.229]	0.795	[0.209]
Manufacturing (refcat)						
Year						
1995	1	[0.000]				
1999 (refcat)			1			
2005				[0.000]	1	[0.000]
Stock listing	0.919	[0.175]	1.008	[0.203]	0.694	[0.171]
Lnsize	1.172*	[0.078]	1.025	[0.071]	1.146	[0.101]
Headquarters company						
Nationals (refcat)						
EU-based HQ	1.262	[0.218]	1.289	[0.247]	1.222	[0.365]
US-based HQ	1.412	[0.406]	1.144	[0.364]		

(continued)

Appendix Table 9.4a Continued

Financial participation	PS 1995 Narrow-based	Robust SE	PS 1999 Narrow-based	Robust SE	PS 2005 Narrow-based	Robust SE
Joint Consultative Council						
No JCC (refcat)						
JCC	1.038	[0.270]	1.265	[0.379]	0.97	[0.262]
JCC (missing)	1.8	[1.012]	2.225	[1.600]	1.422	[1.286]
Unionization (proportion)						
0% (refcat)						
13%	1.212	[0.479]	0.664	[0.252]	1.001	[0.347]
38%	1.208	[0.483]	0.779	[0.318]	1.082	[0.430]
63%	0.686	[0.289]	0.836	[0.373]	1.519	[0.649]
88%	1.032	[0.448]	0.619	[0.280]	0.719	[0.346]
missing unionization	1.294	[0.572]	0.677	[0.257]	0.783	[0.310]
Financial participation						
Narrow-based PS						
Broad-based PS						
Narrow-based ESO	3.890**	[1.064]	1.840*	[0.512]	2.091*	[0.639]
Broad-based ESO	1.902**	[0.457]	1.02	[0.261]	1.574	[0.449]
Communication practices	0.996	[0.030]	0.989	[0.033]	0.982	[0.037]
Constant	0.023**	[0.013]	0.072**	[0.038]	0.057**	[0.036]
Model statistics						
Observations	2531		1903		1406	
log likelihood (model)	-1751		-1427		-1023	
df_m	52		52		50	
chi2	846.5		32674		12140	
p-value	0.000		0.000		0.000	
Cragg-Uhler (Nagelkerke) R2	0.433		0.398		0.402	

Note: ** p < 0.01, * p < 0.05.

Appendix Table 9.4b Determinants of the use of broad-based profit sharing (PS) per year – see Table 9.4a for the model statistics

Financial participation	PS 1995 Broad-based	Robust SE	PS 1999 Broad-based	Robust SE	PS 2005 Broad-based	Robust SE
Country						
Finland	0.581	[0.162]	1.065	[0.299]	32.777**	[13.509]
Sweden	0.796	[0.393]	0.632	[0.178]	1.29	[0.335]
Netherlands	1.345	[0.291]	2.690**	[0.773]	4.171**	[1.170]
Germany	4.238**	[1.998]	4.024**	[0.742]	14.192**	[3.877]
Belgium	0.341**	[0.084]	0.358**	[0.106]	0.597	[0.194]
France	13.088**	[2.749]	17.455**	[4.307]	51.906**	[22.945]
Spain	0.348**	[0.097]	0.460**	[0.121]	1.645	[0.621]
United Kingdom (refcat)						
Industry						
Construction	1.753*	[0.437]	2.244**	[0.686]	1.731	[0.609]
Transportation	0.466**	[0.131]	0.598	[0.178]	0.388**	[0.138]
Banking, Finance	1.758**	[0.314]	1.331	[0.271]	1.501	[0.380]
Chemicals	1.137	[0.193]	0.743	[0.158]	1.017	[0.288]
Other industries (e.g., services)	0.686*	[0.101]	0.987	[0.151]	0.648*	[0.121]
Manufacturing (refcat)						
Year						
1995	1	[0.000]				
1999 (refcat)			1	[0.000]		
2005					1	[0.000]
Stock listing	1.466**	[0.199]	1.423*	[0.199]	1.254	[0.207]
Lnsize	1.129*	[0.053]	1.014	[0.053]	1.242**	[0.077]
Headquarters company						
Nationals (refcat)						
EU-based HQ	1.294*	[0.154]	1.016	[0.136]		
US-based HQ	0.906	[0.164]	0.68	[0.142]	0.823	[0.171]

(continued)

Appendix Table 9.4b Continued

Financial participation	PS 1995 Broad-based	Robust SE	PS 1999 Broad-based	Robust SE	PS 2005 Broad-based	Robust SE
Joint Consultative Council						
No JCC (refcat)						
JCC	1.193	[0.190]	1.153	[0.197]	0.91	[0.183]
JCC (missing)	0.957	[0.425]	0.823	[0.376]	1.515	[1.020]
Unionization (proportion)						
0% (refcat)						
13%	0.733	[0.141]	0.83	[0.171]	1.493	[0.393]
38%	0.552**	[0.123]	0.506*	[0.134]	1.136	[0.353]
63%	0.518**	[0.116]	0.538*	[0.143]	2.023*	[0.643]
88%	0.532**	[0.129]	0.572*	[0.160]	1.041	[0.372]
missing unionization	0.697	[0.174]	0.698	[0.160]	1.009	[0.309]
Financial participation						
Narrow-based PS						
Broad-based PS						
Narrow-based ESO	3.841**	[0.720]	1.634**	[0.306]	1.524	[0.339]
Broad-based ESO	2.076**	[0.324]	1.884**	[0.294]	1.509*	[0.297]
Communication practices	1.097**	[0.023]	1.125**	[0.027]	1.111**	[0.033]
Constant	0.064**	[0.023]	0.130**	[0.049]	0.022**	[0.011]

Note: ** p < 0.01, * p < 0.05.

Notes

1. This section is based on Poutsma (2001) and Pendleton & Poutsma (2004). We refer the reader to these sources for further details about legislative arrangements, policies of governments and social partners.
2. The information on Finland is based on Sweins & Jussila (2010) and on Jones, Kalmi & Mäkinen (2006).

References

Baisier, L. & Albertijn, M. 1992. *Werken in Kringen, Kwaliteit in Overleg.* Brussels: Stichting Technologie Vlaanderen.

Blasi, J, 1988. *Employee Ownership: Revolution or Ripoff?* New York: Harper Collins-Ballinger.

Blasi, J.R., Conte, M. & Kruse, D. 1996. 'Employee ownership and corporate performance among public corporations'. *Industrial and Labor Relations Review*, 50(1): 60–79.

Blinder, A. (ed.). 1990. *Paying for Productivity – A Look at the Evidence.* Washington DC: The Brookings Institute.

Bryson, A. & Freeman, R.B. 2010. 'How does shared capitalism affect economic performance in the United Kingdom?' In D.L. Kruse, R.B. Freeman & J.R. Blasi (eds), *Shared Capitalism at Work: Employee Ownership, Profit and Gain Sharing, and Broad-Based Stock Options.* Chicago: University of Chicago Press, 201–24.

Cheadle, A. 1989. 'Explaining patterns of profit sharing activity'. *Industrial Relations*, 28(3): 398–400.

Conyon, M.J. & Leech, D. 1994. 'Top pay, company performance and corporate governance'. *Oxford Bulletin of Economics and Statistics*, 56(3): 229–47.

Eisenhardt, K.M., 1989. 'Agency theory: An assessment and review'. *Academy of Management Review*, 14(1): 57–74.

Fakhfakh, F. & Pérotin, V. 2000. 'The effects of profit-sharing schemes on enterprise performance in France'. *Economic Analysis*, 3(2): 93–111.

Festing, M., Groening, Y. Kabst, R. & Weber, W. 1999. 'Financial participation in Europe – determinants and outcomes'. *Economic and Industrial Democracy*, 20(2): 295–329.

FitzRoy, F.R. & Kraft, K. 1987. 'Cooperation, productivity and profit sharing'. *The Quarterly Journal of Economics*, 102: 23–35.

Gospel, H. & Pendleton, A. 2004. *Corporate Governance and Labour Management.* Oxford: Oxford University Press.

Gregg, P. & Machin, S. 1988. 'Unions and the incidence of performance linked pay schemes in Britain'. *International Journal of Industrial Organisation*, 6(1): 91–109.

Hall, B.J. 1998. *The Pay to Performance Incentives of Executive Stock Options.* NBER Working Paper Series, 6674.

Heywood, J., Hubler, O. & Jirjahn, U. 1997. 'Use of variable payment schemes: Evidence from Germany'. *Kyklos*, 51(2): 237–58.

Incomes Data Services. 2001. *Pay and Conditions in France 2001.* London: IDS.

IPSE. 1997. *Le partage de profit en Europe: Institutions et effets comparés.* Paris: Cahier Travail et Emploi.

Jensen, M. & Meckling, W. 1976. 'Theory of the firm: Managerial behavior, agency costs and ownership structure'. *Journal of Financial Economics*, 3: 305–60.

Jones, D.C. Kalmi, P. & Mäkinen, M. 2006. 'The determinants of stock options: Evidence from Finland'. *Industrial Relations: A Journal of Economy and Society*, 45(3): 437–68.

Kaarsemaker, E. & Poutsma, E. 2006. 'The fit of employee ownership with other human resource management practices: Theoretical and empirical suggestions regarding the existence of an ownership high-performance work system, or Theory O'. *Economic and Industrial Democracy*, 27(2): 669–85.

Kato, T. & Morishima, M. 2002. 'The productivity effects of participatory employment practices: Evidence from new Japanese panel data'. *Industrial Relations*, 41: 487–520.

Kraft, K. & Ugarković, M. 2006. 'Profit sharing and the financial performance of firms: Evidence from Germany'. *Economic Letters*, 92: 333–8.

Kruse, D. 1993. *Profit Sharing: Does it Make a Difference?* Kalamazoo. MI: Upjohn Institute.

Kruse, D. 1996. 'Why do firms adopt profit sharing and employee ownership plans?' *British Journal of Industrial Relations*, 34: 515–38.

Kruse, D.L., Freeman, R.B. & Blasi, J.R. (eds), 2010. *Shared Capitalism at Work: Employee Ownership, Profit and Gain Sharing, and Broad-Based Stock Options*. Chicago: University of Chicago Press.

Lowitsch, J., Hashi, I. & Woodward, 2009. *The PEPPER IV Report: Benchmarking of Employee Participation in Profits and Enterprise Results in the Member and Candidate Countries of the European Union*. Institute for Eastern European Studies, Free University of Berlin, Berlin.

Mabile, S. 1998. 'Intéressement et salaries: Complementarite or substitution?' *Economie et statistique*, 67(316–17): 45–61.

Murphy, K.J. 1999. 'Executive compensation'. In O. Ashenfelter & D. Card (eds), *Handbook of Labor Economics*. Amsterdam: North-Holland, Vol. 3, 2485–563.

Pendleton, A. 1997. 'Characteristics of workplaces with financial participation: Evidence from the WIRS'. *Industrial Relations Journal*, 28: 103–19.

Pendleton, A. & Perotin, V. 2001. *Profit Sharing in Europe: The Characteristics and Impact of Profit Sharing in France, Germany, Italy and the United Kingdom*. Cheltenham: Edward Elgar.

Pendleton, A. & Poutsma, E. 2004. *Financial Participation: The Role of Governments and Social Partners*. Luxembourg: Office for the Official Publications of the European Communities.

Pendleton, A. & Poutsma, E. 2012. 'Financial participation'. In C. Brewster & W. Mayrhofer (eds), *Handbook of Research in Comparative Human Resource Management*. Cheltenham: Edward Elgar.

Pendleton, A. & Robinson, A. 2010. 'Employee stock ownership, involvement, and productivity: An interaction-based approach'. *Industrial & Labor Relations Review*, 64(1): article 1.

Pendleton, A. & Robinson, A. 2011. 'Employee share ownership and human capital development: Complementarity in theory and practice'. *Economic and Industrial Democracy*, 32(3): 439–57.

Pendleton, A.D., Poutsma, E. & Brewster, C. 2003. 'The incidence and determinants of employee share ownership and profit sharing in Europe'. In T. Kato & J. Pliskin (eds), *The Determinants of the Incidence and Effects of Participatory Organisations*. Advances of the Economic Analysis of Participatory and Labor-Managed Firms, Vol. 7. Oxford: Elsevier Science.

Pérotin, V. & Robinson, A. 2003. *Employee Participation in Profit and Ownership: A Review of the Issues and Evidence*. Luxembourg: European Parliament.

Poole, M. 1989. *The Origins of Economic Democracy*. London: Routledge.

Poole, M. & Whitfield, K. 1994. 'Theories and evidence on the growth and distribution of profit sharing and employee shareholding schemes'. *Human Systems Management*, 13(3): 209–20.

Poutsma, E. 2001. *Recent Trends in Employee Financial Participation in the European Union*. Luxembourg: Office for the Official Publications of the European Communities.

Poutsma, E. & Huijgen, F. 1999. 'European diversity in the use of participation schemes'. *Economic and Industrial Democracy*, 20(2): 197–224.

Poutsma, F., Hendrickx, J.A.M. & Huijgen, F. 2003. 'Employee participation in Europe: In search of the participative workplace'. *Economic and Industrial Democracy*, 24(1): 45–76.

Poutsma, E, Ligthart, P.E.M. & Schoutete, R. 2005. 'Employee share schemes in Europe: A case of Anglo-Saxonisation'. *Management Revue*, 16, (1): 99–122.

Robinson, A. & Wilson, N. 2006. 'Employee financial participation and productivity: An empirical reappraisal'. *British Journal of Industrial Relations*, 44(1): 31–50.

Sweins, C. & Jussila, I. 2010. 'Employee knowledge and the effects of a deferred profit-sharing system: A longitudinal case study of personnel funds in Finland'. *Thunderbird International Business Review*, 52(3): 232–47.

Tihanyi, L., Hoskisson, R.E., Johnson, R.A. & Wan, W. 2009. 'Technological competence and international diversification: The role of managerial incentives'. *Management International Review*, 49: 409–31.

Uvalic, M. 1991. 'Pepper Report: Promotion of employee participation in profits and enterprise results'. In *Social Europe*, Supplement 3/91, Commission of the European Communities.

Vaughan-Whitehead, D. 1995. *Workers' Financial Participation: East–West Experiences*. ILO Labour Management Series No. 80. Geneva: ILO.

Wilson, N. & Peel, M.J. 1991. 'The impact on absenteeism and quits of profit-sharing and other forms of employee participation'. *Industrial and Labor Relations Review*, 44(3): 454–68.

10
Information Technology Systems in the Human Resource Management Area

Hilla Peretz

Introduction

In an era striving for excellence, human resource management (HRM) has become a crucial source of competitiveness (Peretz & Fried, 2012). An important development in improving the effectiveness of HR in organizations is the incorporation of information technology systems for the purposes of collecting, organizing and disseminating HRM-related information to users and decision-makers (Lin, 1998; Ngai & Wat, 2006).

A human resource information system (HRIS) is 'the composite of databases, computer applications, hardware and software necessary to collect/record, store, manage, deliver, present and manipulate data for human resources' (Broderick & Boudreau, 1992). HRIS have grown in popularity since the 1960s (Ngai & Wat, 2006). A survey conducted in 1998 (Ball, 2001) showed that 60 per cent of Fortune 500 companies used HRIS to support daily HRM operations. HRIS are now used not only for administrative tasks but also for strategic and business decision-making purposes (Kovach et al., 2002).

At its beginning, HRIS were seen mostly as a special form of office automation systems, the emphasis being on reducing costs and staff while making standard HR tasks more efficient (Leidner & Kayworth, 2006). In today's workplace, HR tasks have become more complex. That being the case, today's HR professionals rely heavily on HRIS to fulfil their job functions, even the most elementary ones. Therefore, from the administrative perspective, by providing powerful computing capabilities, HRIS are changing and improving procedures and processes that were carried out less efficiently before, such as regulatory reporting and compliance, payroll, pension and benefits administration (Hendrickson, 2003).

HRIS can be classified into two general categories: 'simple' or 'non-sophisticated' and 'advanced' or 'sophisticated' (Ball, 2001). Usually, 'simple' HRIS deals with administrative activities such as payroll and absence recording, while 'advanced' HRIS is more analytic in nature and deals with manipulation of information about the human resources in the organization, such as choosing benefits and training sessions. Because of its nature, advanced HRIS use sophisticated IT tools, such as the integration of the HRIS to a wider IT system in the organization, and complex HRIS communication systems between the managers and the employees. Using advanced HRIS often leads to the provision of timely and quick access to information, the ability to produce a greater number and variety of HR-related reports, and reduced costs (Ngai & Wat, 2006). Finally, as noted by Mayfield, Mayfield and Lunce (2003), successful HRIS support the planning and implementation of managerial key processes in the organization, such as executive decision-making, technology selection, interdepartmental integration and organizational reporting structures. By implementing successful HRIS, HR can potentially become more actively involved in setting and executing corporate strategy.

Although HRIS can provide both administrative and strategic advantages, it should be noted that there are some challenges in the adoption and implementation of HRIS. From a financial perspective, HRIS are usually expensive systems to purchase and implement (Shani & Tesone, 2010). In addition, another relatively common problem concerning both the implementation and the flowing management of HRIS is the question of who is in charge of the system. Since the successful development of HRIS requires the input of both IT and the HR departments, it is not uncommon for disputes over areas of responsibility to break out between these departments (Targowski & Deshande, 2001). In addition, as was broadly discussed by Hubbard, Forcht & Thomas (1998), the implementation of HRIS raises both ethical and legal issues that need to be addressed by the organization. Finally, Roberts (2004) suggests that for a successful implementation of HRIS, it is no less important to obtain the support of managers and employees in the organization. Ngai & Wat (2006) state that lack of commitment from management is one of the most important factors in the successful implementation of HRIS. Although advanced HRIS offer clear advantages to managers, the implementation of such systems is likely to be followed by a certain level of resentment on the part of the managers, depending on the culture of the organization (Ngai & Wat, 2006).

Although the advantages and challenges of HRIS are well established in the literature, most of this research has been conducted in the US and other Western, mostly developed nations. Relatively little research has been conducted on the role of HRIS in the global economy (e.g. Aycan, 2005; Agourram & Ingham, 2007; Ribiere, Haddad & Weile, 2010). The increase in globalization and multinational operations have raised timely and interesting questions about: (1) the degree to which companies located in countries with different cultures tend to implement advanced HRIS programs, and the characteristics of these programs; and (2) how the characteristics of the HRIS together with national culture affect organizational performance outcomes in the organizations (cf. Aycan, 2005). The current research is aimed at remedying these gaps in the literature. Specifically, the main two research questions of this study are: (1) do organizations in specific national cultures tend to implement advanced HRIS programs? And (2) does congruence between HRIS and national culture lead to less absenteeism and turnover?

National values and HRIS

Culture has been defined in many ways. One well-known anthropological definition is that culture consists of patterned ways of thinking, feeling and reacting, acquired and transmitted mainly by symbols, constituting the distinctive achievements of human groups (Kluckhohn, 1951: 86). Since then, researchers have made several attempts to define and classify cultural values (e.g. Aycan et al., 2000; Hofstede, 1991; Schwartz, 1999). Common themes in most of these definitions and classifications are that cultural values are typically shared by members of a society, are passed from older to younger members, and shape a collective perception of the world. Many studies have shown that national culture plays a critical role in individuals' behaviour (e.g. Bajdo & Dickson, 2002, showed that GLOBE national values accounted for 40 per cent of the variance in women's advancement in organizations).

In a thorough review of HRM literature, Aycan (2005) showed that most theories have emphasized the organizational and environmental determinants of HRM practices, while few have explicitly discussed the socio-cultural context. However, growing evidence suggests that national cultures significantly affect the HR practices that organizations are likely to adopt and emphasize, as well as the characteristics of these HR practices (see, for example, Aycan, 2005; Peretz & Rosenblatt, 2011; Peretz & Fried, 2012).

Numerous studies have established the impact of national values on managerial behaviour and actions. Within the theoretical framework offered by Hofstede (1980) and Project GLOBE (e.g. House et al., 2004), societal values, often described as national values, have a strong impact on organizations that overrides other organizational (e.g. size, sector) and environmental (e.g. market) influences. Studies provide some support for this logical link. For example, Dickson, Aditya and Chhokar (2000) reported that societal values accounted for up to 50 per cent of the variance in organizational culture. Drawing on this evidence, we expect that societal values influence the likelihood that organizations adopt HRIS, and the characteristics of these systems, if they do adopt them.

Our expectation is based on the Model of Culture Fit (MCF), which was proposed by Kanungo and his associates (Kanungo & Jaeger, 1990; Mendonca & Kanungo, 1994; Aycan, Sinha & Kanungo, 1999). The MCF assesses culture at two levels: societal (i.e. the socio-cultural context) and organizational (i.e. internal work culture). The model asserts that the internal work culture consists of managerial beliefs and assumptions about two fundamental organizational elements: the task and the employees. The MCF suggests that national culture affects organizational culture, which in turn, affects managerial practices such as human resource practices (Aycan, 2005). Concerning HRIS, national culture may influence the degree of advanced HRIS, for example, the type of HRIS managers choose to implement (none, independent or integrated in a wider system), and the communication design of HRIS if implemented (one way, two way, etc.). The wider the HRIS and the more complex the communication design, the more advanced the HRIS.

In addition, the MCF also suggests that, if employees are exposed to an HR activity that does not fit the national culture, they will tend to respond negatively (Aycan, 2005; Aycan et al., 2000). When the negative reactions are combined across all employees, they are expected to contribute to negative outcomes in the organization such as high levels of absenteeism and turnover. Conversely, when employees are exposed to an HR activity that fits the national culture, they will respond positively, which will help produce positive organizational outcomes (Aycan, 2005).

In this study, we rely on four widely studied cultural values at the national level: power distance, institutional individualism/collectivism, uncertainty avoidance, and future orientation (Hofstede, 1980; House et al., 2004). Empirical studies have shown that these national values predict organizational processes and managerial practices in general (Communal & Senior 1999; Hofstede & Peterson, 2000), and HR practices specifically (e.g. Peretz & Rosenblatt, 2011; Peretz & Fried, 2012). In addition, several studies on information systems and on the use of advanced technologies have also shown that these four cultural values have the most impact on usage and implementation (Ribiere et al., 2010; Png, Tan & Wee, 2001; Chow, Deng & Ho, 2000; Hasan & Ditsa, 1999; Kitchell, 1995).

The values used in the present study reflected reported practices ('*as is*') and they tell us about the current perceptions of each culture (as opposed to *feelings* about cultural aspirations). Aspiration values refer to the society's ideal values, while practical values measure the society's actual engagement in a particular value. In the professional literature, while measuring the effects of societal culture, it is common to use practical values and not aspiration values (e.g. Brodbeck et al., 2004).

We will first discuss how national values are expected to affect the way in which the HRIS is conducted in diverse nations differing on such values. We will then discuss how the level of fit between national values and the different patterns of HRIS contribute to organizational performance, based on the two criteria of absenteeism and turnover.

Power distance

Power distance is the degree to which members of a collective expect power to be distributed equally (House et al., 2002, 2004). In high power distance societies, hierarchy is rigidly adhered to and privileges are distributed unequally. In such societies, higher-level members are expected to preserve their relative advantage in status and power. Thus, with respect to such societies, it is reasonable to expect that organizations will typically design HRIS in which employees have little access to information and in which the communication provided to the employees by the organization is non-interactive in nature. In contrast, in societies low in power distance, one can expect that organizations will be more inclined to establish advanced HRIS characterized by integration of the HRIS into a wider management information system (e.g. ERP, enterprise resource planning). Moreover, these organizations are also more likely to design the HRIS as an interactive system, which allows the user employees to perform complex activities directly on the computer, such as selecting particular fringe benefits, and being approved/disapproved by the computer program (cf. Aycan, 2005). In a field study of 10 organizations in the Middle East, Africa and Australia, Hasan & Ditsa (1999) found that successful adoption of information systems technology was higher in low power distance societies than in high power distance societies. This suggests that:

Hypothesis 1a: *Organizations are more likely to adopt an integrated HRIS system (in which the system is integrated into a wider management information system) in low power distance societies than in high power distance societies.*

Hypothesis 1b: *Organizations are more likely to adopt an interactive HRIS communication design in low power distance societies than in high power distance societies.*

Future orientation

Future orientation is the degree to which individuals engage in future-oriented behaviours such as planning, investing in the future and delaying gratification (House et al., 2002). Future orientation in HRM means investment and development to prepare the workforce to meet future organizational needs. This suggests that organizations embedded in future-oriented societies are more likely, relative to organizations embedded in present- or less future-oriented societies, to adopt advanced HRIS. Kitchell (1995) found that organizations in cultures having a long-term orientation were more likely to adopt advanced manufacturing technology.

Hypothesis 2a: *Organizations are more likely to adopt an integrated HRIS in highly future-oriented societies rather than in present- or less future-oriented societies.*

Hypothesis 2b: *Organizations are more likely to adopt an interactive HRIS communication design in highly future-oriented societies rather than in present- or less future-oriented societies.*

Institutional individualism/collectivism

Institutional individualism/collectivism refers to the degree to which societies value individual rights and opportunities versus group success and individual loyalty to the group. In collectivistic societies individuals are expected to subordinate themselves to the group's goals and success. Therefore, organizations in collectivist societies are likely to avoid individual-based systems because of their potentially adverse effect on group, unit or organizational solidarity and morale (e.g. Kovach, 1995; Vallance, 1999). Rather, organizations embedded in collectivistic societies are likely to design and implement HRIS for purposes that would generally benefit all employees, such as human resource planning or identification of needs for training and development. Chow et al. (2000), in a study comparing American and Chinese managers found that Chinese respondents were more likely to share knowledge, since this was consistent with their collectivistic value system.

Hypothesis 3a: *Organizations in collectivistic societies are more likely to establish interactive HRIS than are organizations in individualistic societies.*

Hypothesis 3b: *Organizations in collectivistic societies are more likely to establish an interactive HRIS than are organizations in individualistic societies.*

Uncertainty avoidance

Uncertainty avoidance is defined as the extent to which a society, organization or group relies on social norms, rules and procedures to alleviate the unpredictability of future events (House et al., 2002, 2004). Organizations embedded in societies characterized by high uncertainty avoidance are more likely, relative to organizations embedded in societies low in uncertainty avoidance, to reduce the use of HRIS, because of a loss of control. Png et al. (2001), in a multinational survey of 153 businesses, found that uncertainty avoidance affected information systems adoption. Businesses in high uncertainty avoidance countries were less likely to adopt information technology infrastructure.

Hypothesis 4a: *Organizations in low uncertainty avoidance societies are more likely to establish interactive HRIS than will organizations in high uncertainty avoidance societies.*

Hypothesis 4b: *Organizations in low uncertainty avoidance societies are more likely to establish an interactive HRIS than will organizations in high uncertainty avoidance societies.*

National values, HRIS and organizational outcomes

The effect of HRIS can be discussed on the basis of two alternative approaches: the universalistic approach and the contingent approach.

The *universalistic* approach to strategic HRM posits that certain HRM practices are universally related to higher organizational performance (Delery & Doty, 1996). This relationship is derived from the resource-based view of the firm proposed by Barney (1991) and colleagues. However, other scholars, such as Rousseau and Fried (2001), have argued for a *contingent* impact of HRM practices on organizational outcomes. Rogers and Wright (1998) suggested that despite evidence supporting the relationship between HRM practices and organizational performance, this relationship is not universal or consistent across all settings. In order to fully understand the effect of HRM activities on organizational outcomes, it is necessary to understand the context in which the organization exists. One key contextual variable that can affect the impact of HRM activities is culture.

Understanding the expected level of fit (consistency) between national culture and the HRIS in organizations is important as a basis for understanding the effects of such systems on organizational performance (cf. Leidner & Kayworth, 2006). Overall, we expect that if organizations adopt HRIS according to the culture in which they are embedded, the results will be more positive performance indicators, such as lower turnover and absenteeism. Conversely, if organizations adopt HRIS that deviate from the dominant societal culture, the results will be more negative performance indicators.

To support our arguments, we draw on the literature on fit that emphasizes the important effect of compatibility between national (societal) culture and organizational human resource practices on organizational performance (see, for example, Aycan, 2005; Kanungo & Jaeger, 1990; Mendonca & Kanungo, 1994). Drawing from the literature on fit, it follows that when employees are exposed to HRM activities that do not fit the national culture, they will tend to respond negatively (Aycan, 2005; Aycan et al., 2000). Conversely, when employees are exposed to HRM activities that fit the national culture, they will be satisfied with the atmosphere in the organization, hence they will respond positively, which will lead to positive aggregate organizational outcomes (Aycan, 2005).

Drawing on these assumptions, we propose that consistency versus inconsistency between the national values and the HRIS the organization adopts will contribute to the organizational outcomes of absenteeism and turnover. Our hypotheses, which follow, are based on the earlier discussion on the expected consistency between national culture and organizational HRIS. More specifically, our earlier reasoning concerning the fit between societies low in power distance and HRIS leads us to the following hypothesis:

Hypothesis 5:   *In low power distance societies, organizations are likely to have lower rates of turnover and absenteeism if they adopt an advanced HRIS in terms of type and communication design (in which the system is integrated into a wider management information system and is interactive in nature).*

Our earlier analysis discussed the fit between future-oriented societal values and advanced HRIS. Extending this reasoning, we hypothesize:

Hypothesis 6:   *In future-oriented societies, organizations will have lower rates of absenteeism and turnover if they use an advanced HRIS in terms of type and communication (in which the system is integrated into a wider management information system and is interactive in nature).*

We further discussed the fit level between individualism/collectivism and advanced HRIS. This leads us to the following hypothesis:

Hypothesis 7:   *In collectivistic societies, organizations will have lower rates of absenteeism and turnover if they use an advanced HRIS in terms of type and communication (in which the system is integrated into a wider management information system and is interactive in nature).*

Finally, we discussed the fit between societies high on uncertainty avoidance and advanced HRIS. Therefore we hypothesize:

Hypothesis 8:   *In low uncertainty avoidance societies, organizations will have lower rates of absenteeism and turnover if they use an advanced HRIS in terms of type and communication (in which the system is integrated into a wider management information system and is interactive in nature).*

Method

Sample

The study was conducted on a sample drawn from the 2009 Cranet data set. The sample consisted of 4740 organizations from 21 countries: Australia (110), Austria (203), Denmark (362), Germany (420), Greece (214), Hungary (139), Israel (114), Japan (389), Finland (136), France (157), The Netherlands (116), Philippines (33), Russia (56), Slovenia (219), South Africa (192), Sweden (282), Switzerland (99), Taiwan (229), the USA (1052), and the UK (218).

Data sources

Data for the study were obtained from two independent sources:

1. Organizational-level data: The data collection tool was a standardized questionnaire, addressed to the most senior HR/personnel specialist in each organization. Questions focused on the organizational level, and covered

major areas of HRM policies and practices. Questions were not designed to tap personal opinions, but to seek factual answers (numbers or percentages) or a yes/no response to factual questions (e.g. Do you use...?). The data were collected in 2009 by international researchers who are part of the Cranet project. The criteria for selecting organizations for the present study were: (1) they had provided full data on HRIS variables; and (2) participation of the respective country in the GLOBE Project (see below).

2. The GLOBE (Global Leadership and Organizational Behavior Effectiveness) 2004 database. GLOBE is a multi-phase, multi-method project, in which investigators spanning the world examine interrelationships between national (societal) culture, organizational culture and organizational leadership. The GLOBE Project began in 1993; today, scholars from 61 countries, representing all major regions of the world, are engaged in this long-term programmatic series of cross-cultural leadership studies. The meta-goal of the GLOBE research programme is to develop empirically based theory and measurement tools to describe, understand and predict the impact of cultural variables on leadership and organizational processes and the effectiveness of these processes.

Variables and measurement

Indices of HRIS

The following measures were obtained from the 2009 Cranet database:

1. Type of HRIS: This measure described the type of computerized HR system in the organization on a 1 to 3 scale, with 1 = do not have computerized HRIS (17.6%); 2 = independent HRIS (48.8%); and 3 = HRIS integrated with wider management system (33.6%).

2. Communication design of HRIS: This measure described the degree to which the computerized HR system was designed to disseminate information unidimensionally or interactively. The measurement used a 1 to 5 scale, with 1 = one-way communication to the entire group of employees (e.g. publishing information for the use of all the employees) (25.4%); 2 = one-way communication to a specific individual (e.g. benefits and schedule) (16.5%); 3 = two-way communication with simple update by the employee on his/her records (e.g. bank record) (25%); 4 = two-way communication with complex transaction in which the employee is able to select items such as preferred benefits, which can be approved/disapproved by the computerized system (23.7%); and 5 = more complex two-way communication system (9.4%).

Cultural practical values

The following measures were obtained from the GLOBE database (House et al., 2004). These data reflected the national values of the participating countries.

1. Power distance: the degree to which members of a collective expect power to be equally distributed.
2. Future orientation: the degree to which individuals engage in future-oriented behaviours such as planning, investing in the future and postponing gratification.
3. Uncertainty avoidance: the extent to which a society, organization or group relies on social norms, rules and procedures used to alleviate the unpredictability of future events.
4. Institutional collectivism: the degree to which organizational and societal institutional practices encourage and reward collective distribution of resources and collective action (House et al., 2004).

Scores for the four cultural values ranged between 1 (lowest) and 7 (highest).

Organizational outcomes

Two variables were taken from the Cranet 2009 database:

1. Absenteeism: this variable indicated the average annual absenteeism (number of days) in the organization.
2. Turnover: this variable indicated the average yearly turnover percentage in the organization.

Covariates – organizational background

Data on three organizational background variables were taken from the Cranet 2009 database:

1. Organizational size: this variable indicated the total number of employees in a given organization (Range: 200–10,573; Mean: 1408). Because of the non-normal distribution of this variable, we used log transformation of the actual number of employees.
2. Sector: this item indicated whether the organization belongs to the private (1) (78%) or the public (2) sector (22%).
3. Level of globalization: this item indicated whether the organization operates locally (1) (56.8%) or in the global arena (2) (43.2%).

Analytic strategy

We used multi-level analysis (hierarchical linear modelling; HLM) to model the structure of the data (Raudenbush & Bryk, 2002). This is because each organization in our sample was nested under the corresponding country culture in which it operated. In addition, because of range differences among the variables, we converted the scores using standard Z scores.

Analysis was performed in two phases. In phase one, we examined the effects of national culture on HRIS. To test our cross-level hypothesis, we estimated two multi-level models. First, we estimated a one-way ANOVA model (unconditional model). This model revealed how much variation in the outcomes (HRIS variables) lay within and between countries. For the second model (conditional model), we added to the equation organizational characteristics and national culture as predictors. To provide a realistic view of how these cultural practices operate in concert with each other, we included them simultaneously as level-2 predictors in the analysis.

In phase two, we explored the interactive effects of the national culture and HRIS on absenteeism and turnover. Again, we estimated two multi-level models. First, we estimated a one-way ANOVA model (unconditional model). This model revealed how much variation in the outcomes (absenteeism and turnover) lay within and between countries. For the second model (conditional model), we added to the equation organizational characteristics, HRIS practices and national culture as predictors, followed by the multiplicative terms of the focal cultural practices and the HRIS practices.

Results

Means, standard deviations, ranges and correlations for the study's level-1 dependent variables (organizational level) and level-2- independent variables (national level) are presented in Tables 10.1 and 10.2, respectively.

Results at the organizational level showed that the two HRIS measures had low inter-correlations (.07**), and at the national level all four possible inter-correlations (N = 21) had medium to high inter-correlations.

Before investigating the relationship of the cultural values with FWAs, we tested for possible multicollinearity. This test seemed necessary, given the relatively high correlations among the independent variables. We used the Variance Inflation Factor (VIF) index, with OLS stepwise regression, to examine possible multicollinearity. VIF = 5.3 was used as the cut-off point for multicollinearity (Hair et al., 1998). The results showed VIF = 1.04, suggesting

Table 10.1   Means, standard deviations, ranges and correlations among organizational level variables (Level 1)

	Interactive HRIS	Integrated HRIS	Absenteeism	Turnover
Interactive HRIS	–	.07**	–.06*	–.04
Integrated HRIS communication	–	–	–.02	–.03
Absenteeism	–	–	–	.03
Mean	2.06	2.35	8.52	15.26
(SD)	(.69)	(1.35)	(6.61)	(17.25)
Range	1–3	1–5	0–45	0–210

Note: N = 4,740, ** p < .01.

Table 10.2 Means, standard deviations, ranges and correlations among national values variables (Level 2)

	Power distance	Uncertainty avoidance	Future orientation	Collectivism
Power distance	–	–.36*	–.54**	–.10**
Uncertainty avoidance	–	–	.74**	–.41**
Future orientation	–	–	–	–.29**
Mean (SD)	5.01	4.70	4.21	4.46
	(.40)	(.56)	(.41)	(.71)
Range	4.14–5.68	3.26–5.42	3.31–4.80	3.46–6.14

Note: N = 21, * p < .05, ** p < .01.

that there was no multicollinearity in our equation. Thus, the country-level variables could be used in the same HLM equation.

Hypothesis testing

Phase 1: Effects of national culture on HRIS

We examined the relationship between national culture and HRIS using HLM. First, we calculated the Intraclass Correlation Coefficient ($ICC_{(1)}$) for each one of the dependent variables, using the formula τ_{00}/τ_{00+} σ^2, for the unconditional model (without the explained variables) and for the conditional model (with the explained variables) (see Table 10.4). $ICC_{(1)}$ represents the percentage of variance between groups (see Bliese & Ployhart, 2002; Raudenbush & Bryk, 2002). τ_{00} represents the variance of level 2 variables and σ^2 represents the variance of level 1 variables. If the conditional $ICC_{(1)}$ is smaller than the unconditional $ICC_{(1)}$, this means that the specific Level 2 variables added in the conditional model explain the country effect (see Raudenbush & Bryk, 2002).

The results indicated that for all the examined dependent variables (type of HRIS and communication design of HRIS), the $ICC_{(1)}$ for the conditional model was smaller than the $ICC_{(1)}$ for the unconditional model, supporting the effect of national culture on these dependent variables. More specifically, the $ICC_{(1)}$s for the unconditional models for type of HRIS and communication design of HRIS were, respectively, .31 and .29. The $ICC_{(1)}$s for the conditional models for these dependent variables were .25 and .21.

Further, to test which of the main effects of the national cultural values is a predictor of the HRIS, we focused on their predictive coefficients (i.e. γ_{01}, γ_{02}) for the random intercept (β_{00}). The results are presented in Table 10.3.

The results indicated that our hypotheses pertaining to societal values and HRIS (H1 through H4) were generally supported: power distance was negatively related to HRIS interactive communication design ($\beta = -.10**$); future orientation was positively related to the integrated HRIS ($\beta = .06*$)

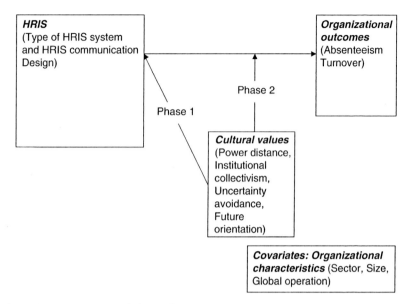

Figure 10.1   Description of the study

Table 10.3   HLM analysis for HRIS outcomes

	Integrated HRIS		Interactive HRIS communication design	
	Coefficient	SE	Coefficient	SE
Level 1 variance (σ^2_{within})	.86**	.21	.75**	.19
Level 2 random intercept (β_{00})				
Intercept (γ_{00})	.69**	.15	.65**	.24
Variance (τ_{00})	.38**	.12	.30**	.14
ICC	.31		.29	
Level 1 variance (σ^2_{within})	.72**	.19	.61**	.16
Size (γ_{10})	.10**	.04	.08**	.04
Sector (γ_{20})	.08**	.04	.02	.01
Globalization (γ_{30})	.07*	.03	.01	.01
Level 2 random intercept (β_{00})				
Intercept (γ_{00})	.50**	.16	.71**	.22
PD (γ_{01})	.04	.03	−.10**	.06
FO (γ_{02})	.06*	.02	.15**	.09
IND/COLL (γ_{03})	.15**	.08	.04	.05
UA (γ_{04})	−.07*	.04	−.03	.01
Variance (τ_{00})	.24**	.07	.16**	.08

(continued)

Table 10.3 Continued

	Integrated HRIS		Interactive HRIS communication design	
	Coefficient	SE	Coefficient	SE
ICC	.25		.21	
Variance Accounted for by:				
Level 1 predictors (%)	16		19	
Level 1 predictors as a % of total variance	11		13	
Level 2 predictors (%)	37		47	
Level 2 predictors as a % of total variance	11		13	
Total ~R² (%)	23		27	

Note: N = 21, *p < .05, **p < .01.

and to HRIS interactive communication design (β = .15**); collectivism was positively related to the integrated HRIS (β = .15**); and uncertainty avoidance was negatively related to the integrated HRIS (β = −.07*). However, uncertainty avoidance and collectivism were not found to be significantly related to HRIS interactive communication design, and power distance was not found to be significantly related to the integrated HRIS.

The results also indicated effects of organization-level variables on HRIS. Specifically, size was positively related to integrated HRIS (β = .10**) and HRIS interactive communication design (β = .08**), with large organizations more likely to use integrated HRIS systems and complex communication design. Sector was positively related to integrated HRIS (β = .08**), suggesting that public sector organizations more likely to use integrated HRIS systems. Finally, globalization level was positively related to integrated HRIS (β = .07*), suggesting that global organizations, as opposed to local organizations, were more likely to use integrated HRIS systems.

Phase 2: Interactive effects of national cultural practices and HRIS on absenteeism and turnover

In the second stage of the analysis, we explored the interactive effects of the national values and HRIS on absenteeism and turnover.

The results indicated that the $ICC_{(1)}$ for the conditional models were smaller than the $ICC_{(1)}$ for the unconditional models, supporting the interactive effect of HRIS and national values on these dependent variables. More specifically, the $ICC_{(1)}$s for the unconditional model for absenteeism was .30 and for turnover was .29. The $ICC_{(1)}$s for the conditional model for absenteeism was .22 and for turnover was .23.

Further, to test which of the interactions was a predictor of the outcomes, we focused on their predictive coefficients (i.e. γ_{31}, γ_{32}, γ_{42},) for the random intercept (β_{00}). The results are presented in Table 10.4.

The results provided partial support to our hypotheses pertaining to the interactions between the national values and the HRIS indicators, such that

Table 10.4 HLM analysis for PA practices, national culture and outcomes

	Absenteeism		Turnover	
	Coefficient	SE	Coefficient	SE
Level 1 variance (σ^2_{within})	.76**	.20	.62**	.14
Level 2 random intercept (β_{00})				
Intercept (γ_{00})	.54**	.12	.45**	.10
Variance (τ_{00})	.34**	.10	.25**	.09
ICC	.30		.29	
Level 1 variance (σ^2_{within})	.68**	.11	.54**	.10
Size (γ_{10})	.08**	.03	.07*	.02
Sector (γ_{20})	.06*	.02	−.05	.02
Globalization (γ_{30})	−.12**	.05	−.10**	.01
Integrated HRIS (γ_{40})	−.07**	.03	−.02	.01
Interactive HRIS communication (γ_{50})	−.02	.02	−.01	.01
Level 2 random intercept (β_{00})				
Intercept (γ_{00})	.20**	.09	.16**	.08
PD (γ_{01})	−.02	.01	−.01	.01
FO (γ_{02})	−.09**	.04	−.09**	.05
COLL (γ_{03})	−.07*	.03	−.09**	.04
UA (γ_{04})	−.02	.03	−.08**	.04
PD * Integrated HRIS (γ_{41})	−.03	.05	−.02	.01
FO * Integrated HRIS (γ_{42})	−.04	.03	−.03	.01
IND/COLL * Integrated HRIS (γ_{43})	−.10**	.07	−.02	.01
UA * Integrated HRIS (γ_{44})	−.10**	.05	−.01	.01
PD * Interactive HRIS (γ_{51})	−.02	.01	−.01	.01
FO * Interactive HRIS (γ_{52})	−.08**	.04	−.03	.02
IND/COLL * Interactive HRIS (γ_{53})	−.02	.02	−.01	.02
UA * Interactive HRIS (γ_{54})	−.09**	.05	−.07*	.04
Variance (τ_{00})	.17**	.07	.14**	.06
ICC	.22		.23	
Variance Accounted for by:				
Level 1 predictors (%)	20		20	
Level 1 predictors as a % of total variance	14		14	
Level 2 predictors (%)	41		36	
Level 2 predictors as a % of total variance	13		10	
Total ~R^2 (%)	26		**24**	

Note: * p < .05, ** p < .01.

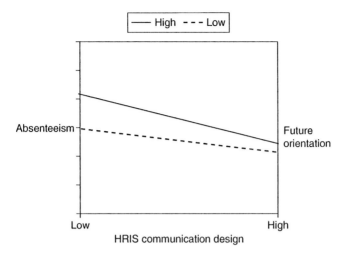

Figure 10.2 Interactive effect of stage of HRIS and future orientation on absenteeism

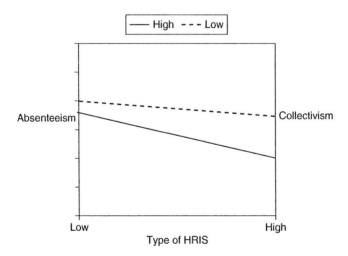

Figure 10.3 Interactive effect of type of HRIS and collectivism on absenteeism

the interactions were significant with regard to absenteeism in 3 of the 4 interactions and for turnover in 1 of the 4 interactions. In order to examine the direction of the interactions more systematically, we graphed the results (see Figures 10.2–10.6). The specific patterns of the interactions supported the direction of our hypotheses.

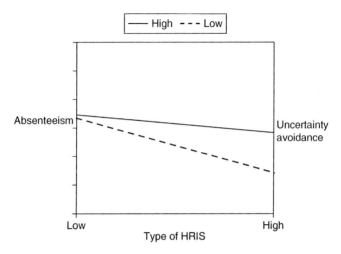

Figure 10.4 Interactive effect of type of HRIS and uncertainty avoidance on absenteeism

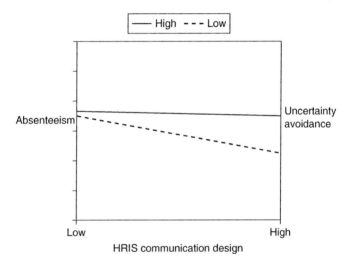

Figure 10.5 Interactive effect of stage of HRIS and uncertainty avoidance on absenteeism

The results failed to support Hypothesis 5, but provided partial confirmation of Hypothesis 6 by supporting the interactive effect of future-orientation and integrated HRIS communication design on absenteeism ($\beta = -.08^{**}$). The figure depicting this interaction (see Figure 10.2) supports the notion that in societies characterized by high future-orientation,

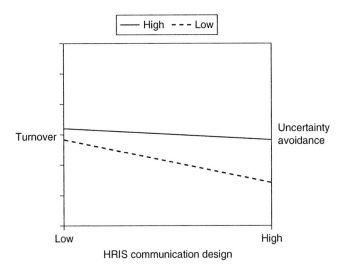

Figure 10.6 Interactive effect of stage of HRIS and uncertainty avoidance on turnover

organizations tend to have lower absenteeism rates if they adopt advanced complex HRIS.

Further, the results pertaining to Hypothesis 7 provided partial support for the hypothesized interactions between collectivism and the interactive HRIS. More specifically, we found an interaction between collectivism and interactive HRIS on absenteeism ($\beta = -.10^{**}$). The pattern shown in Figure 10.3 supported the directions hypothesized by Hypothesis 7, in that it indicates that in collectivistic societies, organizations that adopted a more advanced type of HRIS reported a lower level of absenteeism.

The results pertaining to Hypothesis 8 supported the hypothesized interactive effect of uncertainty avoidance and integrated HRIS communication design on absenteeism and turnover ($\beta = -.09^{**}$ and $-.07^*$ respectively), and of uncertainty avoidance and interactive HRIS on absenteeism ($\beta = -.10^{**}$). As hypothesized, the results indicated that in societies characterized by low uncertainty avoidance, organizations that implement advanced HRIS tended to show lower absenteeism than organizations that did not implement such systems (see Figures 10.5 and 10.6).

In addition, we found several main effects for both national variables and HRIS variables on organizational performance variables (see Table 10.4). Uncertainty avoidance was negatively related to turnover ($\beta = -.08^{**}$); collectivism was negatively related to absenteeism ($\beta = -.07^*$) and to turnover ($\beta = -.09^{**}$); and future-orientation was negatively related to absenteeism and turnover ($\beta = -09^{**}$ to both). With regard to HRIS variables, interactive HRIS was negatively related to absenteeism ($\beta = .-07^*$).

Discussion

The present study focused on the important issue of the relationship between national culture and the use of information technology in the HR area. We focused on two complementary issues: (1) the influence of national values on the implementation practices of information technology in the HRM area (i.e. degree of integration of HRIS into a wider management information system and the degree to which the HRIS was interactive in nature); and (2) the contribution of the level of fit between national values and these HR information technology practices on two key organizational outcomes: absenteeism and turnover. The results generally supported our hypotheses by indicating that national culture affects the information technology practices in the HR area and that absenteeism, and to a lesser degree, turnover tend to be affected by the level of fit between the societal culture and the HR-related information technology practices. The higher the fit, the lower the absenteeism.

These results have important theoretical and practical implications. Theoretically, the results enhance our understanding of the effect of national values on information technology practices in HR and on organizational outcomes. Practically, because of increases in globalization and in the pervasiveness of international business operations, corporations are likely to benefit from research findings on the adaptation of information technology practices under different environmental conditions, and their effects on performance-related outcomes. Thus, the results of this study can enable managers who are responsible for global operations or who are in organizations competing in the global market to decide more effectively which information technology practices to implement in different societal cultures. The study clearly indicates that understanding the fit between HR-related information technology practices and societal values is important in implementing effective information technology practices (cf. Leidner & Kayworth, 2006).

A methodological strength of the present study is the independence of its data sources. While the organizational-level data on information technology practices has been obtained from the Cranet study, the country-level data on cultural values have been obtained from the GLOBE study. The consistent theory-based relationships found in the study, occurring in datasets from different sources, clearly strengthen the conclusions that can be drawn.

Another strength of the study is the multi-level analysis that was conducted. Relatively few studies have examined the interaction between variables at the organizational level and national level, taking into account the nested structure of the data (in the current study, organizations within countries, e.g. Brown, 2005).

Our findings were based on regression analysis, which can enable conclusions about relationships but not necessarily causal direction. However, because the independent variables are national values and 'hard' organizational characteristics, we argue that it is reasonable to interpret the findings in terms of the 'effect' of values on HRIS indicators, and not vice versa. However, it would be useful for future studies to examine regions or subcultures within a nation to avoid generalities and to refine our understanding of contextual influences.

The results pertaining to cultural values support culture-based theories such as those originally advanced by Hofstede (1991) and later developed by the GLOBE study (House et al., 2002), namely that management is influenced not only by organizational culture but also by the culture of the larger society surrounding the organization (Schein, 2000). In a later publication, Hofstede & Peterson (2000) discussed the complex relationships between national and organizational culture. He raised the question of whether management can establish a strong organizational culture that reflects values different from those of the larger national culture and that compete with societal socialization practices. He further argued that even strong organizational cultures of multinational organizations will be subject to local reinterpretations of their 'standard' values when their practices are transferred abroad. Thus, even seemingly identical practices in multinational organizations can produce different nuances in different countries. Understanding the influence of national cultures is therefore of great importance for understanding organizational cultures.

The knowledge derived from the present study about cultural effects is applicable to studies concerning cross-cultural organizational processes, such as globalization, outsourcing and expatriate behaviour. Studies of information technology practices across societal cultures (e.g. Snape et al., 1998) need to consider the separate and the interactive contributions of organizational and national factors. Kim (1999) stated that globalization implies accepting that cultural diversity in management composition and style contributes to the competitive advantage of the firm. The results of the present study suggest that globalization also implies acceptance of both national and organizational diversity. Ultimately, recognition and acceptance of such values should contribute to the successful operation of multinational firms.

Future research should aim to replicate our study over time to test the validity of our results. Future studies should also examine additional organizational performance outcomes, such as productivity, customer service quality and innovation. Finally, an additional, and likely very fruitful, approach would be to include individual-level variables in the analysis, for example, by examining the main and interactive effects of organizational and national values on both HR system-related variables and individuals' perceptions of work values (see Leidner & Kaywort, 2006).

References

Agourram, H. & Ingham, J. 2007. 'The impact of national culture on the meaning of information system success at the user level'. *Journal of Enterprise Information Management*, 20(6): 641–56.

Aycan, Z. 2005. 'The interplay between cultural and institutional/structural contingencies in human resource management practices'. *International Journal of Human Resource Management*, 16(7): 1083–119.

Aycan, Z., Sinha, J.B.P. & Kanungo, R.N. 1999. 'Organizational culture and human resource management practices: The model of culture fit'. *Journal of Cross-Cultural Psychology*, 30(4): 501–26.

Aycan, Z., Kanungo, R.N., Mendonca, M., Yu, K., Deller, J., Stahl, G. & Kurshid, A. 2000. 'Impact of culture on human resource management practices: A 10-country comparison'. *Applied Psychology: An International Review*, 49(1): 192–221.

Bajdo, L.M. & Dickson, M.W. 2002. 'Perceptions of organizational culture and women's advancement in organizations: A cross-cultural examination'. *Sex Roles*, 45: 399–414.

Barney, J. 1991. 'Firm resources and sustained competitive advantage'. *Journal of Management*, 17: 99–120.

Ball, K.S. 2001. 'The use of human resource information systems: A survey'. *Personnel Review*, 30(6): 677–93.

Bliese, P.D. & Ployhart, R.E. 2002. 'Growth modeling using random coefficient models: Model building, testing, and illustrations'. *Organizational Research Methods*, 5: 362–87.

Brodbeck, F.C., Hanges, P.J., Dickson, M.W., Gupta, V. & Dorfman, P.W. 2004. 'Societal culture and industrial sector influences on organizational culture'. In R. House, P. Hanges, M. Javidan, P.W. Dorfman,& V. Gupta (eds), *Culture, Leadership, and Organizations: The GLOBE Study of 62 Societies*. Thousand Oaks, CA: Sage, 654–719.

Broderick, R. & Boudreau, J.W. 1992. 'Human resource management, information technology and the competitive edge'. *Academy of Management Executive*, 6(2): 7–17.

Brown, M. 2005. 'Managing the overload?' *Group & Organization Management*, 30(1): 99–124.

Chow, C.W., Deng, F.J. & Ho, J.L. 2000. 'The openness of knowledge sharing within organizations: A comparative study of the United States and the People's Republic of China'. *Journal of Management Accounting Research*, 12: 65–95.

Communal, C. & Senior, B. 1999. 'National culture and management: Messages conveyed by British, French and German advertisements for managerial appointments'. *Leadership & Organization Development*, 20(1): 26–35.

Delery, J.E. & Doty, D.H. 1996. 'Modes of theorizing in strategic human resource management: Tests of universalistic, contingency and configurationally performance predictions'. *Academy of Management Journal*, 39: 802–35.

Dickson, M.W., Aditya, R.N. & Chhokar, J.S. 2000. 'Definition and interpretation in cross-cultural organizational culture research'. In N.M. Ashkanasy, C.P.M. Wilderom & M.F. Peterson (eds), *Handbook of Organizational Culture and Climate*. Thousand Oaks, CA: Sage, 494–514.

Hair, J.F., Anderson, R.E., Tatham, R.L. & Black, W.C. 1998. *Multivariate Data Analysis*, 5th edn. Upper Saddle River, NJ: Prentice Hall.

Hasan, H. & Ditsa, G. 1999. 'The impact of culture on the adoption of IT: An interpretive study'. *Journal of Global Information Management*, 7(1): 5–15.

Hendrickson, A.R. 2003. 'Human resource information systems: Backbone technology of contemporary human resources'. *Journal of Labor Research*, 24(3): 381–94.

Hofstede, G. 1980. *Culture's Consequences: International Differences in Work-related Values*. Beverly Hills, CA: Sage.

Hofstede, G. 1991. 'Cultural constraints in management theories'. *Academy of Management Executive*, 7: 81–91.

Hofstede, G. & Peterson, M.F. 2000. 'Culture: National values and organizational practices'. In N.M. Ashkanasy, C.P.M. Wilderom & M.F. Peterson (eds), *Handbook of Organizational Culture and Climate*. Thousand Oaks, CA: Sage, 441–62.

House, R., Javidan, M., Hanges, P. & Dorfman, P. 2002. 'Understanding cultures and implicit leadership theories across the globe: An introduction to Project GLOBE'. *Journal of World Business*, 37: 3–10.

House, R., Hanges, P., Javidan, M., Dorfman, P. & Gupta, V. 2004. *Culture, Leadership, and Organizations: The GLOBE Study of 62 Societies*. Thousand Oaks, CA: Sage.

Hubbard, J.C., Forcht, K.A. & Thomas, D.S. 1998. 'Human resource information systems: An overview of current ethical and legal issues'. *Journal of Business Ethics*, 17(12): 1319–23.

Kanungo, R.N. & Jaeger, A.M. 1990. 'Introduction: The need for indigenous management in developing countries'. In A.M. Jaeger & R.N. Kanungo (eds), *Management in Developing Countries*. London: Routledge, 1–22.

Kim, S. 1999. 'Globalization of human resource management: A cross-cultural perspective for the public sector'. *Public Personnel Management*, 28(2): 227–43.

Kitchell, S. 1995. 'Corporate culture, environmental adaptation and innovation adaptation: A qualitative/quantitative approach'. *Journal of the Academy of Marketing Science*, 199: 195–205.

Kluckhohn, C. 1951. 'Values and value-orientations in the theory of action: An exploration in definition and classification'. In T. Parsons & E. Shils (eds), *Toward a General Theory of Action*. Cambridge, MA: Harvard University Press, 159–88.

Kovach, R.C. 1995. 'Matching assumptions to environment in the transfer of management practices'. *International Studies of Management and Organization*, 24: 83–100.

Kovach, K.A., Hughes, A.A., Fagan, P. & Maggitti, P.G. 2002. 'Administrative and strategic advantages of HRIS'. *Employment Relations Today*, 29(2): 43–8.

Leidner, D.E. & Kayworth, T. 2006. 'A review of culture in information systems research: Toward a theory of information technology culture conflict'. *MIS Quarterly*, 30(2): 357–99.

Lin, C.Y. 1998. 'Human resource information systems: Implementation in Taiwan'. *Research and Practices in Human Resource Management*, 5(1): 57–72.

Mayfield, M, Mayfield, D. & Lunce, S. 2003. 'Human resource information systems: A review and model development'. *Advances in Competitiveness Research*, 11(1): 139–51.

Mendonca, M. & Kanungo, R.N. 1994. 'Managing human resources: The issue of cultural fit'. *Journal of Management Inquiry*, 3(2): 189–205.

Ngai, E.W.T. & Wat, F.K.T. 2006. 'Human resource information systems: A review and empirical analysis'. *Personnel Review*, 35(3): 297–314.

Peretz, H. & Fried, Y. 2012. 'A cross-culture examination of performance appraisal and organizational performance'. *Journal of Applied Psychology*, 97(2): 448–59.

Peretz, H. & Rosenblatt, Z. 2011. 'National culture effect on organizational training: A comparative study in 21 countries'. *Journal of Cross-Culture Psychology*, 42(5): 819–33.

Png, I.P.L., Tan, B.C.Y. & Wee, K.L. 2001. 'Dimensions of national culture and corporate adoption of IT infrastructure'. *IEEE Transactions of Engineering Management*, 48(1): 36–45.

Raudenbush, S.W. & Bryk, A.S. 2002. *Hierarchical Linear Models: Applications and Data Analysis Methods*, 2nd edn. Newbury Park, CA: Sage.

Ribiere, V.M., Haddad, M. & Wiele, P.V. 2010. 'The impact of national culture traits on the usage of Web 2.0 technologies'. *The Journal of Information and Knowledge Management Systems*, 40(3/4): 334–61.

Roberts, B. 2004. 'Empowerment or imposition?' *HR Magazine*, 49(6): 157–66.

Rogers, E. W. & Wright, P.M. 1998. 'Measuring organizational performance in strategic human resource management: Problems, prospects, and performance information markets'. *Human Resource Management Review*, 8(3): 311–31.

Rousseau, D.M. & Fried, Y. 2001. 'Location, location, location: Contextualizing organizational research'. *Journal of Organizational Behavior*, 22: 1–13.

Schein, E.H. 2000. *Organizational Culture and Leadership*. San Francisco: Jossey-Bass.

Schwartz, S.H. 1999. 'A theory of cultural values and some implications for work'. *Applied Psychology*, 48(1): 23–47.

Shani, A. & Tesone, D.V. 2010. 'Have human resource information systems evolved into internal e-commerce?' *Worldwide Hospitality and Tourism Themes*, 2(1): 30–48.

Snape, E.D., Thompson D., Yam, F.K. & Redman, T. 1998. 'Performance appraisal and culture: Practice and attitudes in Hong Kong and Great Britain'. *The International Journal of Human Resource Management*, 9(5): 841–61.

Targowski, A.S. & Deshpande, S.P. 2001. 'The utility and selection of an HRIS'. *Advances in Competitiveness Research*, 9(1): 42–56.

Vallance, S. 1999. 'Performance appraisal in Singapore, Thailand and Philippines: A cultural perspective'. *Australian Journal of Public Administration*, 58: 78–86.

11
The Use of Flexible Working across National Contexts and its Relationship to Organizational Performance

Michael Koch

This chapter offers a cross-national examination of popular flexible working arrangements, such as overtime, fixed-term contracts, temporary work and job sharing, and the differences in the use of such methods, before moving on to consider the relationship between flexible working arrangements and organizational performance.

Introduction

Flexible Working Arrangements (FWAs) consist of policies that accommodate the needs of employees and employers in terms of working patterns, times and locations. This includes not only non-standard work schedules such as part-time work or flexi-time, but also measures as diverse as shift work, job sharing, overtime, temporary employment and remote working (Stavrou, 2005; Kossek & Michel, 2010).

Recent years have shown a sustained interest in work flexibility, demonstrated by publications in academic journals and the practitioner press alike (e.g. Hornung, Rousseau & Glaser, 2008; Shockley & Allen, 2010; Kelliher & Anderson, 2010; Coombs, 2011). Legislators appear to have directed their attention to flexible work issues as well. For instance, the Council of the European Union adopted Employment Policy Guidelines that request all member states of the EU to promote 'innovative and adaptable forms of work organization' (Decision 2008/618/EC, OJ L 198, 26.7.2008, p. 52).

The appeal of FWAs stems from their value in a number of contexts. From an employer perspective, the use of flexible work schemes allows organizations to absorb fluctuations in product or service demand by enlarging or decreasing their workforce size. FWAs that include the reduction of staff hours may even help to avoid layoffs and thereby the loss of valuable human capital (Kossek & Michel, 2010). Some FWAs may also enable employees to gain control over their time and place of work, helping them to better balance work and family commitments (Stavrou & Kilaniotis, 2010). In addition, the spread of FWAs is stimulated by a number of broader societal, economic and technological developments. Demographic changes, such as the ageing population in Western economies or the increasing share of women in the workforce, gave rise to a greater need for flexible work (Plantenga & Remery, 2009). Current generations of individuals entering the workforce display a greater awareness of work–life balance, which translates into a higher demand for work flexibility (Scheibl & Dex, 1998). On the demand side of the labour market, difficult macroeconomic conditions and the resulting pressure on payroll costs make workforce flexibility a more vital concern for many business organizations as well. In addition, the availability of new technologies has improved possibilities for working from remote locations.

However, FWAs support two kinds of flexibility that are not necessarily compatible. On the one hand, some FWAs give employers more leeway in terms of hiring and dismissing people. This type of flexibility often runs counter to the interests of employees. For instance, FWAs such as fixed-term contracts benefit employers, but introduce involuntary flexibility for employees. On the other hand, employees mainly benefit from those FWAs that allow them to determine their own working schedule, hours and location (such as teleworking or home-based work; see Kossek & Michel, 2010; Stavrou, Spiliotis & Charalambous, 2010).

The practical relevance of FWAs has been reflected in a substantial body of research. In particular, the relationship between FWAs and different organizational and employee outcomes has been a core interest of scholarship related to flexible work. While there is some evidence for positive performance-related effects of FWAs, the literature as a whole has shown mixed support for a business case for FWAs (Baltes et al., 1999; more recently: de Menezes & Kelliher, 2011). In particular, there is a need for (1) studies based on large and diverse samples that allow more robust generalizations of the performance effects of FWAs, and (2) studies that include effects that could mediate the relationship between FWAs and performance (de Menezes & Kelliher, 2011).

This chapter addresses these needs. Drawing on the most recent data from the Cranet survey, this study first examines the current prevalence of FWAs across major geographies before moving on to an analysis of the relationship between FWAs and different organizational outcomes. By doing so, this chapter not only sheds light on the actual popularity of FWAs, but also contributes to a more thorough understanding of the relationship between FWAs and organizational performance, helping to better assess the effectiveness of this particular management tool.

The remainder of the chapter is organized as follows. The next section describes the popularity of flexible working arrangements, examining which particular practices are more common than others and showing which practices achieve the highest coverage in terms of the proportion of employees concerned. In the second section, the relationship between FWAs and employee turnover, absenteeism and organizational performance is explored using data about private sector companies from the Cranet survey.

Flexible working arrangements in regional context

Recent surveys conducted in the United States and the European Union suggest that the use of FWAs differs strongly among countries and also among different types of FWAs (Plantenga & Remery, 2009; Coombs, 2011). These differences arise from a number of institutional, economic and cultural influences (Brewster & Mayrhofer, 2011). For instance, whereas German law makes flexible work practices an integral part of the German employment system, flexible work in the United States is largely a matter of case-by-case negotiations between employer and employee (Berg, 2008).

While most existing surveys on FWAs are limited to a single country or region, the Cranet survey offers the unique advantage of comparison over a large number of the most important and diverse economies in the world (Parry, Stavrou-Costea & Morley, 2011). The Cranet survey includes factual data on the usage rates of the main flexible working arrangements. The first column of Table 11.1 contains the list of the FWAs for which information was collected in the most recent round (2008–10) of the Cranet survey. Their respective usage rates, expressed as the proportion of companies that employ the particular FWA, are displayed in the subsequent columns for several country clusters. These clusters are for the most part based on the country clusters developed by the GLOBE project (Gupta & Hanges, 2004).[1] They have been shown to provide an appropriate basis for grouping countries according to cultural and institutional similarities (Javidan et al., 2006).

As already observed by other scholars (see Brewster & Mayrhofer, 2011), the Cranet data show that there is an extensive use of FWAs in general. However, important differences exist with regard to (1) the prevalence of different types of FWAs, (2) the coverage achieved by the respective arrangement and, (3) the prevalence of arrangements across different clusters of countries.

Differences between various Flexible Working Arrangements

The second last column ('Global Average') displays the overall usage rate for the examined FWAs across all countries and communities of the Cranet survey. The seven most common arrangements exhibit usage rates of around 60 to 80 per cent. One should notice that these widely popular arrangements mostly address flexibility in the timing of work. Time-based measures such as overtime, fixed-term contracts or part-time often do not require changes in working procedures and can be introduced at reasonable cost. The compressed working week, which lets employees work full-time schedules

Table 11.1 Percentage of companies that use Flexible Working Arrangements

Flexible Working Arrangement	Proportion of companies using FWAs							Global Average	ICC (p < 0.01 for all values)
	Anglo	Confucian Asia	Eastern Europe	Germanic Europe	Latin Europe	Nordic Europe			
Overtime	89%	94%	76%	75%	82%	92%		84%	0,15
Part-time work	83%	64%	55%	98%	94%	95%		76%	0,28
Fixed-term contracts	64%	78%	63%	88%	78%	69%		72%	0,1
Shift work	56%	71%	65%	69%	58%	64%		65%	0,04
Weekend work	61%	43%	69%	80%	61%	61%		63%	0,05
Flexi-time	58%	47%	44%	91%	52%	86%		61%	0,25
Temporary/casual work	72%	35%	44%	72%	74%	84%		59%	0,1
Annual hours contract	24%	25%	24%	39%	30%	42%		30%	0,1
Teleworking	36%	11%	17%	43%	31%	55%		29%	0,13
Job sharing	27%	18%	25%	38%	15%	21%		24%	0,12
Compressed working week	31%	12%	12%	29%	15%	27%		20%	0,13
Home-based work	34%	7%	11%	33%	21%	26%		20%	0,12

in fewer than five days, appears to be the only time-based measure that is considerably less popular. At the bottom of Table 11.1, five FWAs are effectively used to a much lesser extent, displaying usage rates of around 30 per cent or less. Except for the compressed working week, these FWAs involve specific job designs and contracts (job sharing, annual hours contract) or job locations away from the company office (teleworking, home-based work). The relative unpopularity of specific job designs and contracts may be related to their limited applicability, while the low esteem of remote working often stems from a widespread managerial belief that workers need to be in the office in order to be productive (Coombs, 2011). In summary, the usage rates displayed in Table 11.1 suggest that there is a strong divide in popularity of FWAs, with time-based FWAs being vastly more popular than all other measures. This divergence has not been identified in previous work and its causes should be the subject of further investigation.

Regional differences for usage rates of Flexible Work Arrangements

As a consequence of largely different cultural and institutional conditions, the arrangements displayed in Table 11.1 show rather disparate levels of consistency regarding their prevalence across country clusters. By and large, companies in Germanic and Northern European countries seem to make wide usage of FWAs in general, while Eastern European and Asian countries generally exhibit lower usage rates. The most striking differences can be observed for all time-based arrangements. For instance, while a large majority of companies in Germanic and Northern Europe use flexi-time, only about half of the surveyed companies in Asian and Eastern Europe make use of this measure. Differences are also pronounced for teleworking, part-time work and temporary/casual work, which all seem to display a considerable heterogeneity in terms of popularity across country clusters. On the other hand, the most popular and affordable arrangements, such as overtime, shift work and part-time work (with the exception of Southeast Asia), display fairly consistent usage rates across all country clusters, regardless of institutional or cultural context. Expensive and complex arrangements are consequently more often to be found in economically well-developed country clusters.

Significance of national differences

Other than comparing relative usage rates of FWAs across country clusters, one could ask the more fundamental question of how much country effects really account for the differences between FWA usage rates. To address this question, the Intraclass Correlation Coefficient (ICC) was calculated for each FWA as a dependent variable, depicted in the last column of Table 11.1. The ICC 'measures the proportion of variance in the dependent variable that is accounted for by groups' (Luke, 2004: 18) and is accepted as an adequate measure of the importance of country as a predictor of HR practices (Wright & van de Voorde, 2009). In our case, the ICC measures show

how much of the variance of a particular FWA is due to country-specific influences. The higher the ICC for a given FWA, the more of its variance can be explained by the influence of the national context.

Table 11.1 shows that most ICC values float around 0.1, meaning that a mere 10 per cent of the variance in the usage of the concerned FWA can be ascribed to nation-specific influences. By and large, these numbers suggest that country-specific influences may not adequately explain why some FWAs are more popular than others. Part-time work and flexi-time are exceptions in this context. With ICC values of 0.28 and 0.25 respectively, a much more substantial part of the variance in the popularity of these FWAs is due to country effects. Consequently, one can assume that institutional, cultural and structural differences that exist across countries (such as labour law provisions, workforce composition and industry structure) have a significant influence on the use and configuration of these time-based work arrangements, while only having a minor impact on all other arrangements.

Differences in coverage of Flexible Working Arrangements

Table 11.1 shows that several FWAs display high usage rates. For instance, part-time work arrangements are used by 78 per cent of the surveyed companies. However, these usage rates provide no indication about the use of FWAs within companies. A closer look at part-time usage within companies (Figure 11.1) shows that for 37 per cent of the examined companies, part-time schemes are applied to only 5 per cent or less of their workforce. Overtime, and to some degree also flexi-time and shift work, appear to be used for at least moderate proportions of company personnel. Overtime, as the most prevalent arrangement across all firms and country clusters, is also often applied to comparably large proportions of staff. For instance, 17 per cent of all firms included in the Cranet survey use overtime for more than 50 per cent of their workforce. Besides that, most other FWAs are fairly limited in the proportion of staff they cover. With the exception of overtime, shift work and flexi-time, the most frequent coverage is between zero (no usage) and 5 per cent. This implies that although a number FWAs might be widespread *across* companies, their use *within* companies is often restricted to a very small part of the workforce.

Flexible Working Arrangements and organizational outcomes

The relationship between FWAs and organizational outcomes has received considerable attention from researchers (e.g. Dalton & Mesch, 1990; Stavrou, 2005; Giardini & Kabst, 2008; Kossek & Michel, 2010; Stavrou & Kilaniotis, 2010). However, the evidence regarding the performance effects of FWAs has been largely inconclusive (e.g. Stavrou et al., 2010; de Menezes & Kelliher, 2011). In a large-scale cross-sectional study, Konrad & Mangel (2000) examined the relationship between work–life programmes (including a

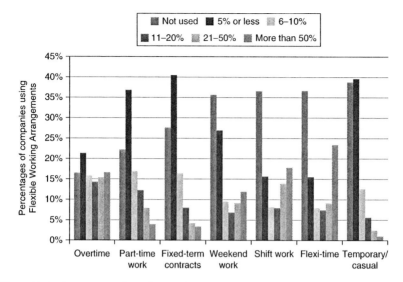

Figure 11.1   Proportion of employees for which the most popular FWAs are used

number of FWAs) and firm productivity. They detected a positive relationship between work–life programmes and productivity, which is stronger for firms with high percentages of highly skilled workers and women (Konrad & Mangel, 2000). Stavrou (2005) examined several bundles of FWAs and found that only one bundle, Work Away from the Office (which includes home-based work and teleworking), had a clear-cut positive relationship to organizational performance. Storey et al. (2002) analysed the relationship between flexible employment contracts and product and process innovation, finding a weak link between the use of flexible contracts and innovation. In a recent longitudinal study, Lee & DeVoe (2012) found that flexitime increases firm profitability, but only when coupled to an employee-centred management strategy. Flextime, when associated to a cost-reduction strategy, was more likely to have a negative impact on profitability (Lee & DeVoe, 2012).

A call has been issued for more robust research to explain the 'why' mechanism of the FWA–performance relationship via modelling possible mediators and is based on large, heterogeneous samples of multiple organizations (de Menezes & Kelliher, 2011). This section addresses these issues by developing and estimating theory on the relationship between FWAs and organizational performance, including mediating effects of two other more proximal outcomes of FWAs, namely absenteeism and turnover. These two variables are among the most salient and widely used outcomes of HR practices in general and FWAs in particular (Dalton & Mesch, 1990; Stavrou & Kilaniotis, 2010). Previous research often examined how FWAs

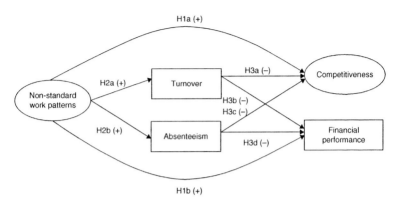

Figure 11.2   Hypothesized model

may influence those variables in isolation, but the mediating role of employee turnover and absenteeism in the relationship between FWAs and organizational performance has not yet been examined. By including these intervening variables, the theory to be developed allows for a simultaneous examination of the direct link between FWAs and organizational outcomes, and also of the indirect performance effects of FWAs that may occur through their impact on employee turnover and absenteeism.

Instead of studying a larger array of FWAs, the following analysis will be focused on one particular bundle of FWAs, namely non-standard work patterns (NSWP). Non-standard work patterns comprise a number of fairly homogeneous and popular arrangements, including annual hour contracts, part-time work, job sharing, flexitime and fixed-term contracts. While the relationship between some non-standard work patterns and individual-level variables such as job attitudes (e.g. Martin & Sinclair, 2007; Kelliher & Anderson, 2010; Wittmer & Martin, 2011), helping behaviours (Broschak & Davis-Blake, 2006), or stress (Jamal, 2004) has been extensively researched (Baltes et al., 1999), their link to organizational-level outcomes has received much less scholarly attention (Stavrou, 2005).

The complete model with all hypothesized relationships is presented in Figure 11.2. Before developing the relationships of this model in detail, previous research on the relationship between non-standard work patterns, absenteeism, turnover and organizational performance is examined.

Non-standard work patterns and organizational performance

Some authors argue that organizations directly reap benefits from FWAs through cost savings or increased workforce effort and productivity (Kossek & Michel, 2010). However, as regards FWAs in general, the evidence for a positive performance effect is mixed (Baltes et al., 1999; de Menezes & Kelliher, 2011). Some empirical studies showed no significant effect (Wood &

de Menezes, 2007), while others reported positive associations of FWAs with performance (Whitehouse et al., 2007).

The diagnosis for non-standard work patterns is similar. Labour flexibility theory suggests that non-standard work patterns should increase performance by offering employers more discretion in dealing with demand fluctuations and making labour costs more variable (Valverde, Tregaskis & Brewster, 2000). This contractual flexibility, which characterizes non-standard work patterns, has been positively associated with organizational performance (Nikandrou, Campose Cunha & Papalexandris, 2006). In addition, while Stavrou (2005), examining organizations from the public and private sectors, found no significant relationship between non-standard work patterns and organizational performance, other authors were able to link related flexible work schedules with increased productivity (Shepard, Clifton & Kruse, 1996). Consistent with the latter stream of research, the following is hypothesized:

Hypothesis 1a: *The use of non-standard work patterns is positively related to competitiveness.*
Hypothesis 1b: *The use of non-standard work patterns is positively related to financial performance.*

Non-standard work patterns, turnover and absenteeism

Employee turnover and absenteeism have been extensively researched as outcomes of FWAs. Authors have argued that, in general, FWAs give employees more freedom to organize their work and family commitments, which in turn leads to greater loyalty and better retention rates (Stavrou, 2005; Kossek & Michel, 2010). In an early field experiment, Dalton & Mesch (1990) recorded reduced levels of absenteeism, but no change of turnover, after the introduction of a flexible scheduling system. In a more recent study, teleworking, home-based work and flexi-time were also found to be correlated with lower levels of absenteeism and turnover in a cluster of Nordic countries (Stavrou & Kilaniotis, 2010). However, the curbing effect of FWAs on turnover and absenteeism does not hold in all country and industry settings. It applies even less to FWAs universally. By contrast, some particular FWAs can even be associated with higher turnover and absenteeism (Stavrou, 2005; Stavrou et al., 2010). Turnover and retention effects of particular FWAs appear to be contingent on whether arrangement participation is voluntary or involuntary, and whether employees exercise control over work scheduling or not (Kossek & Michel, 2010). Stavrou & Kilaniotis (2010) divide FWAs into employee-centred and employer-centred measures. The former mostly involve voluntary participation and do not impose working schedules on employees; they have been shown to decrease turnover (Stavrou, 2005; Stavrou & Kilaniotis, 2010). The latter, such as shift work, overtime and weekend work, often constrain the working schedules of employees and create role conflicts, leading to increased rates of turnover and absenteeism (Stavrou, 2005; Stavrou & Kilaniotis, 2010; Stavrou et al., 2010).

In this respect, non-standard work patterns such as fixed-term contracts are perhaps suitable for organizations, but not necessarily for employees. Indeed, recent studies seem to confirm that some non-standard work patterns have detrimental effects on turnover and absenteeism. Besides the studies by Stavrou and colleagues on a number of non-standard work patterns, Martin et al. (2012) provided evidence for detrimental effects of shift work schedules on the retention rates of workers. The mechanism underlying this phenomenon is partly attributable to normative pressure. Non-standard work schedules create conflicts between work and family role expectations, which lead to the family exercising pressure on the employee to quit (Martin et al., 2012).

Non-standard work patterns also intensify work, for example by forcing part-timers to handle the same workload in less time or by creating expectations of greater effort in exchange for granted flexibility (Kelliher & Anderson, 2010). Finally, they are often imposed and may effectively introduce working schedules that cannot be controlled by employees. This may induce employees to quit or call in sick. Accordingly the following relationship is expected to occur:

Hypothesis 2a: *The use of non-standard work patterns is positively related to employee turnover.*

Hypothesis 2b: *The use of non-standard work patterns is positively related to absenteeism.*

Turnover, absenteeism and organizational performance

The negative impact of employee turnover on multiple facets of organizational performance is well established (Hausknecht & Trevor, 2011). Hancock et al. (in press) conducted a meta-analysis on the effect of turnover on firm performance, finding evidence for a negative relationship with a magnitude of –.03. Absenteeism is also known to negatively impact firm performance via reduced productivity and customer service quality as well as costs of paid sick leave and employee replacement (Harrison & Martocchio, 1998). According to a survey of management consultancy Mercer, the cost of absenteeism can account for up to 36 per cent of the payroll expenses of a company (Mercer, 2008). By consequence, it is expected that:

Hypothesis 3a: *Turnover is negatively related to competiveness.*

Hypothesis 3b: *Turnover is negatively related to financial performance.*

Hypothesis 3c: *Absenteeism is negatively related to competiveness.*

Hypothesis 3d: *Absenteeism is negatively related to financial performance.*

Sample

All measures and data were extracted from the current (2008/2010) round of the Cranet survey. The Cranet project provides a large and diverse sample that lends itself well to an examination of HR practices as predictors of organizational performance (Dany, Guedri & Hatt, 2008; Gooderham, Parry & Ringdal, 2008; Gooderham & Nordhaug, 2011). Specifically, the model was tested using a sample of all private sector firms in the survey, coming from a variety of industries and operating in a large number of economically and institutionally diverse countries. Public sector companies were excluded to avoid the influence of institutional contexts, which are vastly different from the private sector. The sample includes 3630 firms with a mean size of 2117 employees (Median = 375, SD = 13,323). The most frequently represented industries are Metallurgy (18%), Manufacturing (15%), Financial and Professional Services (13%), and Retailing and Distribution (12%).

Measures

The *non-standard work patterns* bundle was constructed as a latent variable that is measured by the indicator variables: annual hour contracts, part-time work, job-sharing, flexitime and fixed-term contracts. This factor structure has already been validated by Stavrou (2005). For each indicator of the bundle, usage rates were measured on a 6-point Likert scale, ranging from (1) 'not used at all', to (2) 'used for 1–5% of the workforce' up to (6) 'used for more than 50% of the workforce'.

Two measures were employed for firm performance. The first measure assessed self-reported *financial performance*, measured as estimated gross revenues over the last three years. The 5-point Likert scale ranges from (1) 'So low as to produce large losses' to (5) 'Well in excess of costs'. The second measure of performance was assessed with six subjective, self-reported indicators of industry competitiveness, including quality, productivity, profitability, innovativeness, stock market performance and sustainable development. The items for this scale were also measured with a 5-point Likert scale, ranging from (1) 'Poor' to (5) 'Superior'. All items were aggregated to one latent construct.

Turnover was measured as the annual quit rate for the organization. *Absenteeism* was measured as the average number of absence days per employee. Turnover, absenteeism and the indicator variables for the examined non-standard work pattern bundle were subjected to a logarithmic transformation in order to improve their distributional properties. Descriptive statistics, including means, standard deviations and intercorrelations are displayed in Table 11.2.

Results

The hypothesized model (Figure 11.2) was estimated in a Structural Equation Modeling (SEM) framework. The use of SEM for analysing Human Resource Management practices has been advocated by management scholars (Steinmetz et al., 2010), notably because it provides more robust results than standard OLS

Table 11.2 Descriptive statistics

	Mean	SD	Annual hour contr.	Part-time work	Job sharing	Flexi-time	Fixed-term contr.	Turn-over	Abs.	Fin. perf.	Quality	Prod.	Prof.	Innov.	Stock market perf.	Sust dev. perf.
Annual hour contract	0.38	0.64	1													
Part-time work	0.76	0.53	0.15*	1												
Job sharing	0.23	0.44	0.12*	0.12*	1											
Flexi-time	0.83	0.75	0.07*	0.25*	0.09*	1										
Fixed-term contracts	0.69	0.52	0.13*	0.18*	0.07*	0.09*	1									
Turnover	2.24	0.99	0.01	0.09*	-0.05*	-0.13*	0.06*	1								
Absenteeism	1.88	0.73	0.07*	0.17*	0.02	0.07*	0.08*	0.12*	1							
Financial performance	4.09	0.99	-0.05*	0.02	0.05*	0.17*	-0.02	-0.08*	0.002	1						
Quality	3.94	0.76	-0.04*	-0.02	0.04*	0.05*	-0.06*	-0.07*	-0.03*	0.23*	1					
Productivity	3.66	0.82	-0.03	-0.05*	0.02	0.05*	-0.07*	-0.11*	-0.06*	0.27*	0.52*	1				
Profitability	3.49	0.93	-0.001*	-0.005	0.02	0.05*	-0.04*	-0.04*	-0.004	0.48*	0.37*	0.56*	1			
Innovativeness	3.48	0.96	-0.001	-0.02	0.04*	0.07*	-0.01	-0.08*	-0.03	0.22*	0.40*	0.43*	0.4*	1		
Stock market performance	3.03	1.1	0.01	0.05*	0.01	0.06*	0.01	0.04	-0.02	0.28*	0.25*	0.33*	0.48*	0.43*	1	
Sustainable development	3.45	0.91	0.01	-0.05*	0.02	0.04*	0.01	-0.08*	-0.01	0.14*	0.30*	0.3*	0.24*	0.34*	0.33*	1

Note: * indicates p < 0.05.

regression approaches that are typically employed in the analysis of FWAs (Dany et al., 2008). In particular, SEM estimations provide for multiple goodness-of-fit indices, allow researchers to incorporate multiple dependent and latent variables, and control for measurement error (Kline, 2010). Taken together, a fine-grained mediation model, the unique sample drawn from the Cranet survey, and a robust methodology should allow for more conclusive results regarding the relationship between flexible work and firm-level outcomes.

Following convention, a measurement model and a structural model were estimated in a two-step procedure (Anderson & Gerbing, 1988). Measurement and structural models were estimated with Mplus version 6.1 and using Maximum Likelihood estimation. By default, Mplus employs list-wise deletion for missing cases in the independent variables and Full Maximum Likelihood estimation for missing cases in the dependent variable (Muthén & Muthén, 2010).

Measurement model

A measurement model at the item level was tested in order to determine whether scale items were adequate indicators of their underlying constructs. It included two latent variables (competitiveness and non-standard work patterns) and 11 indicators (six indicators for competitiveness and five indicators for non-standard work patterns). This model showed a good fit to the data (N = 3,621): χ^2 = 542.36 (p < 0.0000); df = 43; Comparative Fit Index (CFI) = 0.894; Root Mean Square Error Of Approximation (RMSEA) = 0.057; Standardized Root Mean Square Residual (SRMR) = 0.04. All factor loadings were positive and significant.

Structural model

The structural model included all hypothesized relationships. In addition, the error terms for financial performance and competitiveness were allowed to correlate. The model estimation provided a good fit (N = 3,629): χ^2 = 793.162 (p < 0.0000); df = 71; CFI = 0.882; RMSEA = 0.053; SRMR = 0.039. The hypothesized model with all estimated effects is depicted in Figure 11.3.

The path coefficients indicated that non-standard work patterns had a significant impact on financial performance and competitiveness, supporting Hypothesis 1a and Hypothesis 1b. However, the positive influence of non-standard work patterns appeared to be stronger for competitiveness.

The results also showed that the use of non-standard work patterns considerably increased turnover, as predicted by Hypothesis 2a. However, the hypothesized impact of non-standard work patterns on absenteeism (Hypothesis 2b) received only very weak support.

As hypothesized by Hypothesis 3a and Hypothesis 3b, turnover had a significant (albeit weak) relationship with financial performance and competitiveness. On the other hand, the paths between absenteeism and both

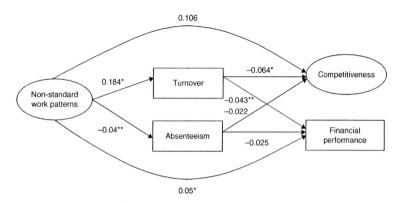

Figure 11.3   Model with standardized direct path coefficients
Note: * indicates p < 0.05, ** indicates p < 0.1.

performance constructs were not significant, implying that Hypothesis 3c and Hypothesis 3d were not supported.

An interesting question arises in the context of these results: Non-standard work patterns positively impact performance and simultaneously increase turnover, which in turn decreases performance. What can be inferred about the total effect of non-standard work practices on both performance measures? This question warrants an investigation of specific indirect, total indirect and total effects of the model. These are displayed in Table 11.3.

Table 11.3 shows that the total effect for the impact of non-standard work patterns on competitiveness (0.095) was smaller than its direct effect (path H1a = 0.106), but still positive. One possible explanation is that the positive direct impact that non-standard work patterns have on competitiveness (e.g. through improved labour productivity), is somewhat diminished by the undesirable performance effect of higher turnover that comes with an increased use of non-standard work patterns. However, the difference between total effect and direct effect was rather small. In more basic terms, this implies that although employees may be displeased with unsocial working hours or imposed working schedules and quit organizations in greater numbers, non-standard work patterns may still pay off for organizations.

A similar observation can be made for the relationship between non-standard work patterns and financial performance (direct effect from path H1b = 0.05; total effect including mediation = 0.043).

Discussion and conclusion

Flexible working arrangements comprise a large and heterogeneous number of measures whose effects are often hard to disentangle. Stavrou et al. (2010) noted that the question whether FWAs benefit mainly employers or both employers and employees is still not thoroughly answered. The empirical investigation outlined above attempted to answer this question for one

Table 11.3   Standardized total, total indirect and specific indirect effects

	Effects (Two-tailed P-values in parentheses)	
	From NSWP to competitiveness	From NSWP to financial performance
Specific Indirect (NSWP → Turnover → Competitiveness)	−0.012 *(0.028)*	
Specific Indirect (NSWP → Absenteeism → Competitiveness)	0.001 *(0.326)*	
Specific Indirect (NSWP → Turnover → Fin.Performance)		−0.008 *(0.076)*
Specific Indirect (NSWP → Absenteeism → Fin. Performance)		0.001 *(0.265)*
Total Indirect Effect	−0.011 *(0.047)*	−0.007 *(0.129)*
Total Effect	0.095 *(0.001)*	0.043 *(0.066)*

particular bundle of FWA, non-standard work patterns. The modelling approach allowed for a comprehensive estimation of direct and indirect effects that non-standard work patterns have on several outcomes measures, reflecting their impact on employees as well as on firm performance in general. The results showed that non-standard work patterns do have a positive impact on multiple measures of organizational performance. Yet, their positive direct impact on organizational performance is partially cancelled out by increased levels of turnover, which affect organizational performance negatively.

Non-standard work patterns can be viewed as a double-edged sword: on one hand, they improve workforce flexibility for employers, which ultimately translates into better firm performance; on the other hand, they may put strain on employees, reduce their job security, limit their working schedule flexibility and finally even induce them to quit. In fact, the value of non-standard work patterns for employees mainly depends on the amount of control they have over organizing their work (Kossek & Michel, 2010). If non-standard work patterns only introduce flexibility for employers, but no flexibility that employees can control, their value to employees is likely to be reduced. As a consequence, firms should be able to reduce employee turnover resulting from the use of non-standard work patterns by giving employees a greater amount of control over organizing work. This, in turn, would also increase the overall positive impact of non-standard work on firm competitiveness.

The comparably large influence that non-standard work patterns have on turnover might not only stem from its negative impact on perceived job control or employee stress. It might also simply reflect the fact that those practices are more frequently used for employees who are not part of a company's core staff, but who are considered to be peripheral workers that come and go more often. More research is needed that actually examines how the impact of non-standard work patterns on outcomes such as turnover varies with the proportion and types of employees that work under a non-standard work pattern regime. Likewise, as opposed to examining mainly firm-level variables, future research should also better account for outcomes of non-standard work patterns that are directly relevant to employees. It is also worth noting that while turnover is the most strongly affected outcome of non-standard work, very little influence on absenteeism can be detected. Absenteeism itself also has no tangible bearing on both measures of firm performance.

Even though the overall effect of non-standard work patterns is positive, its magnitude is rather small and practically negligible for financial performance. Therefore, a strong business case for non-standard work patterns is difficult to support. Besides the small size of the total effect of non-standard work patterns on both financial performance and competitiveness, one should note that the relationship is somewhat stronger for competitiveness. Firms might associate the use of non-standard work with improved levels of competitiveness, but the tangible financial performance outcomes of non-standard work are actually much smaller.

Limitations

Some limitations apply to the present study. For the sake of parsimony, the model only included effects of non-standard work patterns on turnover, absenteeism and two measures of organizational performance, not controlling for other factors that have previously been shown to impact those outcomes, such as degree of unionization, firm strategy, market development or industry (Gooderham et al., 2008). Besides modelling these additional effects, more detailed research could also examine specific industries in isolation instead of pooling data over a range of very diverse industries across which the relationship between non-standard work and its outcomes may differ strongly. In assessing the outcome of FWAs, contextual variables such as supervisor support, role conflict or support of women have not been studied in this chapter. However, these context variables are needed to obtain more fine-grained results that do justice to the context embeddedness of FWA (de Menezes & Kelliher, 2011). The Cranet survey does not comprise data on individual-level effects of Human Resource Management practices such as job satisfaction; its data also do not allow for a differentiation between access and usage rates of FWAs. However, these influences are important in understanding the effectiveness of different FWAs (Kossek & Michel, 2010).

Future directions

As mentioned earlier, countries differ in the cultural and institutional environment in which flexible work practices are enacted. The large Intraclass Correlation Coefficient for part time and flexi-time suggests that these arrangements should be examined in a multi-level framework that accounts for country-level influences. The Cranet database, given its multinational scope, provides an appropriate basis for further research on FWAs that might include multi-level models or multi-group comparisons across countries.

Finally, this chapter's examination of the link between FWAs and firm-level outcomes was focused on a particular bundle of FWAs, non-standard work patterns. Other bundles of FWAs might also be subjected to an analysis in a framework similar to the one outlined above. A comparative analysis of the impact of different bundles of FWAs could then be carried out in order to better understand which bundles of FWAs have relatively stronger or weaker relationships to employee turnover, absenteeism, and different measures of firm performance.

Appendix Table 11.1   Countries and communities for which FWAs were analysed

Cluster	Countries and communities
Anglo	Australia South Africa United Kingdom USA
Latin Europe	Belgium France Israel
Nordic Europe	Denmark Finland Iceland Norway Sweden
Germanic Europe	Austria Germany Switzerland
Eastern Europe	Bulgaria Cyprus Czech Republic Estonia Greece Hungary Lithuania Russia Serbia Slovakia Slovenia Turkish Cypriot Community
Confucian Asia	Japan Taiwan

Note

1. Countries that were part of the Cranet survey, but not included in the GLOBE project were matched to existing GLOBE clusters as follows: Bulgaria, Cyprus, Czech Republic, Estonia, Lithuania, Serbia, Slovakia (matched to GLOBE cluster Eastern Europe), Belgium (to cluster Latin Europe), Iceland and Norway (to cluster Nordic Europe). Owing to a lack of corresponding data, the GLOBE cluster "Southeast Asia" has not been retained for the overview. See Appendix Table 11.1 for a list of countries and communities included in the respective clusters.

References

Anderson, J.C. & Gerbing, D.W. 1988. 'Structural equation modeling in practice: A review and recommended two-step approach'. *Psychological Bulletin*, 103(3): 411–23.

Baltes, B.B., Briggs, T.E., Huff, J.W., Wright, J.A. & Neuman, G.A. 1999. 'Flexible and compressed workweek schedules: A meta-analysis of their effects on work-related criteria'. *Journal of Applied Psychology*, 84(4): 496–513.

Berg, P. 2008. 'Working time flexibility in the German employment relations system: Implications for Germany and lessons for the United States'. *Industrielle Beziehungen*, 15(2): 133–50.

Brewster, C. & Mayrhofer, W. 2011. 'Comparative human resource management'. In A.-W.K., Harzing & A. Pinnington (eds), *International Human Resource Management*, 3rd edn. Thousand Oaks, CA: Sage Publications, 47–118.

Broschak, J.P. & Davis-Blake, A. 2006. 'Mixing standard work and nonstandard deals: The consequences of heterogeneity in employment arrangements'. *Academy of Management Journal*, 49(2): 371–93.

Coombs, J. 2011. 'Flexibility still meeting resistance'. *HR Magazine*, 56(7): 72.

Dalton, D.R. & Mesch, D.J. 1990. 'The impact of flexible scheduling on employee attendance and turnover'. *Administrative Science Quarterly*, 35(2): 370–87.

Dany, F., Guedri, Z. & Hatt, F. 2008. 'New insights into the link between HRM integration and organizational performance: The moderating role of influence distribution between HRM specialists and line managers'. *The International Journal of Human Resource Management*, 19(11): 2095–112.

de Menezes, L.M. & Kelliher, C. 2011. 'Flexible working and performance: A systematic review of the evidence for a business case'. *International Journal of Management Reviews*, 13(4): 329–474.

Decision 2008/618/EC, *Official Journal of the European Union* 198, 26.7.2008, 47–54.

Giardini, A. & Kabst, R. 2008. 'Effects of work–family human resource practices: A longitudinal perspective'. *The International Journal of Human Resource Management*, 19(11): 2079–94.

Gooderham, P. & Nordhaug, O. 2011. 'One European model of HRM? Cranet empirical contributions'. *Human Resource Management Review*, 21(1): 27–36.

Gooderham, P., Parry, E. & Ringdal, K. 2008. 'The impact of bundles of strategic human resource management practices on the performance of European firms'. *The International Journal of Human Resource Management*, 19(11): 2041–56.

Gupta, V. & Hanges, P.J. 2004. 'Regional and climate clustering of societal cultures'. In: R.J. House, P.J. Hanges, M. Javidan, P.W. Dorfman & V. Gupta (eds), *Culture, Leadership, and Organizations: The GLOBE Study of 62 Societies*. Thousand Oaks, CA: Sage Publications, 178–218.

Hancock, J.I., Allen, D.G., Bosco, F.A., McDaniel, K.M. & Pierce, C.A. (in press). Meta-analytic review of employee turnover as a predictor of firm performance. *Journal of Management*. doi: 10.1177/0149206311424943.

Harrison, D.A. & Martocchio, J.J. 1998. 'Time for absenteeism: A 20-year review of origins, offshoots, and outcomes'. *Journal of Management*, 24(3): 305–50.

Hausknecht, J.P. & Trevor, C.O. 2011. 'Collective turnover at the group, unit, and organizational levels: Evidence, issues, and implications'. *Journal of Management*, 37: 352–88.

Hornung, S., Rousseau, D.M. & Glaser, J. 2008. 'Creating flexible work arrangements through idiosyncratic deals'. *Journal of Applied Psychology*, 93: 655–64.

Jamal, M. 2004. 'Burnout, stress and health of employees on non-standard work schedules: A study of Canadian workers'. *Stress and Health*, 20(3): 113–19.

Javidan, M., House, R.J., Dorfman, P.W., Hanges, P.J. & De Luque, M.S. 2006. 'Conceptualizing and measuring cultures and their consequences: A comparative review of GLOBE's and Hofstede's approaches'. *Journal of International Business Studies*, 37(6): 897–914.

Kelliher, C. & Anderson, D. 2010. 'Doing more with less? Flexible working practices and the intensification of work'. *Human Relations*, 63(1): 83–106.

Kline, R.B. 2010. *Principles and Practice of Structural Equation Modeling*, 3rd edn. New York: The Guilford Press.

Konrad, A. & Mangel, R. 2000. 'The impact of work-life programs on firm productivity'. *Strategic Management Journal*, 21(12): 1225–37.

Kossek, E.E. & Michel, J.S. 2010. 'Flexible work schedules'. In S. Zedeck (ed.), *APA Handbook of Industrial and Organizational Psychology*, Vol. 1. American Psychological Association, 535–72.

Lee, B.Y. & DeVoe, S.E. 2012. 'Flextime and profitability'. *Industrial Relations*, 51(2): 298–315.

Luke, D.A. 2004. *Multilevel Modeling*. Thousand Oaks, CA: Sage Publications.

Martin, J.E. & Sinclair, R.R. 2007. 'A typology of the part-time workforce: Differences on job attitudes and turnover'. *Journal of Occupational and Organizational Psychology*, 80(2): 301–19.

Martin, J.E., Sinclair, R.R., Lelchook, A., Wittmer, J. & Charles, K.E. 2012. 'Nonstandard work schedules and retention in the entry-level hourly workforce'. *Journal of Occupational and Organizational Psychology*, 85(1): 1–22.

Mercer, 2008. The total financial impact of employee absences. URL: http://www.fmlainsights.com/mercer-survey-highlights%5B1%5D.pdf [accessed Sept. 2011].

Muthén, L.K. & Muthén, B.O. 2010. *Mplus User's Guide*. Los Angeles, CA: Muthén & Muthén.

Nikandrou, I., Campos e Cunha, R. & Papalexandris, N. 2006. 'HRM and organizational performance: Universal and contextual evidence'. In H.H. Larsen & W. Mayrhofer (eds), *Managing Human Resources in Europe: A Thematic Approach*. London: Taylor & Francis, 177–96.

Parry, E., Stavrou-Costea, E. & Morley, M.J. 2011. 'The Cranet International Research Network on human resource management in retrospect and prospect'. *Human Resource Management Review*, 21(1): 1–4.

Plantenga, J. & Remery, C. 2009. *Flexible Working Time Arrangements and Gender Equality: A Comparative Review of 30 European Countries*. European Commission, Directorate-General for Employment, Social Affairs and Equal Opportunities Unit G1.

Scheibl, F. & Dex, S. 1998. 'Should we have more family-friendly policies?' *European Management Journal*, 16(5): 586–99.

Shepard, E., Clifton, T. & Kruse, D. 1996. 'Flexible working hours and productivity: Some evidence from the pharmaceutical industry'. *Industrial Relations: A Journal of Economy and Society*, 35(1): 123–39.

Shockley, K.M. & Allen, T.D. 2010. 'Investigating the missing link in flexible work arrangement utilization: An individual difference perspective'. *Journal of Vocational Behavior*, 76: 131–42.

Stavrou, E.T. 2005. 'Flexible work bundles and organizational competitiveness: A cross-national study of the European work context'. *Journal of Organizational Behavior*, 26: 923–47.

Stavrou, E. & Kilaniotis, C. 2010. 'Flexible work and turnover: An empirical investigation across cultures'. *British Journal of Management*, 21: 541–54.

Stavrou, E.T., Spiliotis, S. & Charalambous, C. 2010. 'Flexible working arrangements in context: An empirical investigation through self-organizing maps'. *European Journal of Operational Research*, 202(3): 893–902.

Steinmetz, H., Schwens, C., Wehner, M. & Kabst, R. 2010. 'Conceptual and methodological issues in comparative HRM research: The Cranet project as an example'. *Human Resource Management Review*, 21(1): 16–26.

Storey, J., Quintas, P., Taylor, P. & Fowle, W. 2002. 'Flexible employment contracts and their implications for product and process innovation'. *The International Journal of Human Resource Management*, 13(1): 1–18.

Valverde, M., Tregaskis, O. & Brewster, C. 2000. 'Labor flexibility and firm performance'. *International Advances in Economic Research*, 6(4): 649–61.

Whitehouse, G., Haynes, M., MacDonald, F. & Arts, D. 2007. *Re-assessing the Family-friendly Workplace: Trends and Influences in Britain 1998–2004*. Employment Relations Research Series, 76. London: Department for Business Enterprise and Regulatory Reform.

Wittmer, J.L.S. & Martin, J.E. 2011. 'Effects of scheduling perceptions on attitudes and mobility in different part-time employee types'. *Journal of Vocational Behavior*, 78(1): 149–58.

Wood, S. & de Menezes, L. 2007. 'Family-friendly, equal opportunity and high-involvement management in Britain'. In P. Boxall, J. Purcell & P. Wright (eds), *Oxford Handbook of Human Resource Management*. Oxford: Oxford University Press, 581–98.

Wright, P. & van de Voorde, K. 2009. 'Multilevel issues in IHRM: Mean differences, explained variance, and moderated relationships'. In P. Sparrow (ed.), *Handbook of International Human Resource Management: Integrating People, Process, and Context*. Oxford: Wiley-Blackwell, 29–40.

Index

Printed and bound in the United States of America